LABOUR EXPLOITATION AND
WORK-BASED HARM

Studies in Social Harm

Series editors: Christina Pantazis, University of Bristol, UK
Simon Pemberton, University of Birmingham, UK

Environmental harm: An eco-justice perspective
by Rob White (2013)

Harmful societies: Understanding social harm
by Simon Pemberton (2015)

Labour exploitation and work-based harm
by Sam Scott (2017)

A sociology of harm
by Lynne Copson (2019)

*Global kitchens and super highways: Social harm and the
political economy of food*
by Reece Walters (2019)

Pharmaceuticals and social harm
by Sarah Payne (2019)

Deviant leisure and social harm
by Oliver Smith and Thomas Raymen (2019

New perspectives on Islamophobia and social harm
by Chris Allen (2020)

See more at http://policypress.co.uk/studies-in-social-harm

Policy Press
UNIVERSITY OF BRISTOL

LABOUR EXPLOITATION AND WORK-BASED HARM

Sam Scott

First published in Great Britain in 2018 by

Policy Press
University of Bristol
1-9 Old Park Hill
Bristol
BS2 8BB
UK
t: +44 (0)117 954 5940
pp-info@bristol.ac.uk
www.policypress.co.uk

North America office:
Policy Press
c/o The University of Chicago Press
1427 East 60th Street
Chicago, IL 60637, USA
t: +1 773 702 7700
f: +1 773-702-9756
sales@press.uchicago.edu
www.press.uchicago.edu

British Library Cataloguing in Publication Data
A catalogue record for this book is available from the British Library

Library of Congress Cataloging-in-Publication Data
A catalog record for this book has been requested

ISBN 978-1-4473-2204-7 paperback
ISBN 978-1-4473-2207-8 ePub
ISBN 978-1-4473-2208-5 Mobi
ISBN 978-1-4473-2206-1 ePDF

Cover design and image by Policy Press
Front cover image: Getty
Printed and bound in Great Britain by by CPI Group (UK) Ltd,
Croydon, CR0 4YY
Policy Press uses environmentally responsible print partners

Contents

List of poems

The nine poems, at the start of each of the nine chapters, are those of Jenny Wrangborg (Wrangborg, 2013) from her collection published in Swedish entitled 'Kitchen' (translated into English by Freke Räihä). Details of Jenny's poetry can be found at: www.jennywrangborg.se/blogg/in-english/

Lists of figures, tables and boxes

Figures

Tables

Boxes

List of abbreviations

CA	Consultancy Association
CAB	UK Citizens Advice Bureau
CEO	Chief Executive Officer
CSR	Corporate Social Responsibility
EASI	UK Employment Agencies Standards Inspectorate
ECJ	European Court of Justice
ETI	Ethical Trading Initiative
EU	European Union
EWCS	European Working Conditions Survey
FLA	Fair Labor Association
FRA	European Agency for Fundamental Rights
GLA	UK Gangmasters Licensing Authority
GLAA	UK Gangmasters and Labour Abuse Authority
HSE	UK Health and Safety Executive
HRW	Human Rights Watch
ICT	Information and communications technology
ILO	International Labour Organization
ITUC	International Trade Union Confederation
JRF	Joseph Rowntree Foundation
LMIs	Labour market intermediaries
NGO	Non-governmental organisation
ODWs	Oversees domestic workers
OECD	Organisation for Economic Cooperation and Development
PWRH	Pay and Work Rights Helpline (UK)
SAP-FL	Special Action Programme to Combat Forced Labour
SAWS	Seasonal Agricultural Workers Scheme (UK)
SEIU	Service Employees International Union
TUC	Trades Unions Congress (UK)
UK	United Kingdom
UKHTC	UK Human Trafficking Centre
UN	United Nations
Unite	Unite the union (UK)
US	United States

About the author

Sam Scott is a senior lecturer at the University of Gloucestershire, Cheltenham, UK. He began researching issues around labour exploitation and work-based harm via three evaluation reports for the UK Gangmasters Licensing Authority (GLA). These were followed by a Nuffield Foundation small grant looking at employer perspectives on low-wage migrant labour use, two Joseph Rowntree Foundation grants focused on forced labour in the UK and then an Economic and Social Research Council 'follow-on' grant to consolidate this work. The research for the Joseph Rowntree Foundation inspired this book.

Acknowledgements

This book would not have been possible without the support of my employer (University of Gloucestershire), work colleagues and family. Thank you, most of all, to Dagmara Scott for putting up with me throughout the long planning and writing process. This book would not have been completed without your love and support. Thanks also to Duncan Scott, Wendy Scott and Hannah Scott for always being there to put things into perspective. I also owe a debt of gratitude to Jenny Wrangborg who has allowed me to use her inspirational poems at the start of each chapter (see Wrangborg, 2013). This book could also not have come to fruition without the work and encouragement of Christina Pantazis and Simon Pemberton. Of course, the team at Policy Press also deserve a special mention too, particularly Rebecca Tomlinson, Kathryn King and Ruth Harrison. As do the anonymous reviewers who commented on earlier drafts of this book. Thank you also to the Joseph Rowntree Foundation for funding two research projects – *Experiences of forced labour in the UK food industry* (Scott et al, 2012) and *The scope of forced labour in the UK* (Geddes et al, 2013) – that helped to inspire this book and to Dr Alistair Geddes, Professor Gary Craig and the 11 community researchers who worked with me on these two projects. Follow-on funding from the Economic and Social Research Council (grant number: ES/J020567/1) gave me time away from teaching to build upon the Joseph Rowntree Foundation research and to plan this book. Others who helped with ideas and suggestions along the way include Dr Alex Balch and Roger Plant. Finally, I would like to dedicate this book to Dave Holman (1977–2016), a dear friend, who I'll always remember for his warmth, compassion and humour. We miss you, Dave.

Foreword

This is the third book to be published in the Studies in Social Harm series – a series which was established to provide a holistic and multi-disciplinary focus on social harms. When harms – such as pollution, violence and poverty to name a few – are researched from academic disciplinary silos we are often left with partial and distorted assessments of social problems. When such harms are explained solely or predominantly in terms of individual calculus or failure, we fail to connect the manufacture, re-production, and re-configuration of harms to wider social structures and processes. Consequently, we misrecognise how social harms can be prevented by identifying the most relevant policy changes and interventions that are required for the improvement of people's well-being. The series Studies in Social Harm, through a blending of new theoretical and conceptual frameworks, methods, and empirical research, aims to address and rebut these omnipresent short-sightings within contemporary social sciences analyses.

In that vein, Sam Scott's book *Labour exploitation and work-based harm* is both relevant and timely, in a period in which issues – such as trafficked labour at one extreme and zero-hour contracts at the other – have come to the fore of public and policy debates. Casting aside dominant criminological perspectives, with their reliance on legal definitions and remedies, and their tendency to focus on the most extreme forms of labour exploitation occurring as a result of the unscrupulous actions of a criminal minority, Scott develops a framework for understanding work-based harm based on the concept of control. Scott contends that workplace harm arises when controls over workers become exploitative and lead to negative outcomes (for example, with regards to physical or mental health). By identifying work-based harm as resting on a continuum, he invites readers to move beyond the consideration of extreme work-based harms such as slavery which are already criminalised to 'legal and non-coercive employment relationships that are, nevertheless, problematic' (see p 17). Supplementing a vast array of quantitative data provided by international organisations like the International Labour Organization, with original qualitative research including studies involving low-wage migrant workers, Scott provides rich testimonial evidence 'to show how workers may be subject to different types and degrees of control and how this control can become excessive and oppressive' (see p 13). He demonstrates how workers experience direct controls (such as targets, monitoring and surveillance), indirect controls (such as poverty and debt), and exogenous controls (such as ontological insecurity). He traverses 'the edges of acceptability with respect to work-based exploitation and harm' (see p 174) by probing at difficult issues such as worker consent, employer intent and motives, and explores those contexts where exploitation and harm are deemed acceptable. In moving beyond criminological perspectives and developing solutions to worker exploitation, he highlights the role of trade unions, social movements, and reductions in worker inequality as crucial supplements to existing legal baselines and harm reduction strategies employed by a variety of capitalist states.

Previous books in the series are Simon Pemberton's ground-breaking *Harmful societies* and Rob White's innovative *Environmental harm*. Whilst Pemberton provided us with conceptual tools to understand the social production of harm, White developed an analysis of environmental and species degradation through an eco-justice perspective. Forthcoming topics include Islamophobia, the political economy of food, the pharmaceutical industry, deviant leisure and social harm, and utopian approaches. The topics should be key areas of interest to scholars who wish to deepen and extend their knowledge and understanding of both harm production and its amelioration.

Christina Pantazis, Centre for the Study of Poverty and Social Justice,
School for Policy Studies, University of Bristol
Simon Pemberton, School of Social Policy, University of Birmingham

February 2017

I am a human being

I am also human
I need food on the table
a job to go to
dignity
I am not invisible

I am also human
I will break if you send me to war
I will rot if you leave me in a trench
I am fragile goods

I am human
my legs ache after eleven hours between cashier and kitchen
the headache screams after a whole day in a steam-hot kitchen

the human in me says that it is unreasonable
to earn money for someone else
I am not a machine

I am not invisible
I am the one who takes your money at the gas station
building the car you drive, the being that you send off to war
who rots away in your trenches

I am not invisible
I cook for you and your fine dining
clean your houses
take care of your parents
I am so close

I am fragile goods
it hurts when I fall from scaffolds
slip on the greasy floor
lift the old
my body has no spare parts
because I am not a machine
you can not buy a new one, because you can not buy me

the human in me says that you can not claim my surplus value
because nothing is more valuable than humanity
you can not call me to the office and exchange me for a faster model
because I am not a machine

I am a human being
I am so close

ONE

Introduction

This book argues that it is time to define, and in the process identify solutions to, the problems of labour exploitation and work-based harm. The book is clear that extant legal frameworks are a necessary but not a sufficient condition for the successful completion of this task. Put simply, there is a tendency to look at exploitation and harm through a criminological lens. This is fine in so far as it tends to identify extreme forms of coercive exploitation and abuse. However, there are highly complex sets of employment relationships and experiences between the extremes of slavery, on the one hand, and decent work on the other. In order to define and solve the problem of labour exploitation, and the associated issue of work-based harm, one needs to step into this grey area and provoke debate over what is and what is not acceptable. Crucially, such an endeavour requires one to ask critical but highly complex moral questions about largely non-coercive control at, and through, work. To this end, the book sets out to identify the nature of contemporary control over workers as a basis for understanding labour exploitation and work-based harm 'beyond criminology' (see Hillyard et al, 2004). The basic argument is that labour exploitation and work-based harm are problems that are larger than the capitalist system is generally able or willing to articulate. An emphasis on 'social harm' also underlines the point that it is all too often societies – and their constituent political, economic, legal and cultural systems – that cause work-based harm rather than simply individual 'bad egg' employers. The legal system is, however, ill-equipped on its own to deal with such a systemic problem.

Defining the issues: determining the language

The relationship between a worker and his/her employer is one that is infinitely complex. At its core, however, is the simple need of the worker to make a decent living and the simple desire of the capitalist (employer, shareholder, property owner and so on) to make a decent profit. In the pursuit of these objectives hierarchical relationships inevitably emerge. These relationships form the basis of the capitalist system. For most workers, the struggle involves one of advancing incrementally up particular hierarchies such that the pressures of the system are, at least in some small part, lightened over time. In any particular hierarchy, within the overall system, however, there is potential for workers to suffer at the hand of those above them. This potential is heightened in systems where inequality is high.

Suffering at and through work, then, may well be something that is most obvious at the very bottom of the labour market but hierarchies at all levels contain within them the potential to exploit and harm. To be sure, financial rewards, and the status that comes with these, do help to cushion the burdens and pressures of work. Nevertheless, it would be simplistic to assume that only those at the extreme depth of the labour market are being harmed by the inequities of contemporary capitalism. This acknowledgment is an important basis for the book and it is why the book is focused on the language and terminology of work-based 'control', 'exploitation' and 'harm'.

This language is inclusive in the sense that it avoids drawing attention only to extreme cases of worker suffering and instead implicitly and explicitly recognises that hierarchies, wherever they exist in the overall capitalist system, are potentially problematic and worthy of critical investigation by academics interested in worker welfare. Moreover, the language avoids taking *a priori* legal–moral frameworks as a basis for what is acceptable (that is, legal) and unacceptable (that is, illegal) as far as the treatment of workers is concerned. This is important because laws often exist to protect people only from extreme-case scenarios, to protect them only from individual perpetrators (rather than from structures and systems), and to protect dominant interest groups. In all these respects there is a critical logic and rationale for moving beyond crime-based perspectives on worker welfare and worker suffering.

Four main questions are tackled in examining work-based control, exploitation and harm within this book (see Table 1.1):

1. How is the distribution of power between labour and capital changing?
2. How is labour now controlled?
3. What are the negative outcomes of this control?
4. How can these negative outcomes be reduced?

In terms of the first of these questions, considerable academic attention has been directed towards the changing nature of work under advanced capitalism. The prevailing neoliberal political economy has clearly affected the power (im)balance between labour and capital, in favour of the latter (Herod, 2000; Harvey, 2005). We have witnessed the depoliticisation, individualisation, and growing commodification of labour and what Harvey (2005) terms the associated 'accumulation through dispossession'.

In short, neoliberalism has, for many workers, been associated with a decline in overall ontological security and wellbeing, with employment practices a key element in this. More broadly, neoliberalism has been identified by scholars as the key cause of contemporary social harm: 'The neoliberal economic paradigm is fundamentally harmful – it wrecks lives and creates harm on a wide scale – and these features are not some aberration, but integral and necessary aspects of this form of economic and political organisation' (Tombs and Hillyard, 2004, 32).

Table 1.1: Researching work-based control, exploitation and harm

Key questions	Key ideas
1. How is the distribution of power between labour and capital changing?	A number of shifts appear to suggest a growing power asymmetry between labour and capital, in favour of the latter.
2. How is labour now controlled?	There are three types of control that enable power to shift from labour to capital: • Direct: when power is centralised and/ or visible and control explicit • Indirect: when power is fragmented and/ or invisible and control implicit • Exogenous: when control of workers is produced and reproduced outside the workplace in the interests of capital
3. What are the negative outcomes of control?	Control is highly problematic in two instances: • When control becomes excessive and oppressive it can be said to constitute 'exploitation' • When control damages a worker's physical or psychological health, erodes social–communal structures, or damages the environment it can be said to have caused 'harm' • Control, exploitation and harm may also be linked to 'structural violence' and thus reflect social inequalities along class, race, citizenship, ethnic, sexuality and gender lines.
4. How can these negative outcomes be reduced?	Work-based control, exploitation and harm can be tempered through: • national and transnational legal baselines • modifying capitalism • changing labour–capital relations

Arguably, the two prime indicators of neoliberalism as far as workers are concerned have been the shift towards post-Fordist workplace regimes and the associated subcontracting of employment, on the one hand (Peck and Theodore, 1998; 2001; 2007; Wills, 2009), and the search by employers, via international migration, for an ever-expanding pool of labour, on the other (Castles and Kosack, 1973; Cohen, 1987; Wills et al, 2010; Lewis et al, 2015a; Schierup et al, 2015). Thus, across a range of contexts, employment has become more flexible and fragmented and employees have become more diverse. Some have rightly celebrated the positive sides to these shifts; but one cannot ignore the fact that they have also been about an economic logic linked to capital's desire to gain ever more control over labour.

The dominance of the neoliberal orthodoxy and the associated shift to post-Fordist and post-national labour markets have, according to some, resulted in a worsening of worker experiences. As Hillyard et al (2004, 3) argue 'much harm is the social wreckage of neoliberal globalisation'. More specifically, Rogaly (2008a), talks of 'intensification': with the work effort required of labour by capital growing over time. Similarly, Scott (forthcoming) uses the concept of 'informalisation' to capture the increasing blurring of the boundary between formal and informal work, as formal low-wage employment deteriorates. Others talk of 'deproletarianisation' (Brass, 1999; 2014) to underline the fragmentation and loss of collective political consciousness of the workforce or of 'precarity' (Waite, 2009; Standing, 2011; 2014) to point to an increasing proportion of people (the 'precariat') in positions of extreme labour market vulnerability and without a collective voice or any real political might.

Crucially, it seems that, whatever the nomenclature, low-wage migrants are particularly susceptible to labour exploitation and work-based harm. In other words, they are all too often the archetypal 'good' workers under neoliberalism and enable dominant interests to maintain, and gain, power and control over labour. This is why, throughout the book, empirical evidence is drawn from communities of low-wage migrants. To be sure, labour exploitation and work-based harm are problems for workers in general. However, they are particularly prevalent problems for low-wage migrants, and it seems that geographical mobility is often used by capital to extract added value from labour (see, for example, Waite et al, 2015).

A large part of this book is orientated towards understanding the architecture of contemporary work-based control over both migrant and non-migrant workers (see Question 2). Essentially, control may be direct, indirect, or exist beyond the workplace (exogenous). Controls in themselves are not necessarily problematic, though they may be. Issues arise when there are particular negative outcomes associated with work-based control that is, 'exploitation' and 'harm' (see Question 3).

Exploitation in its broadest (Marxist) sense occurs when labour provides capitalists with surplus value, thus driving accumulation, which in turn can drive further control, and lead onto even greater accumulation (and exploitation). More narrowly, exploitation is often, in practice, determined by legal frameworks and baselines and is defined by what is deemed to be illegal within a particular political–economic system. It must be noted, though, that legal approaches to defining exploitation have tended to struggle to achieve definitional clarity or consistency and have therefore tended towards 'judicial maximalism' with considerable evidence of illegality needed before an offence is proclaimed (as in the case of the Netherlands, profiled by Clark, 2013, 58–9).

Between the Marxist and the legal definition of exploitation many have argued for a labour exploitation 'continuum' (Andrees, 2008; Skrivánková, 2010; McGrath, 2012; Strauss, 2012; Lewis et al, 2015a; 2015b; Strauss and McGrath, 2017) running from criminal practices through to decent work. What underpins the continuum is the presence of excessive and oppressive control and also, often, the presence of harm. In this respect, the book is partly an attempt to define exploitation beyond the Marxist maximum, on the one hand (which defines the problem as omnipresent), and the judicial maximalism on the other (which defines the problem as extreme and residual).

The benchmark report of the European Agency for Fundamental Rights (FRA, 2015) is useful in this respect as it makes a number of important distinctions when defining and delineating labour exploitation (see Table 1.2). Most notably, there is the division between slavery, servitude and forced labour, on the one hand, and labour exploitation on the other (see also Chapter Two). There is also the distinction between criminal and civil/labour law; and it is often more common to see general notions of labour exploitation linked to civil/labour law (see, for example, BIS, 2016).

This book, however, adopts a more expansive definition of labour exploitation than the FRA, and conceptualises it as something that may occur outside conventional legal frameworks, whether based on criminal or civil/labour law. Thus, it advances a definition of labour exploitation that is not solely anchored to extant legal structures and systems and focuses instead on a continuum between the criminal–legal extremes of slavery, servitude and forced labour, and decent work. Along this continuum labour exploitation may be defined by some criminal and some civil/labour laws, but these laws on their own are not enough to answer the long-standing definitional conundrum of labour exploitation. Additionally, judgements must be made over what constitutes excessive and oppressive work-based control and evidence of work-based harm must also be proffered. Moreover, and this is the crucial point, these controls and harms may exist beyond, and even rendered unproblematic by, conventional legal framings.

Table 1.2: The definition of labour exploitation according to the European Agency for Fundamental Rights

Terminology	Legal status	Key Article from the 'Charter of Fundamental Rights of the EU'
Slavery, servitude and forced labour	Criminal law	Article 5 – Prohibition of slavery and forced labour • No one shall be held in slavery or servitude. • No one shall be required to perform forced or compulsory labour. • Trafficking in human beings is prohibited.
Severe labour exploitation	Criminal law	Article 31 – Fair and just working conditions • Every worker has the right to working conditions which respect his or her health, safety and dignity. • Every worker has the right to limitation of maximum working hours, to daily and weekly rest periods and to an annual period of paid leave.
Labour exploitation	Criminal law (see above) and/or civil and labour law	

Source: FRA (2015, p 34)

Harm is evident at three main levels. There is individual harm that may be associated with a negative impact on one's physical and/or psychological health. There is social–communal harm that undermines cultural systems that would otherwise allow people to flourish outside of their role as worker. Finally, there is environmental harm, that is, damage done to the physical world in the interests of capital that once again reduces the opportunity for human flourishing. In some instances this harm may be specifically directed towards particular groups according to class, race, ethnic, religious, gender, sexuality, citizenship, and so on, status. In other instances, it may be less discriminatory.

These three harm outcomes are distinct from the academic concept of social harm. The term 'social harm' as used in this and other books (Hillyard et al, 2004; Pemberton, 2015) refers to the idea that societies, and their constituent political, economic, legal and cultural systems, cause harm. Correspondingly, solutions to labour exploitation and work-based harm must look beyond the (occasional) criminalisation of the individual 'bad-egg' employer to consider corporate, state and collective responsibility. This requires a 'shift from criminal justice to a broadly defined social policy' (Hillyard and Tombs, 2004, 23).

Reducing the negative outcomes of work-based control (Question 4) should be a key policy priority for anyone interested in advancing the harm agenda. However, relinquishing and redistributing control, even when this control can be clearly linked to exploitation and harm, is likely to be problematic. This is because, as noted above, there is growing power asymmetry between labour and capital, and surplus value to be gained from this. It is also because those being dominated through the inequities of the capitalist system often seek to avoid the full force of this system by cascading controls down onto others; and so workers become co-opted in their own overall control. This said, there are solutions to exploitation and work-based harm that involve: national and transnational legal baselines; the modification of capitalism; and, changing the power relations between labour and capital. These different types of solutions will all be discussed at length in this book (see especially Chapter Eight) but it is the latter two that align particularly closely with a social harm agenda.

A social harm perspective

People experience 'harm' (Hillyard et al, 2004; Hillyard and Tombs, 2007; Pemberton, 2007; Dorling et al, 2008; Lasslett, 2010; Pemberton, 2015) and 'violence' (Bourgois, 2001; Scheper-Hughes and Bourgois, 2003; Mitchell, 2011; Holmes, 2013) as a result of their commodified status as workers. Such negative outcomes of work-based control are about much more than isolated one-to-one bullying by individual colleagues or 'bad-egg' employers and stem from the inequalities and hierarchies inherent in the capitalist system. They are, in short, embedded within the prevailing political economic orthodoxy and, what is important, play a part in sustaining this.

Polanyi (1944) was one of the earliest scholars to show how significantly capitalism is implicated in harm at an individual, societal–communal and environmental level. Most notably, he argues that the way in which industrial capitalism developed in the UK, and especially northern England, caused considerable harm, with the industrial revolution 'accompanied by a catastrophic dislocation of the lives of the common people' (Polanyi, 1944, 35). This was due to the treatment of nature and man as (fictitious) 'commodities' which both 'disjoints man's [sic] relationships and threatens his natural habitat with annihilation' (Polanyi, 1944, 44). In other words, Polanyi argues that capitalism and the 'free market' is hard-wired to artificially treat land and labour as commodities, when in fact they are not, and that it is this basic assumption that underpins harm. As I will argue later in the book (see Chapters Eight and Nine), Polanyi's linking of the political–economy with harm is central to understanding the types and combination of solutions needed to address the problems of labour exploitation and work-based harm (see also Pemberton, 2015).

Critically, when harm occurs, because it is integral to the capitalist system as conventionally organised, it is often either able to cover its tracks and/or it is defined outside of established criminal framing and so rendered relatively unproblematic in a legal (and sometimes by extension moral) sense. In other words, we may be able to feel and even see harm, but we may not easily be able to fix it to causes or even to reference points and a language that problematises it. The notion of crime, with a distinct victim and identifiable perpetrator, is thus often insufficient to address harm given its structural origins and one must look beyond criminology to define and frame the problem (see Hillyard et al, 2004).

Most obviously, a division between cause and effect tends to accompany work-based harm in contemporary capitalist systems, and this makes it almost impossible to assign responsibility to a 'criminal' when controls over workers become exploitative. State and corporate power is certainly not naïve, and recognises that in building up things like control and financial might there is likely to be damage: damage that is ideally collateral and socially or geographically distant and/or diffuse. The challenge, then, lies not only in minimising harm but in also managing harm when it arises in order to limit liability and visibility. Management explains why systems exist and persist that are harmful and why harm may go unchallenged and even unnoticed, and why it may become an accepted and taken-for-granted, rather than criminalised, aspect of the capitalist system.

Given the above, it is easy to see why many experts have called for the establishment of social harm studies 'beyond criminology' (Hillyard et al, 2004; Hillyard and Tombs, 2007; Pemberton, 2007; Dorling et al, 2008; Lasslett, 2010; Pemberton, 2015). This book is a response to this call. I argue that capitalism, via state and corporate structures, is orientated towards, and in some instances obsessed with, worker control. Much of this control is about the production and reproduction of 'good' and 'better' workers (however good and better are defined). The problem with control, however, is that it has a tendency, if left unchecked, to become exploitative and to cause harm.

Whether direct or indirect, whether within the workplace or outside, controls will be in place to serve various fractions and factions of capital.

This does not mean that labour will inevitably suffer, simply that controls over workers are an essential feature of capitalist accumulation and, indeed, a basic element of maintaining social order. The key question, then, is not whether one is for or against worker control but what types and degrees of control are acceptable, and even desirable, in civilised society. It is clear, for example, that there are workers who are suppressed by excessive and oppressive forms of control and that human flourishing (and even productivity) suffers as a result.

At the extreme end of the spectrum work-based controls will be deemed illegal. Chattel slavery is the most striking example of this. In such instances, workers may be affected in different ways by their enslavement, but it is the process of enslavement that defines the problem as a criminal one, alongside the varied physical and psychological outcomes of the process.

Beyond very clear instances of exploitation, however, there is a considerable grey area where criminological approaches have been found wanting. Most obviously, many people are harmed at, or through, work even though they are not subject to enslavement. In such cases, it can sometimes be difficult to define specific processes that are problematic and, instead, it may be more productive to start with outcomes. This approach can lead us to question the treatment of large numbers of workers well beyond the conventional legal protections and it can also lead one towards a radical critique of the modern employment relationship.

The question for most workers today, for instance, is about whether or not they are free from physical and psychological harm, and, whether or not they are in social–communal situations that allow them space to be autonomous agents and give them the opportunity to develop and flourish as human beings and within social groups beyond their role as workers. If they are not, as is the case for many workers, the next question becomes one of whether they are able to buy enough quality leisure and family time in order to make their employment pay in a spiritual as well as a narrow pecuniary sense.

These questions are essentially about freedom, some of the time, from a narrow employment relationship and a definition of workers, for at least some of the time, as more than deferential subjects and mere commodities. It is about recognising individuals' rights to decent physical and psychological health and to a family and social life while valuing workers for more than an ability to follow orders. The problem arises when worker controls compromise this and when humans become valued only in so far as they meet a particular narrow vision of a 'good' worker. When this occurs, it is not just individuals who are at risk of exploitation and harm it is also the wider societies and communities that these individuals are/were a part of: something Polanyi made very clear in relation to the English working-class (Polanyi, 1944).

The above opens up what Pemberton (2015, 5) calls 'an alternative space' to critique employment practices and worker controls more generally. It takes us beyond the very worst employment cases (such as chattel slavery) to critically examine the changing relations between labour and capital more broadly. Thus attention may still be drawn towards illegal processes, such as enslavement, but other employment outcomes are problematised that emerge as a result of a more complex and nuanced arrangement of causal factors (Pemberton, 2015, Chapter Three).

The harm agenda, therefore, is one that is both critical (focusing on underlying structural causes) and pessimistic (the problems are much larger than legal perspectives would have us believe). Or, put another way, and more optimistically, the social harm agenda provides a language that can allow scholars to better capture, and empathise with, the lived experiences of victims who might otherwise be denied a voice, or even language. It teaches us to look at workers at the extreme end of the exploitation spectrum but to not only look in this particular place for evidence of harm.

As a final point, it is worth emphasising that workers, even in extremely vulnerable positions, still possess agency (Scott, 1985; Rogaly, 2009; Mitchell, 2011; Alberti, 2014). When considering work-based control, therefore, it is important not to draw out false dichotomies. In short, excessive and oppressive controls over workers, and associated evidence of exploitation and harm, can often co-exist alongside worker agency. People are infinitely resourceful and, unless they are in extreme slave-like situations, can still wrest some power back from their work situations however controlling these may be. Thus, the existence of agency among workers should not be seen as evidence that there are not issues to be addressed and, consistent with this, the presence of exploitation and harm does not usually render the victim completely powerless. The issue is about the balance between control and agency, and one's ability to avoid and escape exploitation and harm (see Chapter Seven).

Data sources

This book draws upon a range of data sources for inspiration. At the start of each chapter a poem from the perspective of a low-wage hospitality worker is presented. These poems come from Jenny Wrangborg's collection (Wrangborg, 2013) published in Swedish entitled 'Kitchen' (translated into English by Freke Räihä). The poems draw on Jenny's own experience of working in low-paid positions in the Swedish, Norwegian and Canadian hospitality sectors. They offer an alternative narrative to the book, still drawing out themes associated with work-based control, exploitation and harm but in a way that is designed to complement the main academic text. The issues raised in the poems are personal to Wrangborg but at the same time capture broader issues of workplace disempowerment that are key to understanding why workers, often willingly, accept conditions that severely constrain human flourishing. The poems also hint at the division between public and private self that so many workers wrestle with as they perform tasks in conditions which are exploitative or harmful.

Alongside the accompanying poetry, a number of chapters also contain within them testimony evidence from interviews with low-wage migrant workers. This evidence comes from a Joseph Rowntree Foundation (JRF) funded study into migrant labour in the UK food industry (Scott et al, 2012). The study collected 63 interviews from a range of nationalities working in the UK agriculture, food processing and food hospitality sectors. Workers were selected for interview based on them meeting specific 'forced labour' criteria and needed to have experienced some form of work-based harm or exploitation to qualify for interview. All interviews were conducted in the worker's mother tongue using 11 community/peer researchers (for a discussion of the methodology, see Scott and Geddes, 2015). The testimony evidence is used within the book largely to show how workers may be subject to different types and degrees of control and how this control can become excessive and oppressive (see also Scott, forthcoming).

The views of labour market stakeholders are also examined throughout the book. These were collected as part of another JRF study, but this time into the scope of forced labour in the UK (Geddes et al, 2013, Appendix 7). A total of 31 in-depth interviews were carried out with national-level stakeholders. This was supplemented by evidence from 44 local and regional level stakeholders via four focus groups (held in Boston, Bristol, Dundee and London).

Finally, the direct views of employers are also noted at a couple of points within the book (Chapter Five and Chapter Six). These views were gathered as part of a Nuffield Foundation grant (Number SGS/33876.01) which involved 37 in-depth interviews during 2007–09. The interviews covered a total of 30 horticultural salad growers/processors across England. All 30 companies relied upon migrant workers, mainly but not exclusively from central and eastern Europe, to get the harvest in. The interviews were focused on the demand for temporary migrant labour and covered ten themes. The results from this employer-centred research have already been widely published (Scott, 2013a; 2013b; 2013c; 2015a) and so they are used only sparingly within the book.

Outline of the book

The primary aim of this book is to explore the problem of labour exploitation via a social harm perspective. The book is structured in recognition of this aim. The first priority is to identify the nature of the different, potentially problematic, work-orientated controls that now surround labour. The second priority is to visit and review the key debates that exist with respect to these controls and the questions of whether they can be said to be exploitative and harmful. The third priority is to examine the different approaches and options available to the scholar wanting to develop solutions to worker exploitation and harm. Overall, this approach is informed by an underlying recognition that legal perspectives around worker control, exploitation and harm are flawed in the way that they minimise and residualise the problem. To this end, my argument is simple: it is time to focus on labour exploitation in a broad sense and to start with an awareness of this larger problem before focusing attention, as has become fashionable, on particular fragments of severely exploited labour.

The remainder of this book is divided into eight chapters. Chapter Two outlines the different manifestations of work-based harm. It argues that, although one might be tempted to focus on extremes, such as slavery, that it is important to think of exploitation as a 'continuum'. This more nuanced approach leads one away from criminology, and the notion of criminal employers *per se*, to consider, in addition, the broader political economic context within which controls over workers are being developed and deployed. The continuum approach also underlines the point that problems can often be constructed in particularly narrow ways; sometimes to serve the interests of capital and sometimes simply out of a pragmatic response to the limitations of the criminal justice system. Whatever the reason, the chapter argues that it is time to look at the broad mechanics of worker control, mechanics that mean those conventionally defined as 'victims' by the law constitute just one exploited group among many.

Chapter Three contends that we can learn from history with respect to how best to address labour exploitation and associated work-based harm. Most obviously, there are limitations for those seeking to emancipate labour through radical action alone. History, it will be argued, shows the importance of incremental change within overall political–economic structures that, crucially, can be and have been modified. Eight particular lessons of history are emphasised that show both the historic successes, and failures, of those seeking to resist and tackle labour exploitation and work-based harm. These lessons are intended to help one consider the saliency of the contemporary solutions to work-based control, exploitation and harm discussed in Chapter Eight.

Chapters Four to Six focus on work-based controls of different forms and types. The aim is not to identify controls that are always exploitative and always harmful. Instead, the aim is to profile potentially problematic, largely non-coercive and legal controls, that when used in certain combinations and with certain degrees of intensity can be exploitative and cause harm. Chapter Four reviews controls that are direct in the sense that they are specifically and explicitly used within workplaces to discipline labour. Four direct controls are identified: targets, monitoring and surveillance; endemic job insecurity; bullying and mobbing; and excessive hours. All of these are designed to help employers maximise returns from investment in labour and to make the uncertain purchase of labour power more reliable than it might otherwise be.

Employers do not always use direct sanctions against their staff in order to make them into 'good' workers. In many workplaces, it is clear that more complex feedback loops operate to control labour and maximise returns on investment. Chapter Five outlines five particular ways in which an employer can control labour indirectly within a given workplace. First, workers may be kept at arm's-length through the use of labour market intermediaries (LMIs) and sub-contracting arrangements. Second, workers' poverty and indebtedness can tie them to a particular employer and many employers use financial means to ensure loyalty and deference. Third, employers can establish particular workplace norms (such as a long-hours culture) that regulate behaviour without the need for direct control. Fourth, workers are often disciplined by virtue of what happens to fellow workers who step out of line: something referred to in the book as disciplining by proxy. Fifth, layers of bureaucracy exist within any workplace that ensure conformity without the need for direct sanction. In all of these instances, the employer is not actually disciplining a given worker through a direct negative sanction *per se*, but the employer is ensuring worker obedience via indirect means.

In Chapter Six the question considered is whether it is possible to produce and reproduce 'good' workers outside of the immediate employer–employee relationship and beyond the workplace. In essence, can wider structures be used to control workers and would-be workers that serve the interests of capital in general rather than a single employer in particular? The task of the chapter is to convince the reader that this is possible and that, in various ways, social, political, economic, legal and cultural structures help to produce and reproduce 'good' workers. Five examples of exogenous control are discussed, relating to: reduced ontological security; persistent inequality; workers' nuanced legal statuses; cultural and societal norms; and, human enhancement.

Having reviewed three types of worker control, in Chapters Four, Five and Six (see Table 1.3), the book moves on to consider questions of exploitation and specifically how one defines what is acceptable and what is unacceptable employer control. It is argued, in Chapter Seven, that coercion is only a small component in unacceptable employer behaviour and that there are various reasons why workers experience exploitation and harm without force being ostensibly present. The task of defining non-coercive exploitation is then embarked upon. One strategy is to identify what is defined as decent quality work and to then problematise employment falling outside this definition. Another strategy is to look for evidence of harmful outcomes, physical and/ or psychological. Additionally, the knowledge, intent and motives of an employer are also key to determining culpability and apportioning blame for exploitation and harm. The chapter ends by critically examining legal exemptions where force and coercion is permissible by law.

Chapter Eight is the penultimate chapter and has the task of identifying and evidencing various approaches to reducing work-based exploitation and harm. The most prevalent approaches are the national and transnational legal baselines that outlaw things such as slavery, forced labour, human trafficking, child labour and so on. These baselines are very valuable tools in providing the world with basic safety-net protections. However, labour exploitation is much more complex than these safety-nets generally allow for and involves systems of non-coercive control that are often entirely legal. Solutions to exploitation and harm are, therefore, needed that are beyond legal baselines and tied to a social harm agenda. These solutions may involve the modification of capitalism and/or a change in the power relations between labour and capital, with the two obviously related.

The final concluding chapter (Chapter Nine) draws together the analysis. It identifies the key deficiencies in the dominant criminological approach to problematising employment. The argument is that this approach only works as part of a larger and more critical labour exploitation and work-based harm perspective. Such a perspective is mapped out throughout the book and it is hoped it will inspire further research into legal and non-coercive employment relationships that are, nevertheless, problematic.

Table 1.3: Some contemporary facets of work-based control

Type of control	Facets
Direct (Chapter 4)	Targets, monitoring and surveillance
	Endemic job insecurity
	Bullying and mobbing
	Excessive hours
Indirect (Chapter 5)	Labour market intermediaries
	Poverty and debt
	Norms, expectations and workplace culture
	Disciplining by proxy
	Management by bureaucracy
Exogenous (Chapter 6)	Reduced ontological security
	Persistent inequality
	Workers' nuanced legal statuses
	Cultural and societal norms
	Human enhancement

Equals

The greatest weariness
does not come from manual labour,
the bottle trays lifted up narrow aisles,
muscles screaming of the burden
during impossible balancing acts
with the dishes through the café

it is not the steam from the ovens
the dull knives
or the slippery floors that hurts the most

the labour does not consist of
cooking the food or serving the guests

no, it is the
manager's words
after weeks of unpaid overtime

the gazes
from the affluent
ladies

and countless smiles
that hide the fact
that there is no hope that
we will ever
meet as equals

TWO

The labour exploitation continuum

The purpose of this chapter is to outline the various forms of labour exploitation that exist. At the extreme end of the 'continuum' (Andrees, 2008; Skrivánková, 2010; McGrath, 2012; Strauss, 2012; Lewis et al, 2015a; 2015b; Strauss and McGrath, 2017) there is worker fatality both at work and through work. There are then extreme forms of non-fatal harm, including: chattel slavery; modern slavery; forced labour; human trafficking; and child labour. All of these extremes have criminal–legal frameworks associated with them that are designed to minimise their prevalence. Often, however, these criminal–legal frameworks are either inadequate or are not enforced, and so extreme forms of exploitation and harm go unpunished. Moreover, a great deal of exploitation and harm, as argued in the introduction, goes on above these criminal–legal baseline definitions. This book, is particularly interested in the labour exploitation continuum that includes, but is certainly not limited to, illegal employer practice.

Fatalities at work

Death at or through work is perhaps the most obvious starting point for one interested in social harm (see also Slapper, 1999; Pemberton, 2015, 1). The problem, however, is that official statistics 'must be treated sceptically' (Tombs, 1999, 364). In the case of the UK, for example, it has been estimated that workplace fatalities are around five times more than the rate officially recorded (Tombs, 1999, 345).

Data is often simply not fit for purpose and the chronic under-reporting of workplace fatalities has its routes within a particular political–economic context, whereby the emphasis has very much been on de-regulation and on only exceptional employer criminalisation (Slapper and Tombs, 1999; Tombs, 2007; 2008; Tombs and Whyte, 2010). The onus, to a large extent, and across a range of countries, is on employers, industrial sectors, labour markets and supply chains 'self-regulating'. Associated with this, there is a commensurate discourse around the 'burdens' of regulation and a pressing need to reduce these burdens to a minimum. Clearly related to this has been the neoliberal undermining of external state action, on the one hand, and internal union organising on the other. Thus, even worker fatalities need not always enter the realm of official statistics and, even when they do, the criminalisation of the employer responsible is unlikely (Slapper and Tombs, 1999). For instance, the offence of corporate manslaughter in the UK led to only two convictions between 1965 and 2000, despite 20,000 deaths (Slapper, 1999).

In terms of how widespread worker fatalities are, and notwithstanding the problems of accurate and reliable data collection and recording, the ILO estimates that: 2.3 million people die every year through their work; that there is a worker death every 15 seconds; and that every 15 seconds 153 workers have a work-related accident. Financially, this means that: 'more than 4% of the world's annual GDP is lost as a consequence of occupational accidents and diseases' (ILO, 2015).

Some of the best international comparative statistics available come from the EU and Eurostat (HSE, 2014a; 2014b).[1] Table 2.1 shows annual and average standardised fatality rates (per 100,000 workers) for the 2006–11 period, covering selected EU member states. The EU-15 (the 15 pre-2004 EU member states) average in the 2006–10 period was 1.85 fatalities per 100,000 workers. Although this figure is likely to have risen with recent EU enlargements, the long-term EU trend is downward with respect to workplace fatalities (HSE, 2014b, 2). Global data on fatal occupational injuries is also available through

Table 2.1: Level of workplace fatalities in selected EU member states

Selected EU country	Standardised fatality rate (2011, per 100,000 workers)	Average (2006–10, per 100,000 workers)
Latvia	4.43	3.19
Lithuania	3.77	4.00
Romania	3.21	5.14
Czech Republic	2.90	1.81
Portugal	2.77	4.42
France	2.74	2.13
Spain	2.16	2.48
Italy	1.50	2.12
EU-15 Average	1.39	1.85
Germany	0.94	1.30
UK	0.74	0.91
Slovakia	0.68	0.21
Netherlands	0.63	1.22

Source: HSE (2014a, pp 7–9; 2014b)

the ILO though, once again, a certain degree of caution is required when making international comparisons (see Hämäläinen et al, 2009).

In some cases, worker fatalities are cruel accidents that no one could have predicted. In other instances, they are a result of employer negligence. With respect to the focus of this book – on work-based control, exploitation and harm – this is a very important distinction. Fatalities at work become an issue for the book only when workers have been forced to take, or have let others take, unnecessary health risks because of the controls exerted over them from both the individuals and the institutions they serve. In other words, while tragic, workplace fatalities *per se* do not always indicate that there is a problem of excessive and oppressive control.

Recently, two particularly tragic events have propelled the issue of work-based harm into the public spotlight. First, on 24 April 2013 the Rana Plaza complex in the Savar district of Dhaka, Bangladesh collapsed. There were 3,100+ workers in the building at the time and over 1,100 of these workers died. This was no accident. The day before the collapse cracks had appeared in the building and it was evacuated for a short time, before then being declared safe. Workers, on as little as €38 per month, were threatened with pay cuts unless they returned. Reasons for the cracks included: the building being constructed on unsuitable terrain; the building's use shifting from commercial to industrial without appropriate checks; three upper floors being added without a permit; overcrowding; and, the use of sub-standard materials in building construction. Attention has focused mainly on the link between an unsafe building and the associated negligence of the building's owners and government inspectors. In addition, some responsibility has also been directed towards the 28 western brands being supplied through Rana Plaza. These brands apparently upped their volume requirements and reduced the margins paid to suppliers in an attempt to increase both the supply of, and demand for, their clothing.

This industrial strategy has been premised on a 'double win'. On the one hand, there is Bangladesh's growing working population and need for employment: in 2004 there were 2 million workers in Bangladesh's 4,000 factories but by 2013 there were 4 million workers in 5,600 factories (Burke, 2014). On the other hand, there is the western consumer's love of cheap branded fashion. The problem is that this industrial system – premised on mass cheap labour and businesses operating to higher volumes with falling profit margins – can be harmful. On 1 May 2013 Pope Francis linked what had happened at Rana Plaza to modern slavery:

'A headline that really struck me on the day of the tragedy in Bangladesh was "Living on €38 a month". That is what the people who died were being paid. This is called slave labour. Today in the world this slavery is being committed against something beautiful that God has given us – the capacity to create, to work, to have dignity. How many brothers and sisters find themselves in this situation! Not paying fairly, not giving a job because you are only looking at balance sheets, only looking at how to make a profit. That goes against God!' (quoted in Pitta, 2015)

The issue of having dignity at work and being employed as more than a figure (employee number) linked to another figure (profit) is something that goes to the heart of this book and underlines the reason for focusing on the relationship between work-based control, exploitation and harm. In the case of Rana Plaza, these controls over workers were financial (low pay) and psychological (job insecurity) and they meant that those doing the hiring and firing at the factory, and beyond, could effectively operate without appropriate regard for workers' wellbeing. Moreover, the workers were not in a position to reduce the risks that they faced, even though these risks were known to be excessive before the tragedy occurred.

A little over a year on from Rana Plaza another large-scale employment tragedy struck that was also widely covered in the global mass media. On 13 May 2014, there was a fire at the Soma mine in Turkey leading to the death of 301 miners. As with Rana Plaza, this tragedy was no isolated accident. There had been miners' protests in Turkey in 2013 over working conditions and, following on from this, the opposition requested a Parliamentary Inquiry into the mines around Soma in 2014, but this was rejected by the ruling AKP (Justice and Development Party). Immediately after the disaster, the Prime Minister Recip Tayyip Erdogan said: 'Explosions like this in these mines happen all the time. It's not like these don't happen elsewhere in the world' (14 May 2014). In trying to underplay the fatalities – that made Soma the worst industrial 'accident' in modern Turkish history – the Prime Minister drew criticism from those who noted both the inaction of regulators (who had visited the mine in March 2014) and the closeness between the mine owner (Soma Holdings) and the ruling AKP (see, for example, Erimtan, 2014).

The Soma mine had entered private hands in 2005 as part of a wider coalfield privatisation programme. This programme signalled a fall in the cost of coal and also the rising importance of Turkish coal within

Turkey. It is this specific structural economic backdrop, that appears to have had a detrimental impact upon miners' working conditions, within which the events of 2014 need to be embedded. Alongside this, Turkey in general has lax regulation and low levels of regulatory adherence. What is interesting about Soma is that, following the Prime Minister's attempt to underplay the tragedy, 45 managers and employees in the mine have been brought to trial, with eight senior managers facing murder charges. However, some argue that questions should also be asked in Turkey around the failings of the labour inspectorate, the links between private companies and the AKP ruling party, and the motives behind, and beneficiaries of, the 2005 privatisation of the Soma coalfield.

In both the Rana Plaza (Bangladesh, Manufacturing) and Soma (Turkey, Mining) tragedies the death of workers resulted not out of chance but out of neglect, and the fact that workers were too weak to contest this downward spiral of neglect. In both cases too, it has subsequently become difficult to pin-point exactly who, and what, is to blame for the workplace fatalities. Both examples in this respect are indicative of the contemporary workplace where the pressures facing workers, financial and beyond, come from systems of control and responsibility that are as complex as they are fragmentary. Moreover, it is clearly not enough to leave workers' safety to nation-state regulatory regimes, given that in both Rana Plaza and Soma regulators were evident but failed to have the necessary 'teeth' to prevent mass workplace fatalities, that were certainly not unexpected. At the same time the potential of the 'Corporate Social Responsibility' (CSR) agenda (see Chapter Eight) to fill any state regulatory void also appears unfulfilled (Lund-Thomsen and Lindgreen, 2014).[2]

Overall, then, fatalities at work are all too often about social harm and this is as true in the developed world as it is in the developing world. It is important, therefore, to ask questions about the political, economic, legal and cultural *milieus* within which tragedies occur. Related to this, death at work (and indeed lesser forms of abuse) is all too often explained by both an unscrupulous employer *and* a wider structural context.

Fatalities through work

Not all work-based fatalities are caused directly at work and within the workplace. Employee suicides are the main form of indirect fatality. Data on these horrific events, that are often isolated and very difficult to link to work-based harm, is incredibly patchy and work-based suicides only really come to light when apparent 'clusters' emerge around a given firm or single work site. The most obvious recent cluster occurred at Foxconn's manufacturing factories in China (Chan and Pun, 2010).[3] Foxconn is a Taiwanese company employing over 1.4 million Chinese workers with a $3.2 billion annual profit (2013) and a CEO worth an estimated $5.5 billion (Chan et al, 2013). The company, in other words, is big and the profits it makes are commensurate with its size. Notwithstanding its size and profitability, Foxconn has also come to light because it supplies Apple and Apple posted a record $18 billion quarterly profit in January 2015 with its Chief Executive's pay more than doubling in 2014 to $9.22 million per annum (Rushe, 2015). Money for these companies, and Apple in particular, appears plentiful.

In light of the above, whether or not the attempted suicides (an estimated 18 in 2010) and the actual suicides (said to be 27 between 2010 and 2013) of Foxconn workers in China represents a genuine statistical cluster (the company employs 1.4 million people in China) is to an extent an academic question. The real issue is that Foxconn has experienced suicides at a time of record profits and that, during this time, working conditions have apparently intensified, arguably driven by Apple.

To elucidate, the main concerns around the Foxconn suicides have been that they have occurred at a time when the pace of work has risen and that they are related to the use of labour market intermediaries and a largely migrant workforce housed in barrack-style accommodation. To a large degree, the experience of Foxconn workers conforms to what Rogaly (2008a) has termed an 'intensification of workplace regimes' and it appears that some workers have felt that the only way to contest such intensification has been suicide.

The pace of work at Foxconn appears to be severe and relentless. Workers have seen productivity targets rise, they are set hourly quotas against these, they are watched and monitored very closely, conversations are limited, and shifts are routinely 12 hours long (SACOM, 2011; China Labor Watch, 2012). The driving force behind such labour force discipline has been productivity and efficiency. In one factory, for instance, there were 150 workers assembling 2,000 computers per day in 2006, but by 2011 the same number of workers were assembling 3,500 computers. True, much of this efficiency is down to automation, but there has also been a 'dramatically increased intensity of work' (China Labor Watch, 2012, 4).

Other than the increased pace of work, the second big issue has been the use of labour market intermediaries or what are called 'labour dispatch companies' in China. These companies create a third-party contractual arrangement with workers so that they become at least one step removed from the employer/employee workplace relationship. The arrangement effectively means that workers' employers (the labour dispatch companies) are not responsible for the pay and conditions that ultimately emerge. The workers are contractually obligated to their dispatching company, but this company cannot affect pay and conditions. Moreover, the dispatch company will post workers to a site on an 'as and when needed' basis and so, as well as the chain of command being more convoluted, employment security is often also lower. Further, it is the case that dispatched workers, even when doing the same job as those directly employed, are treated more harshly, with lower wages, poorer benefits and a greater pace of work (China Labor Watch, 2012, 11).

Both the growing pace of work and the use dispatched workers have been highlighted as reasons why China's Foxconn workforce has experienced unease and frustration and why, for some, this has translated into stress, depression, self-harm and, for a few, suicide. The workforce is largely migratory and often housed in tied accommodation, as part of what Lucas et al (2013) terms an 'all-encompassing...total institution structure', and it is among this group that recent Foxconn preventative attention has been directed. In 2011–12 suicide nets and fences were widely installed. Labelled '*ai xin wang*', which translates as 'nets of a loving heart', these are 10ft high wire fences (on the roofs) and 15ft wide nets (at the base of buildings).

The onus has been very much on suicide as a problem among the workforce rather than as a problem related to the intensification of working regimes. In a similar vein, an 'Anti-Suicide Pledge' was established that workers were expected to sign. The pledge included the following text relating to workers' own responsibilities: 'In the event of non-accidental injuries (including suicide, self-mutilation and so on), I agree that the company has acted properly in accordance with relevant laws and regulations, and will not sue the company.' In the face of protest, this pledge was eventually dropped. Instead, social workers, doctors and spiritual healers were brought in to help stressed and depressed workers.

What is interesting about all the above is that work-based harm has been linked by Foxconn (and Apple) to the individual worker and his/her own personal failings. Structural questions, especially those around inequality between workers and managers, and between different parts of product value chains, have not been visited to any concerted degree. As Table 2.2 makes clear, the money filtering through to Chinese labour from Apple–Foxconn is a paltry 1.8% of total value (for an iPhone in 2011). Additionally, the direction of change – towards the intensification of workplace regimes and associated need for greater and/or more nuanced worker control – has not been problematised or halted. In other words, blame and responsibility has been devolved down the global value chain onto the workers: and even onto workers once they are dead.

Table 2.2: Distribution of value for the Apple iPhone, 2011

Part of global value chain	Per cent share
Apple profits	58.5
Materials	21.9
Suppliers' profits	14.3
Non-China manufacturing labour	3.5
China manufacturing labour	1.8

Source: Chan et al (2013, p 107); Kraemer et al (2011, p 5)

In addition to worker suicides, it is also occasionally true that employees are killed outside of the workplace by employers or by the state. This usually occurs when workers protest against pay or conditions and these protests turn violent. A recent example of this occurred in South Africa in 2012, when striking miners from the platinum mine at Marikana (80 miles north of Johannesburg) were shot at by police. A total of 34 miners were killed and 78 injured.

Lonmin, the British company that owns the mines at Marikana, were involved along with the South African government in the subsequent 'Marikana Commission of Inquiry'. This reported in 2015 and found that the trade unions did not do enough to prevent worker violence in the lead up to the massacre. The Inquiry found no government or corporate actor responsible for the massacre and there was no compensation for victims' families. Controversially, the South African deputy president at the time (Cyril Ramaphosa) was a Lonmin mine board member and this, among other issues, caused some to question the independence of an Inquiry looking into the actions of the state and Lonmin (Bell, 2016; Munusamy, 2015). Once again, this case underlines the fact that where harm arises through work, blame is often fixed in particular directions and away from dominant interest groups. A focus on social harm, however, inevitably challenges this kind of response.

Non-fatal work-based harm

Fatalities at work and fatalities through work are, mercifully, rare. Instead, for most victims, work-based harm manifests itself more subtly. Thus, one may well feel most anger towards work that kills, but there is a danger that in focusing only on worst-case scenarios equally problematic forms of work-based control are overlooked.

To use an historic example, slavery did involve worker fatalities, especially during the middle passage, but the issue people had with slavery was about the conditions people endured in their working and 'private' lives, and the lack of decency and freedom in both. Slavery has been described as 'social death' (Patterson, 1982) and debates around abolition were, arguably, less driven by the issue of worker fatality and more the product of deep moral and philosophical objection to the excessive, oppressive and exploitative control of workers both at work and in their private lives (if they had any). It is for this reason that this book focuses on worker control and why, while it is concerned with worker fatality, this tragic phenomenon is positioned at the extreme end of a much larger labour exploitation continuum.

The question that follows, then, is what does this continuum look like beyond fatalities at and through work? An obvious way to introduce the labour exploitation continuum is to review the main (criminal–legal) terminology used within the literature. The first, and most commonly used, term with respect to the excessive, oppressive and exploitative control of workers is 'slavery' both chattel slavery, from a largely historical perspective (see for example Meltzer, 1993), and, in contemporary society, what has been termed modern slavery (see for example Craig et al, 2007). Beyond slavery, there are a number of other closely related terms such as forced labour, human trafficking and child labour. Although often used interchangeably (Strauss, 2012; Box 2.1) these different terms nevertheless capture different types of worker control, exploitation and harm.

Box 2.1: Varied use of terminology: the case of the UK

Terms pertaining to excessive and oppressive worker control, and therefore work-based harm, have been variously used in the UK and this, some would argue confusion, is reflected in recent legislation:

1. The UK Immigration and Asylum (Treatment of Claimants etc.) Act 2004 refers to 'trafficking' and 'exploitation' (drawing on Article 3 of the United Nations Protocol to Prevent, Suppress and Punish Trafficking in Persons, Especially Women and Children);
2. Section 71 of the 2009 Coroners and Justice Act refers to 'forced labour' (drawing on Article 4 of the 1950 European Convention on Human Rights)
3. The 2015 Modern Slavery Act refers largely to 'slavery' and also to 'exploitation'.
4. The 2016 Immigration Act refers to 'abuse' and 'exploitation' in its creation of the new 'Gangmasters and Labour Abuse Authority' (GLAA).

Chattel slavery

For large parts of modern history the idea that humans can be owned and traded like animals has prevailed (Black, 2011, 14). Pseudo-science has sometimes been used to justify this now, largely debunked, formal idea of slavery. The idea of there being a natural order, with some men masters and others slaves (Meltzer, 1993, 5), was key to the justification, and hierarchies were premised on ideas of breeding and inferior/superior races. In short, the theory of 'polygenism' (albeit in different guises) prevailed exactly at the time when Europeans were seeking to conquer other territories and peoples. Polygenism was associated with an 'othering' of non-white 'races' who were said to be of a different 'breed' and therefore legitimate targets for conquest and enslavement: though the term 'slave', ironically, actually has white European origins from the Slavic people (Slavs) of central and eastern Europe who were once commonly enslaved within southern Europe.

Looking beyond the pseudo-scientific justifications for slavery, it is clear that the conventional 'chattel' form of slavery is much less prevalent now than in the past. Chattel slavery, based on the possession of an individual, has been abolished and reinstated many times throughout history, but the last big push – to abolish Colonial slavery – began in sixteenth-century Spain and then eventually spread throughout Europe and North America.

Chattel slaves in Colonial times, under plantation capitalism, had no separate social identity and no workplace or civic rights. They could not profit from their own labour. Most could not marry or, if this was allowed were prevented from choosing their spouse. They were also totally dependent upon their owners and their bondage was life-long and usually hereditary. The last country to outlaw chattel slavery was Oman in 1970, though the practice does continue in some, largely pre-capitalist, labour markets in parts of Africa. Mauritania, for instance, is usually cited in the literature as being the last outpost as far as traditional chattel slavery is concerned, and it is estimated that, out of a total population of 3.2 million in 2007, there were 1 million enslaved (Black, 2011, 240).

Modern slavery

The fact that traditional forms of chattel slavery have largely disappeared since the Abolitionist movement is certainly very positive and marks considerable progression, especially when positioned in an historic perspective. Nonetheless, it is clear that one of the reasons for the success of the Abolitionist movement was the fact that a new stage in capitalist development was emerging at the time of this movement, and indeed was facilitated by its very success. The shift I am referring to is from conventional plantation capitalism (involving the triangular slave trade) to colonial, and then onto post-colonial, capitalism. This shift enabled power to be amassed, and projected, in ways other than through enslavement. Put another way, capitalism became more progressive following the outrages stirred up by the Abolitionist movement, but, crucially, this movement succeeded only because capitalism was able to find ways to control workers that did not require actual legal ownership or physical enslavement. Black (2011, 255), for instance, notes: 'the often cynical merger of anti-slavery with imperialism' and this is why, in contemporary worker research, scholars have argued that slavery may have been abolished but that, amoeba-like, slavery remains via new manifestations.

The 'modern slavery' argument advances this idea (focusing on things like debt-bondage and psychological holds over workers). It states that working relations, and specifically the balance of power between labour and capital, has simply evolved as capitalism has changed but that the pressures for worker control remain strong. Thus Abolitionists may have succeeded in problematising the worst outcomes of this pressure for control but forms of 'modern' slavery persist and these are not simply vestiges of an agrarian pre-modern society. One of the main strengths of the 'modern slavery' agenda is that it teaches us not to assume that in problematising and criminalising the worst forms of exploitation (that is, chattel slavery) that exploitation and harm *per se* will go away. Quite the opposite, there is often a displacement effect when actions are outlawed but the pressure for such actions remains.

Few would now dispute the view that the world is a better place following the abolition of slavery. Critical scholars, however, would counter that slavery never actually ended and that abolition cannot ever be a one-off victory or event. The battle against modern slavery, then, is different to the Abolitionist fight in that it is not a battle to be won forever, nor is it a battle that humanity can afford to lose. Moreover, once one recognises that modern slavery has emerged as a response to the problematisation and criminalisation of chattel slavery, so one can begin to see modern slavery in many different guises and across many different places and forms of capitalism.

One of the dangers of the slavery terminology is that it tends to be traditionally and conventionally understood – as chattel slavery – and so has assumed a special status that draws in only special or exceptional cases. To elucidate, other forms of worker exploitation are rendered relatively minor when compared against images of enslavement from the pre-Abolitionist era, that tend to be evoked by the use of the term 'slavery'. This residualising effect does seem to occur when the term modern or contemporary slavery is used by policy makers or by the press. There is a drive, it seems, to parcel together the very worst-case scenarios through the language used and this in turn, often implicitly, reduces the capacity for other forms of apparently 'lesser' exploitation to be contested (Lerche, 2007; Rogaly, 2008b; Davidson, 2010). Related to this, there has been a tendency to see modern slavery as something only occurring in the developing world that those in the developed world have the potential solve (Strauss, 2012, 141).

Kevin Bales (Bales, 1999; Walk Free Foundation, 2013; Datta and Bales, 2013; 2014; Walk Free Foundation, 2016) is perhaps the most ardent user of the term 'slavery' in a contemporary context (see also Craig et al, 2007; Miers, 2003). He has estimated that there are 27 million modern 'slaves' worldwide (Bales, 1999). Following this initial estimate Bales, via the Walk Free Foundation, has now produced the Global Slavery Index.[4] Published for the first time in 2013 this put the global estimate for modern slavery at 29.8 million (Walk Free Foundation, 2013). The 2016 updated index then put the number of people subject to some form of modern slavery at 45.8 million (Walk Free Foundation, 2016). The 45.8 million figure is considerably above the ILO's 'forced labour' estimate (see below); though both the 'modern slavery' and 'forced labour' calculations have been revised upwards by a considerable degree over recent years (see Table 2.3).

The 2016 Global Slavery Index contains details of the main countries where modern slavery is prevalent. One can look at prevalence in terms of absolute numbers or the proportion of the population who are victims of modern slavery (see Tables 2.4 and 2.5). In terms of the absolute measure, over half (58%) of all modern slavery victims are concentrated in just five countries. Aside from the number/proportion of people enslaved, the Walk Free Foundation also scores governments based on 98 good practice indicators taking into account factors such as the laws in place and the level of victim support in a given country (see Tables 8.1 and 8.2).

Table 2.3: Modern slavery and forced labour estimates compared

	First estimate	Latest estimate	Overall percentage increase	Average annual increase
Modern slavery	27 million (1999)	45.8 million (2016)	70	1.11 million per year
Forced labour	12.3 million (2005)	21 million (2014)	63	0.86 million per year

Source: Bales (1999); Walk Free Foundation (2016); ILO (2005a); ILO (2014).

Table 2.4: The absolute number of modern slavery victims (2016 estimate)

Country	Number of victims (million)	Proportion of population (%)
India	18.4	1.4
China	3.4	0.25
Pakistan	2.1	1.13
Bangladesh	1.5	0.95
Uzbekistan	1.2	3.97

Source: Walk Free Foundation (2016).

Table 2.5: The proportion of the population who are modern slavery victims (2016 estimates)

Country	Proportion of population (%)	Number of victims
North Korea	4.37	1.1 million
Uzbekistan	3.97	1.2 million
Cambodia	1.65	257,000
India	1.40	18.4 million
Qatar	1.36	30,000

Source: Walk Free Foundation (2016).

Forced labour

Most of the worlds employers now do not step over the traditional (chattel) slavery definitional Rubicon in the sense that they do not engage in the coercive control and confinement of workers. The problem, however, is that this traditional definitional Rubicon does still shape and flavour the use of the 'modern' and 'contemporary' slavery terms. In addition, these latter terms have often been rather loosely deployed to the extent that enforcement action against modern or contemporary slavery has not had a solid definitional, political or legal basis. The International Labour Organization (ILO) has attempted to widen the debate about contemporary worker control and resultant exploitation and harm beyond 'slavery' and has developed a very strong global agenda against what it terms 'forced labour' (ILO, 1998a; ILO, 2005a). Although this agenda has been criticised (Lerche, 2007; Rogaly 2008b), I would argue that it further builds on the progress made by the modern slavery discourse.

If modern slavery taught us that the Abolitionist victory was not an end-point, then the forced labour agenda has taught us a great deal about the practical power of a global criminal–legal baseline, or safety-net, to prevent a downward spiral in working conditions. The ILO 'Forced Labour Convention, 1930' (Convention Number 29) and 'Abolition of Forced Labour Convention, 1957' (Convention Number 105) outlaw forced labour and have garnered unprecedented global consensus.[5] These two conventions have been ratified by a record number of the world's nation-states (Convention Number 29: 177 countries; Convention Number 105: 174 countries) and, with this global consensus, an internationally robust forced labour definition has also emerged (see Box 2.2).

Box 2.2: The ILO definition of forced labour

In 2005 the ILO defined forced labour around six core indicators (ILO, 2005b, pp 20–1):

1. Physical or sexual violence or the threat of such violence
2. Restriction of movement of the worker
3. Debt bondage or bonded labour
4. Withholding wages or refusing to pay the worker at all
5. Retention of passports and identity documents
6. Threat of denunciation to the authorities

In 2011 the ILO subsequently expanded the list to eleven indicators (ILO, 2012a):

1. Physical or sexual violence
2. Restriction of movement
3. Debt bondage
4. Withholding of wages
5. Retention of identity documents
6. Intimidation and threats
7. Excessive overtime
8. Isolation
9. Abusive working and living conditions
10. Abuse of vulnerability
11. Deception

The above definition of forced labour means that there are particular indicators that can now be used to determine whether or not a person is a victim of exploitation but is not what one might traditionally and conventionally call a 'slave'. These indicators do have historic roots, however, and the forced labour definition is certainly reflective of both past and present forms of worker control. Under plantation and early imperial capitalism, for instance, there were large numbers of white indentured labourers who paid for their passage to the New World through years of subsequent labour, and were thus trapped in what today the ILO would term debt-bondage.

It is important when using the, now widely accepted, definition of forced labour that one takes into account the experiences of the worker in so far as he or she is likely to have experienced a number of indicators to different degrees. The issue of defining a forced labour situation, then, is about both the severity (for example, how much debt) and the combination of indicators experienced. It would be erroneous to conclude, for example, that a small amount of debt-based employment alone is sufficient for forced labour to occur. The six and eleven indicators in Box 2.2, therefore, should be seen as a guiding framework to enable case-by-case decisions to be made.

Since reigniting the fight against forced labour via the establishment of the 'Special Action Programme to Combat Forced Labour' (SAP-FL) in 2001 (ILO, 2005a), the ILO has provided various estimates of the scale of the problem globally (ILO, 2009a; 2012a; 2012b; 2012c; 2014) and the latest estimates from the organisation are summarised in Box 2.3. There are 21 million forced labour victims at any one time and with a global population of 7.3 billion (at the time of writing) this means that one person in every 348 in the world is experiencing forced labour.[6]

Interestingly, although forced labour was originally seen by the ILO as something of a problem in totalitarian states, most forced labour now occurs in the private economy and is no longer state sponsored, nor is it mainly sexual in nature as many assume.[7] For instance, Table 2.6 shows that there are 14.2 million victims of labour exploitation globally versus 4.5 million victims of sexual exploitation. It is also true that, although concentrated in Africa and Asia, forced labour occurs across both the developed and developing worlds. There are, for example, 1.5 million forced labour victims in the 'developed economies and EU' according to Table 2.6.

Finally, one has to be careful when making comparisons to distinguish between: 1) absolute numbers and (relative) rates of forced labour; and 2) the value of, and profits from, forced labour. In terms of the latter, in 2009, excluding forced sexual exploitation, the total costs of forced labour globally were put at US$21 billion: with the total amount of underpaid wages estimated to be US$19.6 billion and the remaining US$1.4 billion attributed to illegal recruitment fees (ILO, 2009a). More recently (in 2014), the ILO found that: 'the total illegal profits obtained from the use of forced labour worldwide amount to US$150.2 billion per year' (ILO, 2014, 13). This estimate excludes profits from the 2.2 million victims of state-imposed forced labour.[8] Table 2.7 breaks down these profits according to region, with forced labour most lucrative overall in the 'Asia and Pacific' region but, on a *per capita* basis, most lucrative in the 'developed economies and EU'.

Box 2.3: ILO estimates of the scale of forced labour (2014)

- 21 million people are victims of forced labour
- of the 21 million victims, 11.4 million are women and girls and 9.5 million men and boys
- 19 million victims are exploited by private individuals or enterprises and over 2 million by the state or rebel groups
- 4.5 million (of the 21 million) are victims of forced sexual exploitation
- forced labour in the private economy generates US$ 150 billion in illegal profits per year
- domestic work, agriculture, construction, manufacturing and entertainment are among the sectors most concerned
- migrant workers and indigenous minorities are particularly vulnerable to forced labour

Source: ILO (2014)

Table 2.6: The contemporary geography of forced labour, absolute numbers

Region	Sexual Exploitation	Labour Exploitation	State-Imposed Forced Labour	TOTAL	Prevalence Per 1000
Central and South Eastern Europe and Commonwealth of Independent States	300,000	1,100,000	200,000	1,600,000	4.2
Africa	800,000	2,500,000	400,000	3,700,000	4.0
Middle East	100,000	400,000	100,000	600,000	3.4
Asia and Pacific	2,500,000	7,900,000	1,200,000	11,700,000	3.3
Latin America and the Caribbean	400,000	1,200,000	200,000	1,800,000	3.1
Developed Economies and EU	300,000	1,000,000	200,000	1,500,000	3.1
Total	4,500,000	14,200,000	2,200,000	20,900,000	

Source: ILO (2014, p 17)

Table 2.7: The contemporary geography of the illegal profits of forced labour

Region	Total annual profits (US$ billion)	Annual profits per victim of forced labour (US$)
Central & South Eastern Europe & Russian Commonwealth of Independent States	18	12,900
Africa	13.1	3,900
Middle East	8.5	15,000
Asia and Pacific	51.8	5,000
Latin America and the Caribbean	12	7,500
Developed Economies and EU	46.9	34,800

Source: ILO (2014, pp 13–15)

Forced labour, like slavery, does continue to limit the problem of worker control and work-based harm and, in so doing, treats the problem as exceptional and apart from the mainstream capitalist system. Lerche (2007, 431) calls this the 'cocooning of the forced labour issue' which he argues 'makes it relatively safe for governments and international organisations to deal with'. Put another way, both the slavery and forced labour agendas have been progressive in different ways, but both have also failed to challenge the ways in which power flows through the capitalist system and the associated growing divide between labour and capital across developing and developed world economies. This is not to argue that new terms are necessarily needed, just that the language and definitions used to frame a problem do not always capture the full extent of the problem and, in fact, may actually be better off not attempting to do so.

What I mean here is that the ILO's work on forced labour must be taken in context and, while one can criticise it, the ILO must work in a particular way and must also be attentive to the wider international policy environment. It has certainly set a very progressive forced labour agenda, but this has occurred in a context where concerns for worker rights, at global and national levels, are generally very critically received. Most notably, the ILO of the 1980s and 1990s found itself struggling because labour rights did not sit easily alongside the prevailing neoliberal agenda. This agenda then began to thaw – a thawing evidenced through the 'post-Washington consensus' and the associated UN-led Millennium Development Goals and World Bank-led Poverty Reduction Strategy Papers (PRSP) – and the ILO's forced labour programme began. This did not emerge in isolation, however. The 1998 ILO 'Declaration on Fundamental Principles and Rights at Work' (see Box 2.4) was a central early development and it led to the establishment of the 'Special Action Programme to Combat Forced Labour' (SAP-FL) in 2001. Since 2001, and going against the grain of the 1980s and 1990s, the ILO has sought to develop a global approach to forced labour. This approach, though, is still dependent upon an international and national policy context that has thawed but not fully defrosted. In addition, the ILO's tripartite and non-confrontational approach means that in a world still dominated by neoliberal orthodoxy it is still unlikely to be able to respond to the criticism of Lerche (2007), Rogaly (2008b) and others (see Standing, 2010).

Box 2.4: The ILO's 1998 'Declaration on Fundamental Principles and Rights at Work'

The 1998 Declaration covers four fundamental principles and rights at work:

1. freedom of association and the effective recognition of the right to collective bargaining;
2. elimination of all forms of forced or compulsory labour;

3. effective abolition of child labour;

4. elimination of discrimination in respect of employment and occupation.

This declaration led to the development of the 'Special Action Programme to Combat Forced Labour' (SAP-FL) in 2001. SAP-FL put forced labour very squarely back on the global policy agenda and, perhaps most notably, made the point that forced labour was not simply state-imposed but also market-based.

Source: ILO (1998a)

Human trafficking

Since the millennium, human trafficking has arguably commanded the greatest policy attention of all the work-based harm issues. It is certainly where criminal–legal frameworks have been strongest and where victim protection/compensation has been most extensive related to these criminal–legal frameworks (for a pan-European review see Clark, 2013). This trend is related to a shift by the UN from focusing largely on protecting migrant workers' rights (having moved) – evidenced most clearly in the 1990 International Convention on the Protection of the Rights of All Migrant Workers and Members of Their Families – to protecting migrant workers before, during and after they move. In terms of the latter, 2000 saw the UN 'Convention Against Transnational Organised Crime' and three specific protocols, with two targeted at migrants: 1) the 'Protocol to Prevent, Suppress and Punish Trafficking in Persons, Especially Women and Children'; and 2) the 'Protocol Against the Smuggling of Migrants by Land, Air and Sea'.

These protocols – that became known as the Palermo Protocols – signalled the start of a concerted international effort to reduce both human trafficking and smuggling; but it was the former problem that has subsequently garnered most national and international policy and practitioner attention (see, for example, US Department of State, 2014). The Palermo trafficking protocol, for example, led to other transnational instruments such as the Council of Europe 'Convention on Action against Trafficking in Human Beings 2005' and the EU 'Directive on Preventing and Combating Trafficking in Human Beings 2011'. These have then been cascaded down into national anti-trafficking frameworks and approaches.

The now widespread anti-trafficking agenda is noteworthy in a number of respects. First, many today talk of trafficking and modern slavery in the same breath (Datta and Bales, 2013; US Department of

State, 2014, 29; McCarthy, 2014) and this elision gives the impression that trafficking is, or should be, at the heart of anti-slavery campaigning. It also links immigration very closely to modern slavery when, in fact, there is no reason to assume that this link should predominate. Second, the UN-initiated anti-trafficking agenda expressly uses the concept of 'exploitation'. Article 3 of the Palermo Protocol states that:

> Trafficking in persons shall mean the recruitment, transportation, transfer, harbouring or receipt of persons, by means of the threat or use of force or other forms of coercion, of abduction, of fraud, of deception, of the abuse of power or of a position of vulnerability or of the giving or receiving of payments or benefits to achieve the consent of a person having control over another person, for the purpose of exploitation. Exploitation shall include, at a minimum, the exploitation of the prostitution of others or other forms of sexual exploitation, forced labour or services, slavery or practices similar to slavery, servitude or the removal of organs.

In this vein, nation-states have included the notion of exploitation within their own specific anti-trafficking frameworks. The UK, for example, via the 2004 Immigration and Asylum (Treatment of Claimants) Act talks of 'trafficking for labour exploitation'. This use of exploitation as a term, and its specific criminalisation with respect to human trafficking, does not extend into other areas in the sense that international and national strategies tackling excessive and oppressive worker control and resultant work-based harm have tended to avoid the term (though see: FRA, 2015; BIS, 2016). Most still see exploitation as either too vague or broad a concept for it to be meaningful, or, they see it as potentially opening up a 'Pandora's box' that the current criminal–legal nomenclature has tried to avoid.

Why trafficking for labour exploitation has been more widely embraced than the problem of labour exploitation *per se*, and why modern slavery has been seen by many as largely a problem of human trafficking, are both questions that one may legitimately ask given how much resource and support has gone towards the fight against human trafficking post-Palermo. The answer may well be quite simple. The morally-infused anti-trafficking agendas have garnered widespread support because they facilitate other agendas, especially those trying to reduce immigration, prostitution and organised crime (Fitzgerald, 2012; 2016; Yea, 2015).[9] In terms of immigration control, for example, states can use the trafficking agenda to shift policy instruments upward and outward, which both improves control and also diffuses and deflects responsibility (Scott, 2015b).

Whatever the reason for the proliferation in concern over exploited trafficking victims, if not always labour exploitation *per se*, it is clear that states are seeing more and more trafficking cases and that they are increasingly ready to adopt a criminological perspective with regard to these. International data from the annual US *Trafficking in Persons* (TIP) report demonstrates this (see Tables 2.8 and 2.9). In 2008 there were a total of 5,212 prosecutions, 2,983 convictions and 30,961 identified trafficking victims: figures that had risen to 9,466, 5,776 and 44,758 respectively by 2013. However, what is interesting with this global data is that the trafficking agenda, at least when it enters the criminological domain, still seems more focused on sexual exploitation than labour exploitation. Most obviously, labour exploitation makes up only a very small proportion of total trafficking prosecutions and convictions (compare Tables 2.8 and 2.9). Thus, when discussing trafficking there is still a sense in which most attention is directed towards sexual rather than labour exploitation (for a critical perspective, see Agustin, 2007). Related to this, there is a danger that in linking terms like modern slavery with human trafficking that the problem of labour exploitation *per se* becomes artificially constructed, and confined to immigrants only (Davidson, 2010).

Table 2.8: The scale of global human trafficking, 2008–13 estimates, all cases

YEAR	Prosecutions	Convictions	Victims identified
2008	5,212	2,983	30,961
2009	5,606	4,166	49,105
2010	6,017	3,619	33,113
2011	7,909	3,969	42,291
2012	7,705	4,746	46,570
2013	9,460	5,776	44,758

Source: US Department of State (2014, p 45)

Table 2.9: The scale of global human trafficking, 2008–13 estimates, labour exploitation only

YEAR	Prosecutions	Convictions	Victims identified
2008	312	104	NA
2009	432	335	NA
2010	607	237	NA
2011	456	278	15,205
2012	1,153	518	17,368
2013	1,199	470	10,603

Source: US Department of State (2014, p 45)

Child labour

Child labour is the final component in the criminal–legal baseline approach to work-based harm. The ILO have sought to eradicate most forms of child labour and it is one of the four pillars of the 1998 'Declaration on Fundamental Principles and Rights at Work' (see Box 2.4). Following on from this, the ILO passed the convention on the 'Worst Forms of Child Labour, 1999' (Convention Number 182) that built on an earlier 'Minimum Age convention, 1973' (Convention Number 138). The former has been ratified by 179 out of 185 ILO member states (as of 2014) with the notable major exception of India (Phillips, 2013; Phillips et al, 2014).

The ILO (2010a) states that one child in every seven in the world can be classified as a child labourer equating to 215 million workers aged 5–17 years, with 115 million of these working in hazardous conditions (a surrogate for the worst forms of child labour). The geography of child labour is outlined in Table 2.10 with a clear absolute concentration in Asia and the Pacific and a relative concentration in Sub-Saharan Africa. Most forms of child labour involve unpaid agricultural work: only one in five child workers are paid; and 60% of child labour globally is in agriculture.[10]

Table 2.10: The geography of child labour

Region	Child labour population (million)	Proportion of children in child labour (%)
Asia and the Pacific	114	13.3
Latin America and the Caribbean	14	10
Sub-Saharan Africa	65	25.3
Other regions (Middle East and North Africa, the developed countries and the former transition economies of Eastern Europe and Asia)	22	6.7

Source: ILO (2010a)

Above the criminal–legal baselines

Preventing workers dying, preventing chattel slavery, preventing modern slavery, preventing forced labour, preventing human trafficking and preventing child labour, are all very laudable aims. They are each a totemic cause that galvanises opinion and are, if you like, the 'low-hanging fruit' (Standing, 2010, 312) and part of a 'motherhood and apple pie' (Anderson, 2007) moral politics around which most can agree. Who, for instance, would argue against any of the aims listed above? Unfortunately, however, it is only really the prevention of chattel slavery that has so far been accomplished. Some would argue, therefore, that scholars should stay focused on the above baselines to create a very basic 'Plimsoll line' for labour and ensure that the world's workers are protected from the very worst excesses of capitalism. To deviate, so the argument goes, would be to lose focus and to allow these various baselines to escape from view.

This is a persuasive argument that provides ammunition against the 'low hanging fruit' and 'motherhood and apple pie' criticisms of using totemic moral issues to protect workers. The problem is that the establishment of moral consensus and global labour market baselines are not, on their own, sufficient to prevent the excessive, oppressive and exploitative control of workers. They may be part of an approach towards this end, but much more work is required that is potentially more difficult in terms of forging a consensus. Put another way, linking worker exploitation to exceptional circumstances and/or what have been termed 'vestiges of pre-capitalist social relations' (Brass, 2004; 2014; Strauss, 2012, 137) is relatively straightforward. It is much more difficult, however, to define the problem in grander 'exploitation' and 'harm' terms; and this becomes even more difficult because, in enlarging the problem, one inevitably connects it to mainstream economic constellations and interests (see, especially, Lerche, 2007, 430–1; McGrath and Strauss, 2014). One also moves the problem from one associated mainly with the developing world, or developing world migrants, to one with a global basis and of global proportions.

So, an internationally agreed upon 'Plimsoll line' for labour is certainly a desirable aim given we have so far only really managed to tackle the issue of chattel slavery out of the morally totemic list above. Nevertheless, legal safety-nets for workers are unlikely to work, or will be over-worked, if left unconnected to broader problems of which they are a part. They can also create 'deserving and undeserving groups' (Skrivánková, 2010, 4). This is why many have advocated a 'continuum' approach, with problems such as modern slavery and forced labour seen as socially and politically constructed and positioned at the extreme end of the continuum. It is also why the focus of this book is not on one specific 'extreme' type, or term, related to worker exploitation. The aim is not to start with a problem, as already defined and measured (usually within a narrow criminological frame), but to start with the mechanisms and mechanics of contemporary control, inside and outside the workplace, that can sometimes combine to exploit and harm. This approach leaves open space for theoretical and conceptual debate as much as it leaves open the potential for a new language around worker control and work-based exploitation and harm that is 'beyond criminology' (Hillyard et al, 2004; Pemberton, 2015). It has emerged out of a recognition that certain literatures – those focused on modern slavery, forced labour and human trafficking in particular – have advanced our understanding of exploitation, but that they have also restricted the field of view with respect to defining the exact nature (scale, scope, processes, outcomes and so on) of the problem in different contexts and at different times.

Other than opening up the debate over what exactly may be labelled exploitation, a focus on work-based control and harm also gets to the core of the problem that, even under chattel slavery, coercion and force has not always been required. Instead, there is usually a great deal of variety, subtlety and nuance with respect to worker abuse and exploitation. Most contemporary workers, most of the time, are presented with a series of options and try, as best as possible, to take the least-worst route. Choice exists, in this sense, as does apparent free will. The issue, however, is the nature of the choice; and it is this that determines whether free will is in fact evident and meaningful.

If we are free to choose the nature of our exploitation, but not to escape this, then to what extent is that really free will? Moreover, we may feel free to choose but not actually be conscious of the constraints acting upon this apparent freedom. Thus, in a number of respects one needs to move away from the idea of force and coercion to the notion of control. The logical next step then is to define work-based controls.

Put in a slightly different way, slavery has not always been absolute, nor has it always been crudely expressed. Moreover, after abolition the controls on many workers have become increasingly subtle and sophisticated, to the extent that many often cannot see them and are even not conscious of them. This means that a criminal–legal focus on very obviously contemporary 'slave-like' conditions, as has been the recent fashion among policy-makers in particular, poses a danger: that scholars miss large elements of work-based control and overlook large numbers of people who have experienced exploitation and harm. Alongside this, many who experience exploitation and many who experience harm do not align with the criminological perspective of the global baseline approach. As Pemberton (2007, 33) notes: 'The role of the social harm perspective is to help create the discursive spaces where the marginalized can articulate their lived experiences of harm without persistent reference to the notion of "crime"'.

There are two basic ways in which exploitation and harm can be measured statistically beyond the fatality rates and/or baseline definitions reviewed above. The first concerns actual outcomes and the levels of ill-health, physical or psychological, among workers that can be attributed to their role as workers. The second concerns workers' views over the risks they face through employment with respect to their health.

In terms of the former, Eurostat data draws on labour force sample surveys to gauge non-fatal work-related ill-health across the EU. Crucially, this data is contingent upon workers' own reporting and judgements with respect not just to their health but also to the link between this and their employment and associated working conditions. It also requires a worker to have actually taken sick leave in order for their work-related ill-health to be recognised. Latest figures, for 2007, show that 5.5% of EU-27 workers experienced work-related illness resulting in sick leave. The analogous figure for the UK was 2.9%, Germany 3.9%, Spain 4.2% and Poland 11.8% (HSE, 2014b, 4). This data relates to a 12-month period only and only to illness that resulted in actual sick leave, the taking of which is often shaped by specific temporal and spatial contingencies (recessions, employment contracts, social norms, benefits rates, doctors' attitudes and so on). Not only, then, should national comparisons based on this data be embarked upon with caution, it is also the case that the apparent low rates of work-related illness would look much larger were a cumulative measure to be used and/or all illnesses recorded irrespective of whether formal sick leave is taken.

To combat the danger of underestimating the negative health implications of work, the European Working Conditions Survey (EWCS) in 2010 looked at workers' sense of fear and risk with respect to future health and safety. This measure, unlike those so far reviewed, deals with perceptions of harm rather than actual health outcomes, and so must be treated with a degree of caution but is nevertheless a very useful international comparative indicator when thinking about excessive, oppressive and exploitative work-based control. The latest European Working Conditions Survey shows that around 1 in 4 (24%) of EU-27 workers believe that their job risks their health and safety, with a range between 15% and 45% of workers (HSE, 2014b, 5).

Finally, beyond data relating to work-based harm directly, there are a host of indirect employment indicators available to compare the general labour market outcomes and conditions in different nation-states. The ILO and the OECD provide particularly usefully indicators that pertain in various ways to work-based control, exploitation and harm. These are summarised in Tables 2.11 and 2.12. They cover issues such as income inequality, temporary contracts, trade union membership, working time and so on. Their purpose is to give some indication of the grey area between slavery, on the one hand, and decent work on the other. They also allow comparisons to be made between states with respect to employment outcomes and employment policies.

Table 2.11: Pertinent OECD labour market indicators

Indicator	Source
Minimum to Medium Wage Ratio ($ full-time worker)	Earnings Domain
Real Minimum Wage (hourly $)	
Regulation of Individual and Collective Dismissal (regular contracts)	Strictness of Employment Protection Index
Regulation of Temporary Contracts	
Share of Involuntary Part-time Workers in Labour Force	Labour Force Statistics Domain
Temporary Employment as Share of all Employment	
Average Weekly Hours Worked	
Trade Union Density	Trade Union Domain
Working Very Long (50+) Hours (per week)	Better Life Index
Probability of Becoming Unemployed	

Source: http://stats.oecd.org/

Table 2.12: Pertinent ILO labour market indicators

Indicator	Source
Underemployment Rate	Employment Domain
Mean Weekly Hours Worked (per employed person)	Working Time Domain
Earnings Dispersion Among Employees	Earnings and Employment-Related Income Domain
Days Lost due to Occupational Injury	Occupational Injuries Domain
Frequency of Fatal Occupational Injury	
Frequency of Non-Fatal Occupational Injury	
Number of Inspectors	Labour Inspection Domain
Visits to Workplaces in Year	
Visits per Inspector	
Labour Inspectors per 10,000 employed persons	
Trade Union Density	Trade Unions and Collective Bargaining Domain
Collective Bargaining as % of Employees	
Employed Persons Below Nationally Defined Poverty Line	Working Poor Domain

Source: www.ilo.org/global/statistics-and-databases/lang--en/index.htm

Conclusion

It is clear that a criminological approach has been widely adopted towards tackling work–based exploitation and harm. This is a necessary and welcome component in the overall fight to reduce, rather than simply manage, exploitation and harm in the modern economy. Nevertheless, the criminological approach has failings and weaknesses even when faced with the starkest forms of work–based harm: such as death at/through work. Worker fatality statistics, for instance, underestimate the scale of the problem, not to mention the fact that employers are rarely prosecuted for death at/through work. As the benchmark report of the European Agency for Fundamental Rights (FRA, 2015) recently noted, there is a 'current climate of implicit acceptance of severe labour exploitation' (p3) and 'endemic impunity for those who perpetrate severe labour exploitation' (p90). Put another way, the criminological approach to exploitation and harm works in a *de jure* but not always a *de facto* sense.

Aware of this, the chapter has only cautiously welcomed the baseline approach to criminalising the worst forms of exploitation and harm. Not only does this approach suffer from an enforcement gap but, in emphasising the extremes of exploitation and harm, it can render lesser forms of abuse relatively unproblematic and even acceptable. There is also a great deal of work-based harm and exploitation above the criminal–legal baselines. Indeed, the very thrust of the social harm agenda is designed to illuminate these areas not covered by conventional notions of crime. Thus, it is vital that one looks at the problem of work-based exploitation and harm from the perspective of a labour exploitation continuum, rather than solely through legal baseline definitions.

The manager

We could hear the clatter from her keys all the way from the parking lot. She often stood in the kitchen stairs, looking down at us, examining our movements past each other behind the stands. The dance between the coffee machine, the shrimp sandwiches, the muffins and the teas.

Then suddenly, as if she stood in front of the levers to a large machine, she could open her mouth, say something about the speed of our movements, stretching for the speed controls and turning up the pace of the conveyor. Fully aware of our willingness to do a good job.

I can still hear those keys in the manager's voices at staff meetings, in the silence between the lines on the editorial pages and in my own voice when I, in the midst of the stress, ask the temp to please speed things up a bit.

THREE

Lessons of history

As noted in the previous two chapters, traditional approaches to work-based exploitation and harm tend to focus on criminal–legal 'extremes': on cases that are seen as the most deviant and abhorrent. The book is an attempt to move beyond this approach and to widen the definition and debate over what constitutes problematic worker treatment. To this end, in Chapters Four to Six the various ways in which workers may be subject to often legal and non-coercive control in order to make them 'good' and 'better' are mapped. Before embarking upon this endeavour, however, it is important to examine some lessons of history with respect to the control and emancipation of labour.

Specifically, this chapter focuses on eight particular lessons. These are purposefully selective. It is not possible within a book like this to provide a definitive history of work-based control, exploitation and harm. Collectively, the lessons of history show how progress towards reducing work-based exploitation and harm is possible and, indeed, that the world has moved on a long way towards this end. Nevertheless, they also show how difficult it often is to challenge established structures, systems and norms. Related to this, in many instances change has been gradual and incremental; though there are occasional cases (such as the abolition of slavery and development of the trade union movement) where paradigm shifts do occur.

Widespread social stratification

Throughout post-nomadic human history the settled societies that have developed have been stratified. This division, in various ways, has had direct consequences in terms of shaping peoples' employment experiences. Those at or nearest the bottom of the social order have tended to be most at risk of work-based control, exploitation and harm.

In pre-industrial societies access to land was key to determining one's social standing. Following the Norman invasion of England (post 1066), for instance, plots of land were divided roughly into the size of today's English counties. These were then given to the King's noblemen (Barons, Earls, Dukes and so on) who fought for him in battle. These 'Tenants in Chief' then divided the land up further to the Norman knights who had also fought in battle. Below these 'Lords of the Manor' were 'Freemen' who were bequeathed land (about 100 acres) by the Lords. Most of the population, though, were known as 'villeins' (which became a derogatory term) or 'serfs'; who were landworkers and were bound to a particular parcel of land and could be sold along with this land. This status was also hereditary (for a review of the villein/serf system, see Bailey, 2014).

In short, there was an elaborate system of social stratification designed to maintain order. The hierarchies also meant, however, that certain groups of people enjoyed more rights and freedoms than others and that the lives of certain groups were particularly precarious. There was also a cultural hierarchy accompanying this social stratification. Most obviously, the term 'villein' derives from the Latin *villanus* meaning a man employed at a Roman villa. However, while it refers to the feudal majority, it later came on to take on a derogatory meaning. Villein means ugly or naughty in French, rude in Italian, and semi-criminal in English. The corruption of the terms underlines the way in which entrenched class division is not just about a socio-economic divide but also about cultural hierarchy and language. Indeed, from a lofty socio-economic position it appears that throughout history (and to the present day) those less fortunate financially have also been deemed to be less worthy.

Going back much further than 1066, similar hierarchies existed in the Greek Empire. Once again the majority (Helot) population worked the land and supported the minority (Spartan) population. The system was again designed to preserve social order and depended on access to, and ownership of, scarce resources (usually land in the first instance). In both systems, there was extensive evidence of a link between socio-economic stratification, associated cultural hierarchies, and exploitation and harm. The Spartans, for example, were actually permitted at certain times to stalk and hunt the servile Helots in a practice known as *krypteia*.

Such systems of partition have not just been restricted to the class systems of Europe. The Dalits of India (also known as the untouchables or scheduled castes), for instance, show how the adage of 'divide and rule' is a global one. Moreover, the link between the Dalits' social status and employment experiences is an illuminating one within the context of this book. Although the doctrine of untouchability was officially abolished under India's 1950 constitution, the Dalits continue to suffer exploitation as a result of their historically enshrined status at the bottom of the Caste system. The term 'Dalit' actually means broken and ground down and the groups making up the scheduled castes are expected to do work that is degrading and impure and are avoided by society because of the belief that such work is polluting to the individual, mentally and physically.

Today 16.2% of India's population are Dalits.[11] In other words, several hundred million people are confined – because of the caste status inherited at birth – to less favourable occupations across India. What this means for many is a life of very hard work, starting as a child, often characterised by exploitation and debt bondage. The 'Sumangali scheme' in Tamil Nadu, for instance, is one example of this link between caste position and exploitation. Of the workers on this scheme, 60% are Dalits (SOMO/ICN, 2011, 9) and the scheme operates by tying mainly young women into employment within garment factories for a period of three years after which they are promised a lump sum payment that can then be used for the purposes of a dowry (still common among the Dalits and in rural areas). Companies alleged to be involved in Sumangali schemes include: H&M, C&A, M&S, Next, Diesel, Old Navy (GAP), Timberland, Tommy Hilfiger, Primark, Tesco, Mothercare, ASDA-Walmart (FLA, 2012, 4).

Whether a villein/serf, Helot or Dalit, the key point is that throughout history apparently 'natural' class systems have emerged and that it is those at the bottom of these systems who have tended to suffer most. It is also often very difficult to challenge the prevailing social order, even when exploitation and harm is severe. Moreover, when inequality grows to an extreme level, cultural systems and structures are often used to further marginalise victims. This may be something as simple as a label – the corruption of 'villein' to mean semi-criminal, for example – or it may involve a complex pseudo-scientific system, such as that which sustained black transatlantic slavery and later apartheid. The picture, though, is also nuanced and while some groups have remained anchored at the bottom of society there have been instances of social mobility and levels of inequality do change over time.

Plus ça change, plus c'est la même chose

There have been instances throughout history of inequality growing so great as to enslave those at the bottom. Related to this, there have also been instances of reactions against such enslavement, amid a desire to moderate the results of extreme social stratification. The abolition of transatlantic slavery in the nineteenth century is a case of a radical paradigm shift in this respect. However, even as slavery was being abolished, new systems of work-based control were emerging amoeba-like out of its ashes. The message, even when there is an apparent radical paradigm shift, is often one of *plus ça change, plus c'est la même chose.*

The evolution of the relationship between indentured labour and chattel slavery illustrates this point. Indentured labour was one of the initial bedrocks for the development of North America and the Caribbean with a significant proportion of European migrants paying for their journey to these areas through a subsequent tied period of employment (Galenson, 1984; Tomlins, 2001). This colonial labour system was widely practiced by businesses until the more lucrative chattel slavery became possible with the opening up of new trade routes through African colonisation.

In 1807, however, Britain passed the Abolition of Slavery Act, which was a precursor to the 1833 Slavery Abolition Act (for a history of abolition, see Blackburn, 1988). The former outlawed the slave trade while the latter outlawed slavery. Both acts applied only to the British Empire: but the British Empire was the global superpower of the day. Abolition, in one sense, signalled a radical change away from chattel slavery. In another sense, however, it also led to the reestablishment of the indentured labour system.

In the Caribbean, this *volte-face* meant that between the 1830s and the 1910s Indians from British India emigrated to plantations across the Caribbean (and elsewhere) to substitute for the drying-up of chattel slaves (Tinker, 1974; Vertovec, 1995). Contracts were usually for two, five or ten years and the Indian émigrés received free passage, housing, often food and certainly the promise of a much better life, in return for their legal contractual obligation to the plantation owner. The reality of life for the indentured or 'coolie' labour was severe and not dramatically different to the exploitative conditions faced by the chattel slaves. Nevertheless, the system was marginally preferable and so was deemed legal while slavery was outlawed. The use of indentured/coolie labour before and after chattel slavery underlines the point that change is usually incremental in nature and that sometimes hard-won gains are simply about not going any further backwards as far as working conditions are concerned.

The picture of shifts in the nature of labour exploitation, in response to abolition, were not just confined to the British Empire. The coffee and sugar plantations of Brazil were highly dependent upon slave labour and this helps to explain why Brazil was the last American country to abolish slavery (in 1888) (Graham, 1966; Bethell, 1970). In fact, between the sixteenth and nineteenth centuries 4 million of the 9 million African slaves who were shipped to the Americas went through Rio de Janeiro (Bourcier, 2012). However, from the 1830s Brazil slowly started to reduce its reliance on slaves in response to international pressure. In 1831 (the Law of 7 November) Brazil declared the maritime slave trade officially abolished with the importation of slaves from overseas deemed illegal. Although rarely enforced, Brazil came under subsequent pressure from the British abolitionists and in 1850 adopted the Eusébio de Queiróz Act (the Law of 4 September). This effectively strengthened the 1831 laws and made the abolition of the slave trade more of an everyday reality.

Against a backdrop of progressively tighter controls, both the Brazilian government and employers sought to ensure that migrant labour flows to plantations continued. They did this in much the same way as occurred with the indentured/coolie labour system of the Caribbean in the sense that needy, and in many instances tied, migrant workers were sought to replace slave labour. Initially, during the middle/late nineteenth century, a system of subsidised passage was established for Italian emigrants. However, and despite the promises of a new start and new opportunities in Brazil, the Italian government soon became concerned over the conditions Italians were moving into. This culminated in the 'Decree Prinetti' of 1902 that actually prohibited subsidised Italian emigration to Brazil.

As with the abolition of the slave trade, the ending of Italian immigration simply led employers to search for another source of exploitable labour. In 1908 Japanese migration to the Brazilian coffee plantations began. The Japanese were recruited through promises of great riches and the myth of a quick return back to Japan once these riches were amassed. The reality, however, was of chronically low pay and a system of contractual obligations that tied workers, through indebtedness, to their employers. Most commonly, workers not only found themselves having to repay the costs of travel to Brazil but also became dependent upon their employer/landowner for daily necessities. Distances from work to services in towns/villages were usually long and independent accommodation rare. This meant that food and housing was often provided by the employer but that the employer effectively had a monopoly and could charge rates that clawed back a large proportion of the employees' earnings and trapped them within a cycle of poverty, indebtedness and contractual obligations. In extreme cases a 'truck' system (truck derives from the French *troquer*: meaning exchange/barter) operated whereby labour was effectively exchanged for food and accommodation (see, for example, Johnson, 1986; Stevens, 2001).

The battle to end slavery, then, was in one sense won over the course of the eighteenth and nineteenth centuries. However, within the subsequent moral and legal frameworks that established themselves, employers still sought ways to extract maximum value from workers that were exploitative and often harmful, but, crucially, legal. The movement from slave labour to indentured Indian labour in the Caribbean and the shift from slave labour to Italian and then Japanese immigrants on the plantations of Brazil are both indicative of employers' (and governments') resourcefulness in the face of legal constraints. The question is whether such resourcefulness is evident today and, if so, whether it can be said to underpin working conditions that, even if not ostensibly illegal, are nonetheless exploitative and harmful?

Victim blaming

John Milton, the seventeenth-century poet, observed how: 'they who have put out the people's eyes reproach them for their blindness'.[12] This observation is apt in relation to labour exploitation, whereby those at the very bottom of society are often brutalised from above but are then blamed, or they blame themselves, for this. Put another way, throughout history those in positions of power have often found ways to marginalise those below them and to channel any anger or resistance at the prevailing socio-economic inequality inwards. The key outcome of this is that those who are poor feel, and are deemed, responsible for their own marginality (and exploitation). The internalisation of oppression that results tends to then cause considerable physical, psychological and social–communal harm.

In times of slavery, for instance, slave owners who were not despotic could still rationalise the use of humans as possession through recourse to discourses predicated upon ideas of moral or legal superiority and inferiority. There was, in short, an apparent natural order to things with slave owners inherently superior to slaves. Thus, during the trans-Atlantic trade, race and genetics helped slave owners justify and rationalise their behaviour, and even led some to believe that they were being helpful to black Africans by enslaving them.

The same logic, though via very different discourses, applies today in the sense that it is easier to control, exploit and harm workers if one is able to establish natural distance from them; and particularly if one is able to dislike, blame or brutalise the victim. This can actually be quite easy to achieve and need not involve the extensive scientific-backed explanations (based on race, genetics and subsequent superiority/inferiority) that were used during the trans-Atlantic slave trade, the Holocaust and so on. The demonising of the working-class (as 'white trash' in the US and 'chavs' in the UK), of union members (as agitators, Socialists and Communists), of migrant workers (as illegals) are just some of the currently acceptable ways in which certain identifiable groups of workers can be systematically distanced and disliked, usually through the simple use of loaded labels and language (see for example, Jones, 2012).

It is important, therefore, to be careful about stereotyping and assuming that there is a natural order dividing certain groups of people. This is because ways tend to be found for justifying and rationalising the position of those who end up at the bottom of society. This process has occurred throughout history and, worryingly, as society becomes more divided, and as inequality grows, so it appears to be easier to justify this resultant division.

Controlling the poor and the unemployed

Common sense might impel one to see the state as a protector of labour. Experience, however, suggests that the state tends to act in the interests of capital in the first instance, often (but not always) in the hope that this will also work in the interests of labour. One of the classic examples of state labour market intervention comes from the UK 'vagrancy' laws. These emerged in the fourteenth century – via the 1349 Ordinance of Labourers, 1351 Statute of Labourers and 1388 Statute of Cambridge – following the Black Death (1348–50) (Anderson, 2013, 14–15). The Black Death (plague) killed an estimated 30–40% of the population of England, and the idea of vagrancy laws emerged as a response to resultant labour shortages. Collectively, the vagrancy laws had four main elements to them: 1) they curbed excessive wages; 2) they tied workers by contract to their masters; 3) they created compulsory labour for those without work; 4) they made internal mobility dependent upon a 'passport' (a specially sealed and signed letter). In all four instances, it is clear that the state is inclined to intervene only in so far as intervention protects vested (elite) interests. The interests of labour are secondary to this at best and, more accurately, disregarded entirely.

Labour shortages of Black Death proportions are, however, relatively rare and sustained population growth has generally meant that states more often face the issue of a surplus population. Under these circumstances, the problem to be tackled by the state is one of under- and unemployment. The dilemma states face in this respect is that in order to preserve social order some form of relief for the under- and unemployed is usually required. At the same time, however, this relief must be suitably residual and/or stigmatised so as to make it a form of relief of last resort. Put another way, many states have, throughout history, taken on the role of benefactor to the workless poor but where they have done this they have, at the same time, often sought to promote the message that a job at any wage, and under any conditions, is preferable to welfare. In this sense, poor relief throughout history may be said to have regulated labour (Piven and Cloward, 1993) and promoted employment of often dubious quality by virtue of its residual nature and associated stigmatisation.

Aside from regulating labour, state relief to the under- and unemployed has also tended to involve some form of coercion (at least until the twentieth century). The key institution in this respect has been the workhouse. The history of the workhouse across Europe is a long one but the late eighteenth century proved to be a defining period. The case of Bavaria is particularly noteworthy in this respect. The Bavarian Criminal Code of 1751 contained severe punishments for foreign beggars: who were to be punished by branding and expulsion and, if they then returned to Bavaria, execution. However, by 1790 a new and apparently more humane solution to the problem of begging had been established in Bavaria.

The American-born British physicist, inventor and military man Benjamin Thompson (known as 'Count Rumford' of the Holy Roman Empire) proposed to the Bavarian state that all the beggars in Munich be arrested and begging outlawed. The beggars, he advised, should then be sent to a workhouse to make military uniforms and paid according to unit output (piece-rate) while receiving accommodation, one meal daily, and some basic work training. This proposal was put into operation in 1790 and deemed a success: with news spreading across Europe. The Bavarian test-bed for the workhouse model of state intervention spread and perhaps the most (in)famous example of its use came through England's 1834 New Poor Law (the Poor Law Amendment Act). This effectively institutionalised the unemployed and forced them to work within these institutions should they require state relief (for a history of the English workhouse system, see Driver, 1993). Conditions were purposefully intended to be severe, with the aim being to reduce the cost of poor relief and to make the masses fear the workhouse. The workhouse solution of 1834, drawing on the example set in Bavaria in 1790, may have been less severe than the brandings, expulsions and even executions that were tried in some areas of Europe. Nevertheless, workhouses still supported exploitative employment: they themselves involved state-induced forced labour and in addition they acted as an example to the masses of the fate that could await them should unemployment hit. The message they sent was therefore pretty clear: take any job, whatever the pay and conditions, and avoid the workhouse at all costs.

Those in the workhouse were housed, clothed and fed but in the process families were split up (to limit breeding), beneficiaries were often made to wear badges or uniforms, and meals were meagre and starvation-level. The New Poor Laws of 1834 effectively meant imprisonment for being poor and unemployed. Moreover, this imprisonment caused a direct threat to health. One of *The Lancet's* founders, Thomas Wakley, for instance, called on doctors to: 'put a stop to the atrocities of the new Poor-law system' (Wakley, 1841). This call was finally heeded with the beginning of the modern welfare state: most notably the National Insurance Act 1911. This began the process of establishing an independent unemployment benefit (albeit for wage earners in the first instance) and thus started to erode the primacy of the workhouse.

The state's role with respect to the poor and unemployed, then, has certainly not been neutral or benign. Governments have in the past sought to control the poor (through vagrancy laws) and to stigmatise and control the unemployed (through the workhouse). In both cases, the aim has been to control workers and ensure a steady, reliable and cheap flow of labour. To be sure, in the twentieth and twenty-first centuries there have been more alternatives and governments have offered viable escape routes and refuges for the unemployed and exploited (though to different degrees in different welfare contexts). However, the main historic lesson from state intervention in relation to the poor and unemployed appears to be one of empowering capital rather than labour and of making workers 'good' and 'better' in the sense that they are more, rather than less likely, to accept employment on terms most beneficial to employers.

Limiting compensation

When wrong is done to workers a major aspect of addressing injustice is compensation. Is there historical evidence of workers successfully persuading, or forcing, unscrupulous employers to make reparations? The answer to this question is that victims of exploitation and harm have tended to gain a justice of sorts, though in some cases they have been entirely excluded from any compensation.

Most infamously, when slavery was abolished across the British Empire in 1833 the government made no provision to compensate freed slaves. On the contrary, it was felt necessary to compensate slave owners for losses incurred (Draper, 2013). Thus, £20 million was given to around 3,000 slave-owning families in the UK and overseas: equating to around £16.5 billion in today's money (Manning, 2013).[13]

The view at the time was that, to ensure the safe passage of the full abolition of slavery, and avoid any potential protests, delays or conflict, people should receive recompense for their loss of 'property'. The West India lobby network was notable in pressuring for this financial sweetener. To some, such compensation was a shameful act (Manning, 2013); yet others have defended it as a basis for compromise towards the ultimate and, crucially, peaceful abolition of slavery (Hannan, 2013). Whatever one's view, however, there is no denying that to compensate slave owners but not slaves during the abolition of slavery appears unjust by today's standards.

Other, ostensibly more progressive, policies did actually involve freed slaves being compensated. Two particular events in North America are noteworthy in this respect: the American War of Independence (1775– 83) and the American Civil War (1861–65). In the former, the British were desperate for additional troops and in 1775 issued what became known as Lord Dunmore's Proclamation. This was effectively the first mass emancipation of slaves in US history: the proviso being that these slaves had to fight in British regiments during the War of Independence. Having fought for the British, the freed slaves were then promised their own land and thousands were transported to Canada: mainly to Nova Scotia (as recorded in the 'Book of Negroes'). The problem, however, was that both the land and the climate made anything more than survival extremely difficult and the majority of the Black Loyalists, as they are known, subsequently left their unforgiving Nova Scotia home. They were, once again promised land and opportunity 'back home' in Sierra Leone, where they founded Freetown in 1792. Similar compensation schemes existed in the UK where the black population in London at the time (many also Black Loyalists) were encouraged to emigrate to Sierra Leone. The abolitionist Granville Sharp set up the 'Committee for the Relief of the Black Poor' which was made up of British philanthropists who felt 'voluntary return' preferable and more humane to supporting the black communities in the UK. As in Nova Scotia, however, conditions were once again harsh and many of those emancipated Black Loyalists, promised a land of opportunity, ultimately perished (Walker, 1993).

The compensation given to freed Black Loyalists in the late eighteenth century was nothing more than a form of residual benevolence and then opportunism. It involved giving away land that was rocky, remote and inhospitable to those with limited experience of working such land, and then encouraging these beneficiaries to up-sticks again to become pawns in embryonic African colonialism. The irony, of course, is that this policy ultimately involved removing the 'problem' of the black poor from the UK and Canada and was driven by many of the Abolitionists who were economically enmeshed within African colonialism. It was not until the American Civil War (1861–65) that a more genuine form of benevolence emerged in respect to freed slaves.

Specifically, in 1865, black refugees freed and displaced due to the American Civil War benefited from 'Sherman's Special Field Orders Number 15' or what became known as the '40 acres and a mule policy'. This granted 40 acres of land, mainly on the sea islands in Georgia and South Carolina, to freed slaves. At the time many freed black people wanted land redistributed from slave owners to those who had worked the land and this 40 acres and a mule policy was seen as a benchmark. However, Sherman's order was soon reversed (by President Andrew Johnson) and the hopes of mass compensation for freed slaves were dashed. Once again, the story of compensation for former slaves is one of raised hope, ostensible opportunity, but ultimately very limited reparations. The favoured solution to the end of slavery was ultimately to emphasise the emancipatory potential of free wage labour rather than land redistribution with black land ownership and farming in the United States declining significantly over the century that followed the aborted 40 acres and a mule policy (Otabor and Nembhard, 2012).

Effective compensation for the dispossessed appears rare and where it has been trialled the trial has either not lasted (the 40 acres and a mule policy) or has been cynical (the remote Nova Scotia resettlement) or opportunistic (the Sierra Leone colonisation project). The only real successful example of compensation, in fact, has been where those dispossessed of their slaves have been deemed worthy of financial support (in UK after the 1833 abolition). The question, given this rather pessimistic historical diagnosis, is whether the situation can or should be remedied?

Many argue, for instance, that reparations can only realistically extend so far back in time (for example, to within living memory). Nevertheless, this has not stopped the 15 Caribbean countries forming the CARICOM (Caribbean Community and Common Market) alliance from seeking compensation for slavery and its continued legacy. CARICOM outlined, in March 2014, a 10-point reparation plan[14] and has threatened to go to the International Court of Justice in The Hague if European countries refuse to discuss this. Among other things the plan calls for: a full formal apology for slavery and its legacies; assisted repatriation; support for improved public health; support for improved education; and cancelling of international debts. Realistically, however, this pressure for reparations for historic abuse seems unlikely to succeed and the lessons of history as far as worker compensation is concerned are far from emancipatory.

Restrained resistance

What evidence is there, historically, of successful resistance in the face of work-based exploitation and harm? Well, there appear to be two types of resistance. First, some have sought radical system change. Second, some have argued for incremental change within a broadly stable socio-economic system.

The latter, incremental improvements, have been most common throughout history. During the Roman Empire, for example, the Stoics were prominent in supporting the more humane treatment of slaves. Seneca's 'Letter 47' (to Lucilius) is well known in this respect because, while not calling for an end to slavery, it is a rallying call for greater equality. In the letter, Seneca makes the following key point:

> I do not wish to involve myself in too large a question, and to discuss the treatment of slaves, towards whom we Romans are excessively haughty, cruel, and insulting. But this is the kernel of my advice: treat your inferiors as you would be treated by your betters. And as often as you reflect how much power you have over a slave, remember that your master has just as much power over you. (cited in Garnsey, 1996, 56)

He goes on to argue that we are all part of the same stock and that we all are capable of being enslaved albeit in different ways.

The Stoics were particularly important as far as views on slavery were concerned because in essence they promoted the idea of some kind of universal citizenship. In other words, they tried to remind people of their common bonds to others irrespective of social position in the hope that this commonality would underpin moves towards a fairer and more humane society. Crucially, this philosophical position did not inevitably imply the need for slavery to end but, as a minimum, called for better treatment of slaves. Nonetheless, Stoicism was eventually outlawed in the Roman Empire as part of a more general clamp-down on (pagan) philosophy in favour of Christianity.

In the Judaeo-Christian world a similar incremental approach has tended to be adopted towards social stratification and the labour exploitation often resulting from this. Slavery, for instance, has not usually been threatened by religion; more commonly, religious leaders have advocated incremental improvements. The classic example of this is the letter from St Paul to Philemon concerning Philemon's runaway slave Onesimus. The letter indicates Paul's encouragement of Onesimus to return but also shows his commensurate concern that Philemon receives his slave in a Christian (humane) manner. Thus, rather than giving freed/runaway slaves sanctuary, Paul's teaching focuses on the maintenance of a master–servant relationship but on more equal terms. There are certainly hints at the possibilities of freedom in the letter, but freedom for slaves is never actually called for explicitly: it is more a case of granting greater freedoms and more progressive treatment.

Jewish teachings were perhaps the most liberal in respect to slavery. Most obviously, Deuteronomy 24:18 calls for empathy and reminds Jews that they were once slaves in Egypt before the Exodus. Related to this, Jewish religious teachings (most notably through the Law of Moses) establish minimum standards for the treatment of slaves. Among other things, a weekly rest day (on the Sabbath) extends to slaves, as do various festivals and holidays. Slaves injured through employment are also protected: with those responsible for the injury required to provide victim support. There is also provision for the cancelling of debts and freedom from slavery via the seventh-year manumission for Hebrews and 50-year Jubilee period. Moreover, slaves are allowed to be part of the community and have rights to a private and family life. In other words, the system of slavery, although allowed for, is not akin to the chattel-like slavery of plantation capitalism and is moderated by religious advice, laws and doctrine.

From the Greek-rooted Stoic philosophising, to Christian Rome, through to Judaism, it is clear both that certain forms of slavery are rooted in the very foundations of modern western civilisation but also that there has always been a desire among theologians and philosophers to prevent the worst excesses of social stratification. At times, however, there have been instances of more radical reactions against inequality and associated labour exploitation.

The Roman Servile Wars, for example, are some of the most famous early revolts against slavery.[15] The third servile war (73–72 BC) led by Spartacus has been particularly widely studied and replayed. This involved a slave rebellion at a gladiatorial school but ultimately led to a movement involving thousands. Once Spartacus was killed, however, the surviving followers (around 6,000 in number) were very publicly crucified. The authorities wanted to send a clear message to anyone seeking to rebel that such rebellion was futile and would ultimately lead to death. Certainly, this was the last of the servile wars, but it is hard to say who was more fearful after the event: the slaves were certainly fearful of any kind of overt radicalism; at the same time, though, the slave owners were also clearly fearful of revolt.

Examples of slave uprisings are numerous but the threat of eventual recapture and subsequent maltreatment for rebels has loomed large throughout history, as has the uncertainty of 'what and where next?' post-rebellion. In 1831, for instance, there was a significant slave revolt in Southampton County (Virginia, US) known as the Nat Turner Rebellion. This involved 50–70 slaves rebelling and killing white slave owners: they were eventually captured and many were then executed by the state. The revolt also initiated a period of white retribution where slaves were killed by white mobs. In addition, certain states used the rebellion to justify even more repressive laws towards black people. Alabama in 1832, for example, passed the following law: 'Any person or persons who shall endeavour or attempt to teach any free person of colour, or slave to spell, read, or write, shall upon Conviction thereof by indictment, be fined in a sum not less than two hundred and fifty dollars no more than five hundred dollars' (Thirteenth Annual Session of the General Assembly of the State of Alabama, 1831–32).

In fact, even the most successful slave revolt in history can ultimately be judged to have failed. In 1791, in the French colony of Saint-Domingue, Toussaint L'Ouverture, led revolutionary forces against the French and war lasted until 1794 when the French abolished slavery (following the French Revolution and the formation of the First Republic). The rebel leader Toussaint L'Ouverture was then made governor in 1801 but by 1802, under Napoleon Bonaparte, he had been captured and slavery reinstated across the French empire. Another rebel leader emerged in reaction to this, Jean-Jacques Dessalines, and for a second time the French were defeated with a new independent country – Haiti – being established in 1804. In one sense this exceptional case shows that it is possible to overthrow an oppressor. However, the fact that it is the only case in world history where slaves established a new nation-state by an in-situ rebellion is telling. Also telling is the fact that on Haiti international colonial slavery was quickly replaced by new forms of worker exploitation perpetuated by the new domestic elite: 'The black elite who ran the state used forced labour to protect their plantations from the preference of people to live as peasant proprietors' (Black, 2011, 211). Moreover, Haiti has not exactly done well economically since the rebellion. It is one of the world's least developed nations – ranked 161 out of 187 in the UN's Human Development Index (UNDP, 2013, 150) – and remains led by a mulatto (mixed race) elite.

In seeking to challenge work-based control, exploitation and harm there are two main paths that can be taken. The first involves argument and influence from within. The second involves a more radical challenge to authority and to the status quo. In the above examples, it is clear that argument and influence has tended to be more productive than revolt. However, as we will see below (in the section on worker empowerment and collective action), a radical challenge to authority is sometimes needed in order to initiate a paradigm shift.

Social movements

The balance between elite and mass action in order to improve working conditions can be seen in relation to the eighteenth-century UK anti-slavery movement: one of the most important social movements in the history of global labour relations. Here, the key steps to abolition were taken by Quakers, via the formation of the 'Society for Effecting the Abolition of the Slave Trade' in 1787. This society was a London-based, and relatively elite, network but the aim was to make the abolitionist campaign into a mass movement (Jennings, 2013).

One early development, in 1787, was the production (by Josiah Wedgewood) of slave medallions to be worn to promote abolition by supporters. The medallions had the line: 'Am I not a man and a brother?' The work of the 1787 Society for Effecting the Abolition of the Slave Trade was tireless, and, as well as the production of these medallions, various pamphlets were produced to educate the public about the slave trade. This helped to ensure that in 1791 an Abolition Bill was heard in Parliament. The Bill was unsuccessful, and it was quickly realised that the abolitionist campaign needed even broader support. In 1791 an educational pamphlet was produced and this led to a boycott of sugar from slave plantations, drawing in between 300,000 and 400,000 consumers from 1791 to 1792. This is one of the earliest, and ultimately successful, examples of a mass consumer movement (Midgley, 1996).

The sugar boycott was also accompanied by other forms of mass action. Most notably, in 1792, towards the end of the boycott, petitions were signed by around 390,000 people and presented to Parliament. The boycott and associated petitions demonstrated that the tide was turning with respect to abolition, and that the rejection by Parliament of the 1791 Abolition Bill had been short-sighted. This social movement is perhaps one of the most important in terms of labour–capital relations and it shows the importance of cooperation across social hierarchies in order to prevent extreme exploitation and work-based harm.

Following the mass social movement to end slavery one of the next major social movements targeting worker rights emerged again in the UK, in the 1830s, but this time focused on native workers. It had been illegal to form a union in the UK via the Combination Acts (1799/1800) and then legal but in practice very difficult via the Combination Act (1825). Then, in 1834, six men from the county of Dorset in southern England swore a secret oath to form the 'Friendly Society of Agricultural Labourers' in an attempt to try to arrest the decline in agricultural wages caused by the over-supply of labour and emergent mechanisation. This response was seen as more progressive than some earlier violent responses in the UK (such as the 'Swing Rebellion').[16] Although unions were no longer illegal, there was concern once this society was discovered over the implications of worker collectivism. A Dorset landowner, reflective of this unease, wrote to the Home Secretary to complain about the Friendly Society (union) and its attempt to affiliate with the Grand National Consolidated Trades Union. The Home Secretary recommended invoking the relatively obscure Unlawful Oaths Act of 1797 which had been used for naval mutinies and banned secret oaths.

Overall there was general fear in the early nineteenth century of mass insurrection following the French Revolution and Swing Rebellion with some seeing trade unions as part of the problem and others seeing them as part of a new solution. The union members (known as the Tolpuddle Martyrs) were quickly found guilty of taking an illegal oath and sent, in 1834, to Australia for seven years' transportation. In response to this, a protest was organised in London (by the Central Committee of the Metropolitan Trade Unions) with between 35,000 and 100,000 people attending, and 800,000 people signing a related petition. The protest and petition led eventually to the Tolpuddle Martyrs' sentence being commuted, and underlines once again the potential power of social movements to positively affect change.[17]

Worker empowerment and collective action

There are three main ways in which capital's hold over labour may be resisted. First, where labour is highly skilled it is likely to be insulated from many of the problems of vulnerability. Second, the state can, if it chooses, and can afford to do so, offer workers an alternative to potentially exploitative and harmful employment through the benefit system. Third, workers can come together collectively to resist the exploitative tendencies of capital, either violently, or by forming/joining trade unions (see for example, Mason, 2007).[18]

It is the latter union strategy that carries an important historical lesson as far as a social harm perspective is concerned. While the UK was at the forefront of abolishing international slavery in the eighteenth and nineteenth centuries it was to some extent reluctant to see domestic workers' conditions improve because of the lucrative nature of industrial capitalism and the factory system. Thus, when workers tried to organise to fight for improved pay and conditions in the eighteenth and nineteenth centuries, the Combination Acts (1799/1800 and 1825) kept unions at first illegal, and then legal but severely constricted (see, for example, the Tolpuddle Martyrs' case above). At the same time, the 1834 Poor Law (also see above) was brought in to force those unwilling to work within the factory system into much greater hardship. The dominant sentiment among the UK elite was to treat labour as expendable and easily replaceable and to deny workers a collective voice for fear that this voice might have an impact on profitability.

Despite the role of business and the state in limiting workers' power in response to mass protests against the exploitative and harmful factory system, eventually (in 1872) trade unions were broadly accepted (following the 1867 Royal Commission on Trade Unions). This signalled a paradigm shift, and is important historically in order to demonstrate how it is possible for social harms to not only be resisted but to be reduced through collective effort. The period of struggle in the nineteenth century at first appeared futile but eventually lead to important victories not only in relation to enabling trade unions but also in relation to addressing ills such as child labour, excessive working hours, unsafe working conditions, poverty wages and so on. While most of the historic examples used in this chapter point towards the need to make incremental changes from within, the story of the birth of the trade union movement and the subsequent fight for workers' rights more generally shows how sometimes more significant paradigm shifts, underpinned by significant popular resistance and protest, are needed to prevent social harm.

Conclusion

This chapter was not intended to be a definitive history of worker control, exploitation and harm. The eight examples chosen were purposefully selective. The points they make are varied but, on the one hand, they demonstrate a tendency toward a gradual improvement in the plight of the most vulnerable workers. On the other hand, they reveal just how difficult it is for those subjected to exploitation and harm to free themselves from this. In fact, even when capital abuses labour, and even when this abuse is exposed, it is not always labour that is ultimately compensated for such injustice. The example of UK slave owners receiving pay-outs following abolition underlines just how skilfully capital is able to manage its way out of 'difficult' situations. Nevertheless, there are occasions when capital oversteps the mark to such an extent that a paradigm shift is triggered, based on mass social movements and/or radical protest and resistance. The abolition of transatlantic slavery and the development of the trade union movement are two notable examples in this respect.

War alarm

Have you heard coffee cups bang against coffee cups
the murmur of an attacking army
standing with your stomach leaned against the bench
with hands building shrimp sandwiches and feet
aching from the weight
pulled between
the roar of freezers
and the screams of the cash-line
in today's
race against the clock
inexorably ticking past the lunch break
beneath the sizzle from the coffee machine
the pop music from the speakers
families, children screaming on the terrace
to the tweet from the microwave ovens
the machine gun clatter of the order frequency
and the juice presser that presses the last few drops
out of us

FOUR

Direct workplace controls

Workplace control

The focus of this book is on social harm within the context of work and the workplace. Social harm may be linked to 'extreme' processes (such as slavery) and outcomes (such as worker fatality) but it involves much more than this. The book is, therefore, interested in all workers and does not start conceptually with a single group or single problem. Instead, attention is directed towards controls, both from inside and outside the workplace, that are used to produce and reproduce 'good' and 'better' workers (however 'good' and 'better' are defined). The problem, as argued throughout the book, occurs when controls over workers become excessive and oppressive. In such instances the important point is to recognise exploitation and to identify the range of harmful outcomes that may result. The priority in the next three chapters of the book is to outline controls, largely legal and non-coercive, that could be deemed problematic and constitute part of the study of work-based social harm.

Controls over workers can exist within the workplace (this Chapter and Chapter Five) or within wider society (Chapter Six). In terms of the former, there is usually a combination of direct (this Chapter) and indirect (Chapter Five) control within any given workplace. The issue is not that controls exist *per se* but the nature, intensity and combination of control and whether or not it is exploitative or harmful in either intent or outcome.

The mechanisms and mechanics of worker control are complex. They exist because of the need to limit tensions between labour and capital that would be potentially detrimental to productivity. They also exist because of the need to manage labour into a position of strength, whereby work is embraced rather than resisted. Both deference and enthusiasm are required features of modern labour markets, though they are not always co-present, and capital has in its armoury various means to achieve these and to produce and reproduce 'good' and 'better' workers.

The core question, first posed by Lynd and Lynd (1929), is why workers work as hard as they do? An obvious starting point in this respect is to recognise that labour is treated as a 'commodity' (see Polanyi, 1944) but a commodity that is essentially of variable quality before and after its purchase. The challenge for capital, then, has been to reduce the uncertainty and variability of labour recruitment and employment so that a safer return on investment is secured. This is why myriad forms of control have emerged in order to produce and reproduce 'good' and 'better' workers. Put another way, labour must be prepared and willing to relinquish some of the value it creates in order for capital to amass the appropriate profit levels (see Braverman, 1974).

Some (for example, Marxists) would argue that this basic need for labour to produce surplus value is in itself exploitative. However, this is not the definition of exploitation employed in this book. Instead, exploitation is taken back a step and I argue that it is when controls over workers become excessive and oppressive that exploitation exists. Essentially, then, it is not a problem that workers are part of a system where value is created but then relinquished and relocated. The issue is the nature of the system driving this value shift from labour to capital. Capitalism in this light is not exploitative *per se* but certain forms of capitalism, and certain areas within a given capitalist system, can be exploitative. Exploitation also very often leads to physical, psychological, social–communal and environmental harms.

It is important to recognise within this framework that controls over workers within the workplace come from different sources and have different sets of motives attached. This book is not interested in all forms of control. It is only interested in controls over workers that are part of a wider (political–economic) strategy. Thus, conventional bullying, for example, is excluded from this analysis because this form of oppression is largely personal rather than strategic (political–economic) in nature, though I accept that the two may interlink.

Taking workplaces as a whole, there are four core control scenarios:

1. One-to-One Management: This is typical of very small-scale enterprises, or of a 'mentor' being assigned to a specific staff member in a larger enterprise.
2. Hierarchical Management: One person controlling numerous workers at arm's-length is common in most businesses.
3. Network Management: This is when control occurs among peers and is devolved by management into ostensibly flat work teams.
4. Arm's-length Management: This occurs when workers within a given workplace are answerable to, and controlled by, authorities beyond that workplace. The classic example here is of agency and gang labour supplied into a firm for a temporary period.

Each of the above scenarios is likely to co-exist within a workplace and the exact inter-personal nature of control tends to be highly complex. The point is, however, that these scenarios are about strategic rather than personal relationships. They exist because of the need to ensure that workers are deferent and/or enthusiastic and to minimise the risks involved in investing in labour that is, by design, of variable quality.

Taylorism and scientific management

In 1911 Frederick Winslow Taylor published *The Principles of Scientific Management*. This was one of the first comprehensive attempts to develop a science of modern labour control. It arose out of, over the nineteenth century, a shift from craft to mass production and the universal outlawing of slavery. Thus, mass labour was needed in mines and factories but it had to be managed rather than coerced into efficient and productive work. Famously, Taylor observed widespread 'soldiering' whereby workers intentionally work below their maximum capacity. He viewed this as a problem that could be solved through methodical science and associated management to implement the insights from this. Through conducting various experiments Taylor was able to provide employers with insights into how the speed of production could be increased, and related to this, how workers could work more efficiently.

Soldiering was viewed entirely from the perspective of the employer and little was made of the way in which this strategy makes repetitive, and often physically demanding work, bearable. This approach set in motion a dominant tendency, over the twentieth century, to view labour as the problem to be cracked. This book turns this assumption on its head, and is interested in what occurs when the 'labour problem' has been too efficiently solved. Put another way, could soldiering be a practice worth defending if it provides workers with cover and allows them a sufficient degree of humanity in otherwise degrading forms of employment? And, what price is paid for highly successful scientific management that treats workers with the same degree of reverence and respect as machines?

To be sure Taylorism, and the subsequent flood of research on the labour process, was an important component of economic success over the twentieth century. Though, in the end, many of the mass production industries that Taylorism restructured ultimately relocated to where labour was cheapest. Taylorism also established a number of important workplace norms that we now take for granted. These include: 1) the use of science and technology to uncover the most efficient and effective work and production processes; 2) the division of tasks so that workers can become specialist rather than generalists; 3) careful pairing of certain workers to certain jobs; 4) monitoring and supervision of the labour process; 5) specific and specialist management roles overseeing work; 6) financial rewards for efficiency and productivity.

Taylorism underpinned a key part of the Fordist production system, so dominant over the twentieth century, and has been the centre-piece of direct forms of worker control ever since. It is essentially about the highly specialised technical control of labour and this is evident both in the traditional manufacturing of Taylor's day and in post-Fordist work sites.

We have already seen, for example (see Chapter Two), how Foxconn's operations in China have been associated with severe forms of management and control that in the extreme have been said to drive workers to take their own lives. Such direct workplace controls are also evident in the developed world and should not simply be seen as something associated with a particular stage of capitalist development.

In the UK, for example, the company Sports Direct (*the* major sports retail discounter in the country) has recently made headlines for working to a particular business model. This is based upon a specific methodology with respect to worker control that effectively takes scientific management into the twenty-first century.

Sports Direct is made up of 67 separate companies and had a turnover of £3 billion (2014). The sports discounter's main 'engine room' is its distribution centre in the former mining village of Shirebrook, Derbyshire, UK. Here, most workers are employed via labour market intermediaries and most of these are on 'short-hours' contracts. The strategy is to combine the resultant insecurity – there is little guarantee of stable work or a secure income – with constant monitoring, surveillance and associated scrutiny of performance. Workers are searched as they leave a shift and, during the shift, they are continually monitored for their 'picking rate'. They are also checked against a variety of performance and quality criteria during a shift (such as length of toilet break, unscheduled socialising and so on) and if their pick rate is too low, or if they fail to meet or contravene the criteria, workers are given 'strikes': too many strikes over a six-month period and the worker is 'let go'.

There is no soldiering at Sports Direct because it has been successfully managed out (see Box 4.1). The question is whether the resultant levels of control are excessive and oppressive? Locals apparently call the Sports Direct distribution centre 'the gulag' and the union Unite has called it a 'workhouse' (House of Commons, 2016a). The owner of Sports Direct, Mike Ashley, is one of the UK's richest people with wealth of \$5 billion in 2015 according to Forbes. However, when asked in 2015 by Parliament (via the Scottish Affairs Select Committee) to give evidence around his employment and business model he was too busy and 'unavailable'.[19] Instead, the chairman of Sports Direct Dr Keith Hellawell gave evidence.[20] At this hearing he responded to allegations around working conditions, citing the need for corporate 'flexibility' as key to the businesses survival. Eventually, in June 2016, the Sports Direct owner did appear in Parliament at the Business Innovation and Skills Committee (House of Commons, 2016a). He argued that 'the value of Sports Direct is the people' it employs and told the committee that he 'knew and understood' the workers and used agencies because they are 'experts in people'.

It seems, then, that many businesses – whether Foxconn (China, manufacturing) or Sports Direct (UK, distribution and retail) – have become locked into a competitive downward spiral whereby surplus value from already highly controlled workers has become a key aspect of competitiveness. This spiral has driven unparalleled technical control especially in low-wage routine manufacturing and distribution occupations. Put another way, the issues of control, exploitation and harm raised in relation to Sports Direct are about a generic business model now prevalent across the global economy, not about the specific moral fabric of the owner and chairman. Moreover, there is widespread fear that this model is in the ascendancy (see House of Commons, 2016a).

Box 4.1: Work-based controls at the Sports Direct UK distribution centre (according to the Unite union)

- employing the vast majority of staff (circa 3,400) through two agencies on short-hour contracts (336 hours guaranteed per year);
- general culture of fear in the warehouse;
- 'strikes' used to discipline workers: with six strikes allowed in a six-month period;
- no grievance procedure for workers: if they complain then they find that they no longer have work;
- docking pay for turning up as little as a minute late;
- evidence of workers coming into work unwell: with 110 ambulance call-outs noted;
- charging workers for the administration costs involved in the payment of their wages;
- failure to pay workers while they wait to get searched before leaving work;
- disciplining for excessive chatting and breaks;

- workers banned from wearing certain brands of clothing;
- refusal to engage with the unions.

Source: House of Commons (2016a)

New management

Scientific management was initially an attempt to control the mass working-class. However, the big shift in the developed world over the twentieth century was the emergence of a mass white-collar 'middle'-class. By the late 1950s Peter Drucker's *Landmarks of Tomorrow* (1959) had coined the term 'knowledge worker' to reflect this shift and the key question linked to it was how to manage the emergent and growing white-collar class. Direct technical control was part of the solution, but in many workplaces it was seen as only a small part. Instead, management moved from being administered through authority to manipulation, as recognised by Wright Mills (1951):

> Many whips are inside men, who do not know how they got there, or indeed that they are there. In the movement from authority to manipulation, power shifts from the visible to the invisible, from the known to the anonymous. And with rising material standards, exploitation becomes less material and more psychological. (1951, 110)

Thus worker control became more subtle, sophisticated and, arguably, more all-encompassing, during the twentieth century as the nature of mass employment changed. Indeed, an entire industry quickly emerged to cater for this management prerogative. This industry recognised, crucially, that human control need not simply be one way: in the sense that workers work hard due to direct technical control *and* also often through their own choosing.

The fact that controls need not be directly imposed and that workers may be manipulated rather than controlled was a key insight from the 1950s (Baritz, 1960; Wright Mills, 1951). It demonstrated that an understanding of psychology, anthropology, sociology, human resource management and so on were all key to the production and reproduction of 'good' workers and could be used to underpin both worker deference and enthusiasm. Some were fearful of these new insights into workers' psyche. Baritz (1960, 210), for instance, argued that social scientists (whom he called 'servants of power') had given capital tools with: 'implications vaster and more fearful than anything previously hinted'.

Irrespective of one's view over the merits of the new control methodologies, the key fact remains that manipulation and persuasion emerged alongside the more established direct and visible forms of worker control and that this emergence was associated with labour market change. Employers also often preferred the new techniques because they tended to: 'consolidate employer power behind a veneer of consent' (Austin, 1988, 56).

The above shows that worker control is about much more than scientific management and has been since at least the 1950s. An interesting body of work from the 1970s looking at the labour process has demonstrated this point in considerable depth and with considerable skill (Braverman, 1974; Burawoy, 1979; Edwards, 1979). The issue still remains a simple one of how labour is controlled to generate maximum surplus value, but the solutions are more complex than ever. The rest of the chapter will focus on the cruder forms of direct worker control, while more nuanced forms of control both inside and outside of the workplace will be examined in Chapters Five and Six respectively.

Targets, monitoring and surveillance

As noted above, Taylor recognised at the beginning of the twentieth century that workers could be set steeper targets to reduce and even eliminate soldiering. It seems that time for sociability at work has for some time been equated with inefficiency, and that workers are assumed to be able to function in a machine-like fashion, reaching full speed the moment shifts start and only stopping once shifts end. The desire to achieve machine-like efficiency from labour has meant that many workplaces have seen practices intensify as the work effort norm has been ratcheted up. On production lines this may be accompanied by manic conveyor-belt speeds and associated repetitive strain injuries. As Hodson (2001, 120) notes: 'The unceasing pressure of the assembly line allows no relaxation from the demands of the job.' In office contexts stress has become the surrogate for the production line, which appears to be speeding up despite the apparent labour saving advancements of ICT.

Resistance to work intensification is difficult because of the individualised worker model that now prevails within the workplace. Very simply, if employers decide that they would like workers to do something, and the worker is physically and mentally capable of doing this, then there is little to get in the way. Over the 1980s and 1990s

Green (2001, 53) has observed that, associated with this: 'Work effort has been intensified. Intensification was greatest in manufacturing during the 1980s, and in the public sector during the 1990s. Between 1986 and 1997 there have been substantial increases in the number of sources of pressure inducing hard work from employees' (see also Green, 2004). Intensification not only makes work harder but it can also erode the morale and confidence of workers as they fail to meet the targets set. This can add to vulnerability, not to mention contributing to work-based harm.

Targets that are difficult for workers to reach are one thing, but control is also facilitated by the use of targets that are impossible to reach all of the time. The phenomenon of 'rainbow targets' (see Box 4.2) means that workers are forever running to stand still as they struggle to reach the parameters set by management. Newsome (2010, 201), for example, found targets so demanding that 70% of the workforce were on warnings for missing them. The fact that targets are just out of reach or, when reached, drift a little further away, means that workers can never feel truly at ease because in one sense they are always seen to be underperforming or just about performing acceptably. This is not only a psychological hold but it is also a disciplinary hold in the sense that targets missed are often seen as grounds for legitimate disciplinary action.

Box 4.2: Rainbow targets – author's own ethnographic reflection

This is ethnographic reflection inspired by research into migrant worker exploitation (see Scott et al, 2012):

> Rainbow targets do exist in the everyday reality of workers even if they have never quite met them. They are very attractive and bring the promise of riches. They channel workers' energies based on this promise. Then, when the mass of workers approach, they move and re-establish again at a safe distance. After a few chases workers become exhausted and/or realise their task is futile. Even the rainmakers with the job of creating the rainbow never reach it. Their reward, however, is knowing from the start how the game works and being able to sit back and watch the chase.

Alongside intensifying and often unrealistic targets, workers are subject to employers monitoring their performance. This not only ensures that targets are adhered to but also that there is a subtle workplace culture whereby one's performance is subject to self-regulation as a result of the looming spectre of employer monitoring and associated surveillance (Ball, 2010; Thompson, 2002). This monitoring and surveillance also extends to sickness absence where employers' 'frustrations at the indeterminacy of labour's attendance' (Taylor et al, 2010, 283) is often achieved by forcing people back to work or out of employment. New technologies and bureaucratic systems may have enabled more extensive monitoring and surveillance of late but the point remains that it is the basic search for greatest value from labour that drives these mechanisms of control.

In my research on the UK food industry (Scott et al, 2012) one of the most obvious tools of direct technical control was the performance related pay system known as the 'piece-rate'. This is most common on farms, where many workers are paid according to the volume and quality of the produce harvested or packed. (There is less need to pay piece-rate in food-processing factories because the speed of work can be controlled by the speed of the production line). Experiences of the piece-rate system generally revolve around underpayment, inter-worker competition and excessively paced work in order to achieve acceptable wage rates:

"They paid per box. We were paid per box...two pounds or something like that. So if we didn't pick enough boxes then we didn't earn. We didn't even earn enough to pay for an accommodation. As I said, the Romanians were there. There were only five Poles. The Romanians took possession of the farm. And unfortunately they were giving us the worst...so I couldn't pick the strawberries where I wanted. So I couldn't pick enough boxes and then I earned only £10. In the conditions there was mud up to knees. And after all day at work only £10. It was a swindle because they claimed that it was going to be work paid per hour. On the farm, they told us later that it was piecework and that we were paid per box." (female, 53y, Polish)

"Piecework was set to unrealistic standards. Out of 120 pickers only very few (up to ten pickers) could make £2 or £3 per hour! I am aware of the minimum wage, but we did not receive it. We were given only one day to learn how to pick strawberries quickly, which is unrealistic. You cannot learn so quickly...He knew that doing this piecework we will earn only £2 an hour. He knew that.

We worked on piecework and he gave us unreal targets."
(male, 31y, Belarusian)

"We worked on piecework. We were picking strawberries
and raspberries. I was working as fast as I could, but I still
was not able to earn even minimum wage. Sometimes we
did not have many strawberries, but we still had to pick
what was there and earned very little.' (female, 42y, Latvian)

The above quotations clearly, and rather crudely, show how systems of
reward and monitoring can be used to control and discipline workers.
The examples are all drawn from the UK's food production industry
where the system of piecework is sometimes used. Piece-rate targets
are effectively used to ensure workers work harder for the minimum
wage: though in theory they do provide the opportunity to earn well
above the minimum wage level. Employers also use piece-rates to
'weed out' slower workers and, at the same time, discipline the labour
that remains.

Even without the use of piece-rates, it is clear that in certain labour
markets productivity has been raised at the expense of worker welfare
and wellbeing:

"They said I was slow, that I should have been working
faster. They watched me with a stopwatch. That I should
have tied up three chickens per minute, not one as I was
doing. It was not true. They kept a record in a notebook
to be able to prove how many chickens I was managing to
tie up. As far as I saw, they were measuring only my time."
(female, 27y, Polish)

"Supervisor all the time behind your back, and if somebody
is working slowly or want to ask something so there isn't
any talking at all, we are not allowed to talk…I felt his
breath behind my back, it is very stressful, person stiffen
hands straight away, all the time a person is under a threat,
automatically there is no comfortable working." (male,
57y, Polish)

"When you looked at the line you were dizzy. I think
that that speed was forbidden when they turned it on, it
was unlawful. We told them, but they said that we had to
work faster. Yes, they hurried us up all the time. We were

watched, told not to speak with each other, to work faster."
(female, 45y, Polish)

"In reality it was a nearly the prisoner camp, it was the worst
farm I have ever worked in. People were so nervous, there
were rows between people because there was no calmness,
no peace, because everyone was stressed out about keeping
pace or if you do not keep pace you do not earn!" (male,
56y, Polish)

The timing of workers with stopwatches, the breath behind workers'
backs, the outlawing of conversation, and the nervousness of workers
that are all expressed above is indicative of workplace intensification and
the associated heightening of targets and increased use of monitoring
and surveillance.

In industries like food production, though this is not the case in
many workplaces, power was directly visible and oppression directly
traceable. Supervisors on the farm and in the food production line
were likened to Nazi-era guards:

"The supervisors were like prison guards. Among ourselves
we called them Gestapo...Often they shouted at us...I
would say that they did not treat us like humans." (female,
42y, Latvian)

"The speed of work was very quick. In the management
there were a few people who were putting a lot of pressure
on the speed, so this factory was not nice at all. One
manager we called Hitler because he was standing and
hurrying up employees all the time, the people were treated
as things, simply statistics, and you could not say anything,
if you do not like something: 'Bye bye, there will be next
person on your place.'" (male, 34y, Polish)

Associated with this, there were times when workers were under such
control that basic rights to breaks were denied:

"Let's start, for example, from the physiological needs to
use toilet. We could only go twice or once for five minutes
in eight hours. Not everybody does it in five minutes
some needs more time for this. There are things that take
longer. Five minutes was for coming out, washing hands,

going to the toilet, washing again and coming back. It is too short time for doing it this way. There were people like women who…it is a delicate subject for them, you know, to tell a man what for are you going to the toilet. For example, when woman had a period, it is for a woman shy subject explaining yourself to the young man, and those supervisors were laughing at this. These are people with higher positions.' (male, 57y, Polish)

"Company every day is demanding more and more. Now every time we go to the toilet we have to sign a paper, at the end of the week they will deduct this time from our wages. They do not pay for our break times and time we spend in the toilet." (female, 54y, Latvian)

Throughout the above there is very much the sense of workers being seen as inherently problematic unless they are subject to totalitarian-style control that even denies them workplace rights to breaks and conversation.

In terms of explaining the severity of controls experienced above, it is apparent that employers are transferring many aspects of the competitive pressures that they face onto their workers. They are effectively asking already pressurised and low-paid staff to generate even more in efficiency and productivity savings to ensure continued competitiveness as profit margins are squeezed. And so, the uneven power relations of corporate supply chains are eventually burdening those at the bottom (the workers) who are least able to resist. The irony of this situation is that just as one company finds a way to extract more value from workers, so this solution will spread and another solution will eventually be required to achieve a future competitive edge. This is the downward competitive spiral that direct technical control helps to achieve, and that is so feared by workers.

Targets, monitoring and surveillance in the office environment tend to be slightly different to those in the factory, farm or distribution centre. My own experience in higher education, across a number of institutions, is illustrative of the types of ways in which individual and team performance is now measured. Specifically, there are at least 14 domains where performance can be gauged, assessed and usually quantified (see Box 4.3). The argument is that these performance indicators perform both a quality-control and a labour-control function. To be sure, they are used to improve the teaching and research outputs and to acknowledge and incentivise best-practice, but, they are also used as part of a broader management prerogative that is not always conducive to workplace security or worker collectivism.

Box 4.3: Some key performance indicators now used in higher education

1. research excellence framework: rating the quality of individual's research outputs
2. teaching excellence framework: rating the quality of individual's teaching
3. university league tables: ranking the overall quality of the University
4. number of students enrolling on a course or module
5. graduate job destinations and overall student employability
6. national student survey: where students rate their university experience
7. module evaluations: where students rate their module experiences
8. course evaluations: where students rate their course experience
9. student representatives: where students give collective feedback to course meetings
10. peer review of teaching
11. peer review of research
12. annual performance review: a one-to-one meeting with line manager
13. annual workload review: a one-to-one meeting with line manager
14. awards to recognise staff excellence in teaching, administration or research.

Job insecurity

There has been a great deal of recent attention directed towards workplace precarity (Waite, 2009; Standing, 2011; Lewis et al, 2015a; 2015b). It seems that for a particular group of workers, who arguably constitute a distinct yet deproletarianised class, insecurity in work has become the norm. We see this manifest itself in a number of respects from the lottery of daily street hiring and temporary agency work (Peck and Theodore, 2001) through to zero-hours contracts (Lopes and Dewan, 2014; ONS, 2014) and workers' reliance on 'bogus' self-employment opportunities (Behling and Harvey, 2015). For low-wage migrants in particular there is a distinct sense in which work opportunities are concentrated in what are essentially precarious 'secondary' (Piore, 1979) labour markets and this is especially true in countries where temporary guestworker schemes predominate (Lenard and Straehle, 2012).

The economic rationale behind endemic, structural insecurity in labour markets is essentially one of capital seeking to transfer the insecurities of the market onto certain segments, arguably growing segments, of the labour force. The distribution of risks and rewards, as a result, becomes uneven with those gaining least reward taking on a disproportionate level of risk, via job insecurity. Insecurity, however, is also a component in worker control. Thus while it may be true that there are sharp declines in employee commitment and morale related to insecurity (Cappelli, 1995; Burchell et al, 1999), it is also true that these negatives are seen as a price worth paying by businesses in need of both flexible and deferential workers. Put another way, secondary labour markets not only help to absorb market risk, they also help businesses to control workers who may take umbrage at their role as 'shock absorbers' for the ebb and flow of the market.

Recently, the emergence of the 'on-demand' or 'gig' economy in personal services has typified this increasing insecurity within so-called formal labour markets. Providers like Uber (taxis), Deliveroo (take-away delivery), Airbnb (accommodation) and Handy (cleaning) have all emerged that involve the use of sophisticated just-in-time ICT systems, and associated 'Apps', to link the relatively time-rich income-poor self-employed with their relatively time-poor income-rich customers.

Some believe the on-demand economy in personal services is eroding pay and working conditions, reducing the role for trade unions, and leading to a decline in tax revenue as the boundary between the formal and informal economy blurs. Uber, for example, has been subject to litigation in the US for classifying workers as 'contractors' rather than 'employees' (see Chapter Six): something that means workers enjoy fewer rights, protections and entitlements. Others argue, however, that the new on-demand economy in personal services provides, among other things, 'total freedom, total flexibility, and more money'.[21]

Whatever the pros and cons of the ICT revolution, facilitating the supply of what *The Economist* (2015) has termed 'workers on tap', it is clear that insecurity is the bedfellow of flexibility and that one person's on-demand service is another person's on-call labour. There are, as a result, many issues now being raised by workers with respect to service-based careers premised upon ICT shell-companies and self-employment (Khaleeli, 2016). Not least, the worker is prized away from the institutional protections of the corporation, the state and the union and is left working, to some degree, as if in the informal economy. This informalisation process clearly has implications for labour over the short, medium and long term.

Beyond the secondary labour markets of the on-demand economy, insecurity has also spread into ostensibly permanent and once secure primary labour markets. It seems that fear of job losses, organisational change and general job insecurity is now endemic for most wage labour and that this is now a direct tool of control.

Most obviously, a number of professional careers now depend upon protracted periods of early career insecurity. Unpaid internships, for instance, are common (and controversial) in industries like the media, fashion, law and politics (Siebert and Wilson, 2013; Shade and Jacobson, 2015). Furthermore, in the university system it is expected that, for most, a permanent post will only arrive only after a protracted period (paid and unpaid) of job insecurity and often associated geographical mobility (Kimber, 2003; May et al, 2013; Lopes and Dewan, 2014; Forkert and Lopes, 2015; Nadolny and Ryan, 2015). Among other things, this professional career-path fragmentation and associated casualisation has been explained as part of a process of the management of white collar workers, and in relation to cost cutting.

In addition to the casualisation of white collar employment, especially in relation to early career professionals, insecurity also manifests itself in terms of the ongoing fear of job losses and what is euphemistically called 'restructuring'. One infamous term used among management consultants is 'POPed' also known as getting 'people off payroll'. This is accompanied by other job loss jargon from management handbooks such as going for 'low hanging fruit' (job losses) and 'rightsizing' (downsizing) firms. These management tactics are not particularly hidden from view and employees at all levels are allowed to gain insight into the looming spectre of job losses, which it is hoped will make better workers out of those that remain.

A number of recent examples illustrate the point not only that job insecurity is something facing even 'mainstream' employees but that these employers are also treated as easily interchangeable and expendable:

- In 2003, PWC (a management consultancy) sacked Accident Group (a law firm) workers by text message.
- In 2011, the Everything Everywhere (that is, Orange and Tmobile) telecommunications company used a RAG (red, amber, green) traffic light system to let staff know of redundancies.
- In March 2012, 500 KPMG (a management consultancy) staff were sent an email telling them to call a number for a pre-recorded message outlining their redundancy options.

Thus, through texts, email, voicemails, traffic light systems and so on, workers are sent clear messages about their value irrespective of whether or not they lose their job. This endemic insecurity is part of a now flagrant control mechanism. Whether or not the resultant nervousness in the workforce is ultimately good business is, however, open to question.

In terms of statistics, the main international comparative measure of job insecurity is the OECD's 'probability of becoming unemployed' indicator. This is calculated as: the number of people who were unemployed in Year Y, but were employed in Year Y-1, over the total number of employed in Year Y-1. OECD job insecurity figures are presented in Table 4.1, with Spain, Greece and Portugal standing out as having a particularly volatile labour market.

The OECD's headline national figures only take us so far, however. The UK, for example, is near the OECD job security average, and lower than many social democratic states (such as Sweden, Denmark and Finland). We know, though, that in neoliberal states job insecurity tends to be high even when the economy is doing well and people are not actually losing their jobs. The figures, in short, do not give one a flavour of how individual workers, at an everyday level, are disciplined and regulated by a culture of insecurity.

Three key aspects to employment insecurity came out of my empirical research on low-wage migrant employment in the UK food industry: workers being perpetually 'on-call' waiting for work to materialise; workers arriving at the workplace to discover either no or limited employment available; workers being made perpetually aware of their expendability and the associated over-supply of labour.

In terms of workers being perpetually 'on-call' the following quotations are illustrative:

> "We are finding out if we are working or not only a night before. Sometimes if opposite your name is written 'stand by' you know that you have to be ready to go to work from 7:00 am until 11:00 am and you are not allowed to leave your room, just in case they call you for work." (female, 37y, Lithuanian)

> "You cannot organise your private life because every day you have to be ready to work and you never know if you are going to work." (male, 56y, Polish)

Table 4.1: OECD 'Better Life Index' 2014, job security

Country	Probability of Becoming Unemployed (%)
Australia	4.4
Austria	3.4
Belgium	4.5
Canada	6.6
Chile	4.7
Czech Republic	4.2
Denmark	5.8
Estonia	5.3
Finland	6.4
France	6.5
Germany	3.2
Greece	12
Hungary	6.7
Iceland	4.3
Ireland	6.4
Israel	6.5
Italy	5.5
Japan	2.9
Korea	3
Luxembourg	4
Mexico	4.7
Netherlands	3.6
New Zealand	5.8
Norway	2.9
Poland	7.3
Portugal	9.1
Slovak Republic	5.8
Slovenia	5
Spain	17.7
Sweden	6.5
Switzerland	2.8
Turkey	7.8
UK	5.6
USA	6.3
OECD	5.3

Source: OECD Better Life Index (2014), http://stats.oecd.org/Index.aspx?DataSetCode=BLI#

"It was stressful for me, I couldn't plan anything as I never knew how many hours I'll have. If I wanted to do something – like go to the hairdresser – then I'd notify a week in advance that, say, on Monday I want to go to the hairdresser." (female, 36y, Polish)

Moreover, even if migrants are promised work there are often still no guarantees. In fact, some employers call on workers only to then send them home again or to provide them with limited shifts:

"They told to that Lithuanian person to organise 20 people for the morning shift and when they arrived and were standing outside that big gate they were told that they can go home because there is no work!" (female, 44y, Polish)

"There were times when we were taken to X. We sat in the canteen for three hours and waited for orders to come in. We waited from 10:30 am to 1:00 pm just to find out are we needed or not. No one was paying us for this. Sometimes they say 'Sorry we don't need you' but we paid transport to go and sit in the canteen! Next day they, after four hours waiting, they gave us a little bit of work." (female, 37y, Lithuanian)

"In factory A you can come to work, work for 15 minutes and then they tell you 'Thank you, you can go home'. In B factory, even better, you come to work, you sit in the canteen for one or two hours and wait. Finally, they ask you to go to work. You sign in, work for 15 minutes and then they tell you 'Thank you and see you tomorrow'… Usually they send home the newcomers, people they never seen before. Their reason always is the same 'small orders today'. Sometimes I don't understand it. If you have little orders today, why does factory request the workers from agency?" (female, 38y, Lithuanian)

As Standing (2011, 34) observes: 'A life in temping is a curtailment of control over time, as the temp must be on call; the time someone must put aside for labour exceeds the time in it'.

The opportunities for workers to complain in light of this insecurity are often very limited. Most notably, employers often emphasise the expendability of workers in order to regulate their behaviour. The classic tactic in this respect is to stress, explicitly and implicitly, the elasticity of labour supply into a given work role. This can then be used to ensure deference even in the face of worsening employment conditions:

> "If a job used to pay £350 (per week), they'll pay you £200 now. You want it or not? If not, many others are queuing!" (male, 42y, Chinese)

> "They were saying, 'If you don't like it go and look outside the gate, there is 20 or more people waiting to go on your place' and it was like a person subconsciously was telling himself that he has to do it because he is afraid to lose his job." (male, 57y, Polish)

> "He was very critical (and said) that if I can't work faster then he has got people from Romania and from Bulgaria and much cheaper. So I was working like that in huge stress. I heard even some words from him 'Don't play with me because for your place I have many others workers and I will send this work to somebody else to do!'" (female, 58y, Polish)

> "He warned us that if we will be working unsatisfactory, we will lose a job immediately, because there are a lot of unemployed people who can work for him...We got the message...We have to be silent and keep quiet even if we will be unsatisfied with the job." (male, 41y, Lithuanian)

In the classic early UK study of forced labour, Anderson and Rogaly (2005, 50) found: 'a climate of insecurity and fear, a sense that one cannot do anything to protect one's physical integrity if others are willing to exploit it'. This climate of insecurity and fear means that a person need: 'never to have felt the lash to know the consequence of disobedience' (Sutch, 1975, 342 cited in Brass, 2014, 5). This explains why the willingness of workers to complain about issues at work is so low even in the free world. Box 4.4 documents the experiences of UK stakeholders and their frustrations with respect to exploited workers' unwillingness to complain.

Box 4.4: UK stakeholders' experiences of worker fear

- 'A lot of people are afraid to come forward because of fear of losing their job.' (Low Pay Commission representative)
- 'In the current climate there may be some reluctance to complain because, you know, it can make your life quite difficult.' (EASI representative)
- 'I think people are very, very sensitive. Specially at this stage with the recession – people are worried about their jobs, they're willing to put up with the bad practices…and unfortunately the employees, they're so desperate, there's no other jobs…they will just take it.' (MEAD representative)
- 'They're frightened to talk about work, because if they lose the work they lose the housing.' (CAB representative)
- 'They would not want to disclose anything if they thought that it would get back in some way to their employer, who may be their landlord…and of course they can quickly find themselves out on the street. So, consequently, they don't like to complain.' (Centre-Point Outreach representative)
- 'Even if they change their job, they wouldn't make a fuss about it because their reference depends on their employer. They wouldn't make a fuss about it fearing about their reference. It is inevitable as a new employer needs a reference.' (Avon and Bristol Law Centre representative)
- 'You hear of some cases where somebody has tried to enforce their rights, you know and gets dismissed on the spot…and then you've got 200 other sort of fruit pickers who are never going to enforce their rights because they saw what happened to their colleague.' (CAB representative)
- 'It is not unheard of for people who complain to us to say 'No, I haven't felt able to take this up with the management because the last person who did was threatened or sacked'. You know I've heard that quite a lot…it's certainly a comment that I've heard fairly regularly.' (HSE representative)
- 'Very few workers will commit to a statement, very few. I mean we can take action as far as rescinding a licence, revoking a licence goes on that…but obviously as far as a criminal prosecution goes, that's a different kettle of fish.' (GLA[1] representative)

Source: Geddes et al (2013)

Note: [1] In 2016 the GLA (Gangmasters Licensing Authority) was renamed the GLAA (Gangmasters and Labour Abuse Authority).

Bullying and mobbing[22]

Sometimes controls over labour may become personal and adversarial in a way that targets, monitoring, surveillance and workplace insecurity are not. In these instances, agents of power (supervisors, managers and so on) are given the task of transferring pressures onto workers directly and a name and face is given to worker control. Workers will respond to this, if pressure is excessive, by feelings of powerlessness and identifiable bullies may emerge. Moreover, in some cases groups of workers will be co-opted into bullying behaviour against a colleague or small number of colleagues: something known as 'mobbing'.

Both bullying and mobbing are commonplace and this book is interested in them here in so far as they are used strategically by capital as a tool to discipline labour. This caveat is important because bullying and mobbing may also result from dysfunctional personal relationships that have nothing much to do with the need to strategically and systemically control labour (see Beale and Hoel, 2011).

In terms of overall prevalence, Hoel et al (2010, 453) estimate that bullying affects between 5% to 10% of European workers at any one time while Raynor et al (2002) show that, in a five-year period, bullying will affect 25% of workers. Raynor et al (2002) also point out that, in 75% of cases, a manager is responsible for this. Though we know from Pollert (2010, 80) that when bullying does occur the hierarchies involved usually close ranks against the complainant. Mobbing (see Leymann, 1990; Niedl, 1996; Einarsen, 2000) is a network-based variety of bullying that: 'is a much more sophisticated way of doing someone in than murder, and in most countries it has the advantage of being entirely legal' (Duffy and Sperry, 2012, 3). It can involve classic bullying traits – physical abuse, verbal abuse, work overloading, social isolation, entrapment and so on – but it is experienced by a worker as an orchestrated movement against him/her by the employer and through a number of the employers' agents. It is, essentially, a collective and strategic form of workplace control and discipline with the aim often to drive a worker out. It also has the effect of making an example of a particular worker, that others are then scared of and disciplined by. According to Duffy and Sperry mobbers are also: 'masters of impression management, and they deliberately create a negative and misleading image of the target victim' (Duffy and Sperry, 2012, 9). This denies the victim space for complaining and traps them in an inward-looking situation where their own mobbing is not only seen to be their own fault, but is also largely hidden, even if the consequences are not.

There is ample evidence of physical and psychological health problems from bullying and mobbing (Duffy and Sperry, 2012) but in many cases such harm is ascribed to the characteristics of the individual rather than to their regressive work experiences (Leymann, 1990). This is despite the fact that the mental affects from bullying and mobbing can actually be: 'fully comparable with Post Traumatic Stress Disorder from war or prison camp experiences' (Leymann and Gustafsson, 1996, 251).

In my own research on the low-wage food industry I found evidence of visible and direct supervisor bullying; though I did not find evidence of more subtle and hidden forms of mobbing, and it may be that the latter is more common in white-collar work environments. The bullying uncovered was mainly direct verbal abuse such as shouting, name calling and swearing:

> "Supervisors were treating us very badly. They shouted at us, sworn at us. They did not call us by names, we were called by numbers. They treated us like slaves, like slaves. It was very difficult to get used to this, we were treated like livestock. But we did not have a choice as we did not have our passport, no language knowledge and no money, but debts with interest on top. I did not know what to do." (female, 42y, Latvian)

> "Those English who are supervisors are treating us like animals, calling names, rushing us, like in a concentration camp…what they have in the end of their tongue, they don't have any barriers, a person is treated like…dung…a total cesspit, humiliation, there is only work, work, doing the most you can so there will be as much profit from it all. People are only working objects to (the supervisor)." (male, 57y, Polish)

> "Polish and Russian employees were treated the worst. There was a girl Tina who was called names by the boss: 'You are useless, you should go and stand under a street lamp!' Every time she wore make-up she was called a bitch. She was told to go to stand under a street lamp." (female, 32y, Polish)

> "The farmer was treating us terribly. He was swearing at us every five seconds even if it was not our fault, for no apparent reason. He was constantly shouting at us: 'You c★★t, you total and utter s★★t, go away from my farm and do not come back'. He was constantly using phrases like 'you're stupid', 'you idiot'." (male, 31y, Belarusian)

Workers put up with this bullying because they were in no position to complain as relatively powerless individuals against their more powerful employers. For most, this kind of work was about survival with bullying a normal part of this process. Moreover, when workers do complain – and 'whistleblow' (see Chapter Five) or engage with a trade union (see Chapter Eight) – they are often further bullied or mobbed and made an example of.

Excessive hours

Whether one is forced to work long hours by their employer, out of economic necessity, or due to a cultural expectation, the fact remains that such action can be very detrimental in terms of health and wellbeing. There is a link between long hours and job dissatisfaction (Artazcoz et al, 2009), long hours and workplace accidents (Wagstaff and Lie, 2011), long hours and anxiety and depression (Kleppa et al, 2008), and long hours and poor social and family life (Harrington, 2001). Excessive hours are legislated against for these very reasons: such as through the EU Working Time Directive limit of a 48-hour working week (see Chapter Eight). However, OECD data still shows that working 'very long hours' (over 50 hours per week) is a problem (see Table 4.2). It is most prevalent in countries like Mexico, Turkey, Japan and Korea where out of both economic necessity (Mexico, Turkey) and social pressure (Japan, Korea) employers are able to create a long-hours culture.

Perhaps the most well-known recent campaign to resist excessive hours and ensure work breaks has come from domestic workers in Singapore. Here the estimated 200,000 domestic workers were not entitled to even a day's rest until 2013. The law then changed following a campaign for domestic worker rights, though there is still no minimum wage. This campaign developed after Singapore's failure to sign up to the 2011 ILO Convention on Decent Work for Domestic Workers (Convention Number 189), which establishes global standards for the world's 50–100 million domestic workers in those states that ratify it. Progress was slow in Singapore because of how popular and widespread the use of domestic workers has become but, in the event, it was realised that legislation was not in line with the majority world-view. It is telling, however, that in a highly-developed economy like Singapore such labour practices were the norm until the campaigning and state intervention that followed.

Excessive hours are also common when workers are vulnerable, so the employment insecurity talked about above can lead to pressure

Table 4.2: OECD 'Better Life Index' 2014, very long hours

Country	Working Very Long (50+) Hours Per Week (%)
Australia	14.2
Austria	8.6
Belgium	4.4
Canada	4.0
Chile	15.4
Czech Republic	7.1
Denmark	2.1
Estonia	3.6
Finland	3.7
France	8.7
Germany	5.6
Greece	5.7
Hungary	2.9
Iceland	13.7
Ireland	4.2
Israel	18.8
Italy	3.7
Japan	22.6
Korea	27.1
Luxembourg	3.18
Mexico	28.8
Netherlands	0.6
New Zealand	13.1
Norway	3.1
Poland	7.6
Portugal	9.3
Slovak Republic	6.5
Slovenia	5.7
Spain	5.6
Sweden	1.1
Switzerland	7.3
Turkey	43.3
UK	12.3
USA	11.4
OECD	8.8

Source: OECD Better Life Index (2014), http://stats.oecd.org/Index.aspx?DataSetCode=BLI#

on workers simply to work flat-out whenever there is the prospect of earning:

> "There are no established working hours. (If orders are good) you can start at 6 am and finish 12 in the evening. We are working around 60 hours weekly, sometimes 80 hours. There isn't time to do anything. You come home, get shower and go to sleep. In the morning you get up at 6 am again and go to work. That's it!" (female, 24y, Bulgarian)

> "You work from 7:30 am to the evening. You must work till you finish all the work, in the evening…you just keep working…When they tell you that you must make 100 kilogram of bean curd you cannot leave the factory until you actually meet the target. No fixed time." (male, 50y, Chinese)

> "The working hours during the season are usually from 6.15 am until 10, 11 pm. This is constantly during the season. From Monday until Sunday, those are the hours I am working constantly. And I cannot take a day off at all during the season. This is minimum of two and a half months during the season. Yes, two and half months without day off. Yes, I feel very stressed. I just feel very tired and almost falling asleep staring at the fruit." (male, 27y, Slovakian)

Beck (2000, 77) has observed that: 'the boundaries between work and non-work are staring to blur, in respect of time, space and contractual content'. This is true for many of the workers cited above, especially those who are living a very insecure life 'on call' and picking up any scraps of work thrown to them, and with all the deference required of them. For such workers, the need for employment, and the need to be ready for employment whenever it arises, can effectively limit active and independent communal life outside of work (Mitchell, 2011). Excessive hours, in this respect, are more than about time spent in work, they are also about time spent waiting for and worrying about work.

Conclusion

From Taylorism onwards employment research has been directed towards questions of how best to control labour, with the problem of how to minimise labour exploitation and work-based harm receiving scant attention. The science of employment has been largely shaped by the requirements of capital and, as a result, a great deal of knowledge has been amassed to enable employers to maximise their returns on their investment in labour. The emergence of carefully targeted direct workplace controls are the most obvious example of the knowledge that has built up during capital's quest for 'good' and 'better' workers. These controls are designed to make people work harder, and also to be more grateful for the chance to work hard, and they are often implemented without the need for bullying or mobbing.

One clear example of this is the imposition of almost unreachable 'rainbow targets' and the monitoring of employee performance against these. Such targets reduce slackness in the system such that spare time for worker sociability is limited or non-existent, and the treatment of workers as objects and quasi-machines is seen as something to be lauded. Another example of this type of management is the use of endemic insecurity to discipline labour that might otherwise contest the intensification of workplace regimes. In both cases workers are likely to be driven to work hard through direct forms of controls that, crucially, do not involve force *per se* as traditionally defined and understood.

From a social harm perspective, the question is whether individual workers and the societies they are part of suffer from the kinds of direct controls discussed above. If something is lost in the ever-tightening control machinery available to capital, then this raises the question of whether the workers subjected to this machinery are controlled in an excessive and oppressive manner. To be sure, the direct control systems discussed largely fall within the law, but this is the benefit of looking beyond criminology when seeking to question work-based practices that are exploitative and/or harmful. Through a social harm lens, then, we can start to problematise what might otherwise be deemed a normal part of everyday employment and ask, very simply, is there not a better way to do things that might allow workers a chance to flourish both inside and outside the workplace?

The coffee maker

She stood there with tears in the kitchen, coffee under her nails and the fatigue,
tiredness in a body that could not manage any more right now.

She said that now she did not want to be a part any more, now they would
have to find someone else who could work a whole day without
going to the bathroom.

Someone who could face the contempt with infinite patience,
that if they wanted a machine they could buy a regular coffee maker.

Her fist was clutched around the cake slicer with suddenly so sharp edges
that she recoiled when she saw her own gaze in the cutting machine blade.

Someone had called her lazy and rude, asked her to work faster,
it was like watching a machine jarring under pressure, just that there were no
spare parts, they would simply have to buy a new one now that the old one was
worn out.

A coffee maker of the latest model:
quiet, fast and easy to clean.

FIVE

Indirect workplace controls

Network-based control

The previous chapter looked at direct worker controls within the workplace, namely: targets, monitoring and surveillance; job insecurity; bullying and mobbing; and excessive hours. The purpose of this chapter is to profile indirect forms of worker control within the workplace. This is in recognition of the fact that employers may use various mechanisms to produce and reproduce what they recognise as 'good' and 'better' workers but that within these mechanisms there may be elements of obfuscation with respect to both the visibility and origins of control.

This is an important recognition because under the advanced capitalist system power and control has evolved in sophisticated ways. There has been, quite simply, a broad and largely progressive shift away from coercion:

> Whereas feudal property was founded on armed force and sustained and expanded through the power of the sword (though it was also traded and inherited), capitalist property rests upon forms of activity that are intrinsically non-coercive and non-political. (Walzer, 1983, 294)

In other words, power is now gained and maintained more subtly and skilfully than in the past. Controls still exist but they are as likely to be felt as to be seen. At the same time, beneficiaries are likely to be equally evasive with power veiled to a degree not evident in previous phases of capitalism.

The main implication of this is that the capitalist constellations underpinning contemporary accumulation have become complex, multifaceted and multi-dimensional. We see this in the way in which product supply chains are contingent upon sub-contracting and the use of labour market intermediaries. However, while 'circuits may be disconnected, capitalism is neither dead nor disorganised' (Thompson, 2003, 372). On the contrary, the networked dispersion of capitalist functions is about the maintenance of control through indirect means. This enables capital to maintain power but to not be as directly accountable for the implications of this maintenance. In terms of labour, this causes workers to experience distance and dislocation from the mechanisms controlling their time and actions. Most obviously, a worker may be employed by an agency on a temporary contract to work in a firm sub-contracted by a larger company that in turn supplies an even larger organisation. In this instance, it is hard to see the worker ever being able to locate, never mind to challenge or resist, those actually responsible for exploitation and harm when it arises.

Recent investigations into labour exploitation in both the Thai prawn industry (Hodal et al, 2014) and the Indian tea industry (Chamberlain, 2014) have demonstrated very clearly the networked way in which many industries function (See Table 5.1). There is invariably a dominant 'lead firm', with shareholder beneficiaries, towards the consumer end of the supply chain (Gereffi and Korzeniewicz, 1994) and then often equally powerful 'category managers' heading the actual production networks. Below these major firms there are then various networks in and through which exploitation takes place. These might be smaller sub-contracted companies, labour market intermediaries, and so on. The complex corporate networking means that those with most power and control are usually only indirectly accountable for any exploitation and, as such, often assume, somewhat paradoxically, the role of supply chain custodian in order to prevent exploitation from occurring.

Table 5.1: Network-based capitalism and exploitation

Food industry case study	Lead firm(s) at head of global value chain	Category manager	Supplier level 1	Supplier level 2	Workplace exploitation
Thai Prawn Industry (Hodal et al, 2014)	Global Supermarkets	CP Foods (Prawn Supplier)	Fishmeal Producer	Trash Fish Trawlers	Exploitation of Burmese and Cambodian migrant workers in international waters on trash fish trawlers
Indian Tea Plantations (Chamberlain, 2014)	Global Supermarkets and Brand Company (e.g. Tetley)	Assam Tea Estates owned by consortium (including Tata Global Beverages)	Assam Tea Estates		Exploitation of workers on estate who are paid under the Assam state minimum wage. Workers are also taken from estate and sold as domestic servants.

Source: Hodal et al (2014); Chamberlain (2014)

One of the problems with the network base of many modern labour markets is that capitalism is highly organised and incredibly complex but that labour is all too often unorganised and isolated. As Beck (2000, 86) notes: 'Never before have working people, irrespective of their talents and educational achievements, been as dependent and vulnerable as they are today, working in individualised situations without countervailing, collective powers, and within flexible networks whose meaning and rules are impossible for most of them to fathom.' Thus, not only does networked capitalism enable indirect control over labour to flourish but it also makes it harder for labour to come together and to locate and challenge any exploitative and harmful practices.

There are two essential ingredients of the indirect network-based control now so characteristic of modern employment. First, power is achieved and maintained via the functional diffusion of productive roles across intra- and inter-firm networks and by the associated devolution of responsibility down through these networks and eventually onto firms and workers with least power. Edwards (1979) remarks in the opening to his seminal book *Contested Terrain* that what is so impressive about modern organisations is their ability to maintain power by relinquishing it; in the sense that control over workers has increasingly become de-personalised and placeless: there is often no person or group of people who can easily be identified as responsible for changing working conditions and so workers are often left with no-one to blame and no minds to try and change in order to gain more breathing space. Edwards goes on to suggest that 'the workplace is a battleground' (1979, 13) and so it would seem, to continue his analogy, that employers are increasingly using guerrilla warfare against increasingly exposed employees. The ostensible relinquishing of roles and responsibility across corporate networks means that power appears diffuse and so is not left exposed as a visible and monolithic target for resistance (as it has done in the past). Thus, power becomes more nimble, nuanced and thus enduring.

Second, diffusion of roles and devolution of responsibilities across corporate networks does not mean that socio-economic hierarchies are essentially flattening. It means that these hierarchies are becoming more complex and less directly implicated in their own sustenance. This is not particularly new, as Thompson (1993, 43) notes of the eighteenth century: 'the Gentry might profit from the sale of wool, but they were not seen to be in a direct exploitative relation to the clothing workers'. In order for this distance and dislocation to be maintained networks are required, as outlined above, but so too are key agents at each network level within the overall socio-economic hierarchy. These agents are located within a system in which they follow orders and affect livelihoods without being in any position themselves to resist. It is in such systems that agents end up harming others without any alternative option (other than to harm themselves). Back in 1930s Oklahoma, for example, John Steinbeck's *Grapes of Wrath* (Steinbeck, 1939) observed how farmers were being evicted from the land by: 'people caught in something larger than themselves...it's the monster...Men made it, but they can't control it'. This 'monster', gives to those who follow it but it also takes from those who do not. Moreover, it also, sometimes, takes even from those who follow.

The ostensible relinquishing of control through corporate networks and the associated role of agents of power in these networks are important dimensions in understanding workplace controls that often snowball out from power bases, but then become detached from these, while also still sustaining them. Controls in this respect can certainly take on a life of their own and when this means obvious worker exploitation and harm those with power, to be fair, often do try to rein things in. The key challenge for capitalism, given the networked system that now prevails, is to protect those on the edges of the system bearing the full brunt of the pressures and responsibilities that travel down through the various hierarchal structures that sustain it. The problem in this respect is that short-term profits may be lost as a result of cushioning labour; even if, over the medium to long term, labour is likely to be most productive, and the overall system less harmful and more sustainable, when based on more humane forms of control.

Labour market intermediaries

One of the main ways in which labour is kept at 'arm's-length' from capital is through the use of indirect employment, whereby labour market intermediaries (LMIs) are responsible for workers, even though they do not usually determine workers' ultimate conditions of employment. The activity of LMIs has been increasingly examined by academics (Barrientos, 2008; 2013; Coe et al, 2008; Peck and Theodore 1998; 2001; 2007; Purcell et al, 2004) and particularly in relation to migrant labour (Rogaly, 2008a; Pijpers, 2010; Findlay and McCollum, 2013; Sporton, 2013; Jones, 2014). Moreover, the role of LMIs appears to be growing across advanced capitalist societies as standard employment relationships break down. As Strauss and Fudge (2013, 5) observe: 'Two of the key trends in contemporary labour markets are the rise in nonstandard work and new and increasing forms of labour intermediation.'

An important watershed in this rise in non-standard, mediated employment came in 1997 via the ILO's Private Employment Agencies Convention (Convention Number 181). Historically, the ILO had been against private employment agencies because of the fear that they would lead to a downward competitive spiral: with firms moving directly employed workers onto temporary and arm's-length contractual relationships. The ILO's decision to seek to regulate rather than oppose LMIs was, therefore, highly significant and reflected the global pressure towards greater labour market flexibility commensurate with the dominant neoliberal paradigm.

Firms use LMIs for three main reasons. First, the negative impacts of market uncertainty can be at least partly transferred onto temporary workers. Thus, a firm will employ a core staff but then use LMIs to lever the workforce up or down depending upon demand. As the following low-wage employers explained:

> "So it's a phone call to one of our two agencies. And we'll say, depending on which product, and which kind of pack-house, say we need more baby leaf salad, we'll say we need another 50 staff. So we'll phone up the agency and they hopefully have sort of 50 more people on the books who are looking for work. And [they will] pick people up at weird times depending on what time orders come in. And we'll say, you know, can we have 30 staff, can we have them in 20 minutes kind of thing…I saw an email this morning saying that they'd taken on 34 people to do one shift and the orders were, well they were crappy, so they let them all go at one o'clock in the morning kind of thing. So it's literally that. We need them, we don't, we need them, we don't, we need them, we don't." (HR Manager, Lettuce, Onion and Watercress Grower)

> "We use 200 agency staff to top-up during busy periods with 26 languages spoken on-site. Now the traditional model of factory employment involved workers on a Monday to Friday 8 am to 4 pm, or 9 am to 5 pm contract, with the prospect of weekend overtime. This wasn't efficient given when in the week our demand is greatest and we could never meet the demand on Sunday: which meant a backlog into the new week. To survive, we needed to be flexible in the way we worked and turn workers 'on and off' as quickly as the sun comes out. In our industry [salad

produce] the weather drives demand." (HR Manager, UK Salad Producer)

A similar system of flexibility exists in business relationships and specifically sub-contracting along supply chains (Wills, 2009): where large firms contract work out to smaller firms as and when they require their services. The use of both LMIs and sub-contracted firms, then, is about the distribution of risk along the supply chain to where there is least resistance and/or where power is limited.

Second, LMIs are used because they allow firms to use workers but to not be directly responsible for these workers. LMIs effectively make it more difficult to fix blame for exploitation and harm onto any one actor. Third, and as we saw in the previous chapter, insecurity in employment can be a tool to control and discipline labour, and this is true of LMIs offering non-standard employment to precarious workers. In summary, then, LMIs and the workers they post absorb market risk, confuse the chain of corporate command and responsibility, and result in more disciplined and controlled forms of labour (see Box 5.1, and the case study of Atlanco-Rimec in Chapter Eight).

Box 5.1: Sports Direct and agency labour use in the UK

In June 2016 the House of Commons Business, Innovation and Skills Committee collected evidence on agency labour use by Sports Direct at its Shirebrook distribution centre in Derbyshire, UK. It heard from the unions, the agencies supplying labour to Sports Direct, and from Sports Direct (House of Commons, 2016a). Views differed on whether agency labour was exploitative. Reading the evidence provided, four questions on agency labour use by Sports Direct stand out:

- Why is the majority of the Sports Direct workforce (circa 3,400 workers) employed through agencies?
- Why are 'short-hours' (guaranteeing only 336 hours work per year) contracts used by these agencies?
- Why is an attrition rate of 1.5–2% of workers per week not of concern (each week this means 34 staff out of an agency's 1,700 workers will leave, equating to the entire workforce over the course of a year)?
- Why do so few workers take part in consultations (45 responses were received to a survey sent to around 2,000 workers)?

Put another way why could a business model not be developed that means:

- most workers are employed directly;
- most workers have a stable workload and income;
- most workers, over the course of a year, want to remain with their employer;
- most workers have the opportunity to raise concerns over control, exploitation and harm anonymously and to an independent body.

Strauss and Fudge (2013) have drawn direct links between LMIs and what they term 'unfree labour'. One can see, given the above, how these links exist. However, it is important to recognise that the role LMIs play is varied and multifaceted. Many, for example, post skilled workers and there is often little evidence of exploitation at this level of the labour market given the pay these workers receive. Where there are concerns over LMIs is at the bottom end of the labour market, where intermediaries are being used to cut costs and increase profit levels. Relatively little is known, though, about the varied types of LMIs that find employment (and travel, accommodation and so on) for precarious workers.

To address this knowledge gap, and drawing upon my own research (Geddes and Scott, 2010, 210), it is possible to distinguish between various forms and types of temporary labour provision:

- Global versus Local: Many countries have both large and small LMIs and larger global/national firms are often much more conscious of, and exposed to, potential reputation damage than SMEs.
- Communal versus Bureaucratic: The difference here is between LMIs supplying workers through social ties (kin and kith) and those supplying workers based only on professional–contractual ties. The former type of communal LMI tends to operate in the informal economy, but is not necessarily more exploitative.
- External versus Internal: Some labour users operate by having in-house rather than relying on genuinely independent LMIs. This means that they either have very close ties to ostensibly (but not *de facto*) independent firms who are often located on site or adjacent, or, that workers are moved between businesses via a larger parent company to meet temporary requirements. In both cases, the parent firm effectively controls the temporary labour supply, even if quasi-autonomous LMIs exist.
- Formal versus Informal: The classic informal LMI is the smuggler/trafficker who promises migrants travel and employment for a fee. Informal LMIs are generally where government concern is focused.

- Regular versus Task-based: Many firms have a regular (daily, weekly, monthly, seasonal) need for temporary labour and will use LMIs accordingly. There are, however, specific tasks and projects that also require temporary workers but that occur on a more *ad hoc* basis.
- Direct versus Indirect: The deployment of workers from one agency to another agency can sometimes occur so that two or more LMIs are involved in a given placement. In these cases, labour supply would be classed as indirect. This is something that often happens in the case of migrants moving to, and finding their first job within, a host country. When two or more LMIs are used in worker posting, the chain of command and responsibility becomes even more convoluted than normal.
- Domestic versus Foreign: In the case of temporary migrant workers, foreign LMIs are often used to facilitate travel to and find work within a host country.
- Work versus Other Services: LMIs primary role is to provide employment. However, many also provide workers with extras such as travel and accommodation. Deductions for the latter are often more controversial than LMIs' role in supplying work.
- Temporary versus Permanent: There is a distinction between LMIs posting workers who expect to gain permanent employment versus those who will always be temporary. In many cases, the prospect of potential permanent employment is used to incentivise temporary workers.

The above clearly demonstrates the complex nature of temporary labour provision and it would be wrong to conclude, in my view, that all LMIs are by design exploitative. The sector is far too nuanced for this.

What is clear, however, is that excessive and oppressive work-based control is often evident when and where LMIs operate, partly because of the cover LMIs are able to give employers. In short, LMIs are there to absorb responsibility for workplace exploitation and work-based harm because they are ultimately responsible for the workers they post, and, they post some of the most precarious and vulnerable workers in the entire labour market. This explains why the ILO was reluctant to acknowledge the role of LMIs until quite recently (1997) and why the focus of many investigations into sub-standard working conditions has been centred on LMIs. Phillips and Mieres (2011, 20), for instance, argue that: 'the prevalence of labour contractors is a strong contributing factor to the conditions in which unfree labour relations and forced labour practices are enabled to flourish' and this is a point that Fudge and Strauss (2013) demonstrate very clearly in their recent book *Temporary Work, Agencies and Unfree Labour*.

Commonly, the link between LMIs and exploitation takes one of two main forms. First, it involves LMIs recruiting and then supplying vulnerable migrant labour across international borders; usually from poorer peripheral areas to more affluent core economies. An example highlighted by Human Rights Watch (HRW, 2011) was of Cambodian migrants moving to Thailand for domestic work. Agents in Cambodia would recruit, train and place the would-be migrants and then organise their journeys to Thailand for employment. However, charges for these services purposefully created a debt-bondage situation, whereby it soon became impossible for a worker to withdraw consent from the scheme regardless of how bad conditions got. Effectively LMIs were manufacturing migrants' compliance through elaborate systems of indebtedness and the migrants then became heavily dependent upon whatever work was on offer.

Second, LMIs are used within a national labour market in order to allow core companies to distance themselves from the 'dirty work'. Sharma (2006) cites the example of the indigenous Quechua people in Bolivia to illustrate this process. In the Bolivian sugar cane industry the main companies employ sub-contractors in order to achieve a particular output every fortnight. These sub-contractors then employ LMIs to hire enough labour to meet their target, and they usually recruit the more vulnerable Quechua people. However, the LMI is only commissioned by the sub-contractor and not by the big sugar companies. Thus, the big sugar companies can claim that they are not responsible for working conditions, even while benefiting from these conditions.

Whether LMIs are used in migrant labour markets (as in Cambodia/ Thailand) or in convoluted domestic supply chains (as in Bolivia) the point remains that LMIs are where control over labour appears to be most intense. One of the moral–legal dilemmas is whether LMIs are entirely to blame for the resultant exploitation and harm that workers experience. Put another way, to what extent are the users of domestic labour (in Thailand) and the large sugar companies (in Bolivia) responsible for the actions of the LMIs on whom they ultimately rely?

My own UK-based research uncovered various issues with LMIs. Principally, there was a pattern of underpayment due to excessive deductions, with this underpayment then leading on to indebtedness and desperation for work. One of the main (illegal) tactics was to ask workers to pay for the chance to get a temporary job:

"We paid [X] £250 each for providing work for us. It was
not for accommodation. It was for the opportunity to work.
If we did not pay, we would sit without work. She did not
request money straight away. We started to work, earned
some money and then she demanded £250 from each
person. If you do not pay, you would sit without work."
(female, 50y, Lithuanian)

"We were working maximum of 25 hours per week, but
more often we worked only for 10 to 12 hours per week.
No work, no work, no work, no work. Later on he came
to us and said, 'If you would like to work more, you will
have to pay me again. If you refuse to pay me, you would
not get any work.' We did not pay the owner of the agency
but a Latvian woman who was the agency manager's wife.
We were made aware if we pay them, we will have work
in the future…If you pay them, they have an expression:
these are 'our people'. They will provide work in the first
place to 'our people'. They provide work to those who
paid them." (female, 60y, Latvian)

The fact that LMIs required informal payments in order to provide
migrants with work is in itself illegal in the UK. What this lead on to,
however, was equally problematic: migrants got into debt because of
the need to pay to get work and this indebtedness made them all the
more desperate and deferential. This is classic debt-bondage but for
modern times and was something directly orchestrated by the LMIs
via the charges levied.

LMIs also controlled migrants in other ways, most obviously through
the provision of tied accommodation. This type of accommodation
provision is not illegal. Nevertheless, tied accommodation was often
expensive relative to what workers got paid and/or was overcrowded
and sub-standard:

"Can you imagine that my wife and I had to sleep in a
single bed? Our two sons were in a bunk bed that both of
them could sleep in. The whole family was in one room."
(male, 43y, Chinese)

"I was shocked [sighs]. Very small accommodation, we were
five people. The caravan is for five people…We have two
rooms, a common, a living room and a kitchen…One of

the girls sleeps in the living room, two of us are living in one of the rooms and the two girls live in the other room." (female, 21y, Bulgarian)

"All of us [eight people] with lots of baggage were placed in a tiny room [by the agency]…One person slept on the bed, but the rest of us [seven] slept on mattresses on the floor." (male, 27y, Lithuanian)

"I worked for a bit. Then I was not working for two months. Later we worked, but agency requested all the money for accommodation. So we were sitting without any money at all. It was like that…When we get our salary, we had to pay for accommodation. They purposely gave us enough work to pay for accommodation and that was it." (female, 61y, Estonian)

Thus, once again additional fees levied by LMIs were creating situations of indebtedness for migrants. Such situations are very difficult to escape. Moreover, when you are reliant on LMIs for work and for accommodation you are also in vulnerable and precarious positions irrespective of the debt you owe to them. It is due to these circumstances than many argue that there is a direct relationship between LMIs and unfreedom (Strauss and Fudge, 2013).

Poverty and debt

Debt-bondage is one of the key indicators of forced labour (Box 2.2). It arises when workers find themselves dependent upon their employer for work and also indebted to them. It is one of the classic forms of indirect control in the sense that, through debt, an employer does not actually have to tell a worker to work, and to work hard. This simply becomes a necessity in order to survive.

Indebtedness through employment comes about in a number of ways: through insufficient work; through low pay; through excessive deductions; and via inherited debt. One of the big questions is why workers do not simply walk away from their job in order to escape their debt? The answer to this is complex. If you are poor and dependent upon work, then walking away might actually mean destitution and starvation. In such contexts, debt bondage is often seen as the least-worst option. It is also the case that failure to pay debts often leads to further trouble via informal reprisals or legal action. The 'lender' also often provides indebted workers with essential money to cover seasonal downturns in work, for healthcare, weddings, funerals and so on when no other source of finance would be available. Finally, escaping debt would likely mean moving house and area, something that takes considerable psychological strength (and money). Related to this, there are complex social and cultural networks that tie workers to particular places, and to particular labour markets, despite debt being prevalent.

Temporary and seasonal workers are the most vulnerable to debt bondage because of their need for money during slack periods of employment. In India, for example, it is common for prospective seasonal labourers to tie themselves to an employer through the advancement of loans to cover the slack period until paid work becomes available. In some cases the prospective labourer receives a small allowance until the seasonal work arrives, with all debts to be settled at the end of the season. The workers is, therefore, tied to the employer for the season. Debts can, however, be so great that they either leave workers with little actual pay or are carried over into the next season. Paradoxically, many workers actually express support for this system because their debt allows them to survive the off-season and also provides a guarantee that employment will eventually arrive.

Financial dependence on LMIs and employers is also created in other ways. Anderson and Rogaly's benchmark study (2005, 38–42), for instance, found that debt and deductions are common in forced labour cases and come in various guises. There are charges for migrants for travelling to a country: their travel, documentation and so on There are fees for actually finding people employment. There are charges for tied accommodation. And, there are charges for work-related services such as uniform and equipment provision, travelling to work and so on. These various types of deductions, as with the seasonal advancements that are common in India, mean that the wage workers received is in reality much lower than officially advertised. Moreover, the real wage can actually fall so low as to underpin indebtedness.

One particularly long-standing mechanism of indebtedness is known as the 'truck' system. This is common on remote ranches and plantations where workers (often indigenous minorities) are paid, but they are then charged excessive prices for basic foodstuffs, clothes and medicines. The employer is effectively capturing back the wages paid by making sizeable profits from supplying workers in remote locations with essential goods. He/she has both an employment and retail monopoly and is able to indirectly squeeze workers via the latter. This truck system often leads to worker indebtedness and has been closely linked in the literature to exploitation and forced labour.

The question of why exploited workers, in any country, accept indebtedness as a permanent shadow over them is complex. Crudely, workers have no choice, and their choices are even more limited when in debt. There is still, however, the question of why workers do not rise up against indebtedness and this, according to the ILO, is linked to prevailing moral–legal norms:

> Modern-day slavery relies on the workers' code of ethics, a code that prevents them from leaving their jobs before they have paid off their debts. Although the debt may have been incurred as a result of fraud, the debtor is imprisoned by this common code of ethics and feels morally obliged to repay the sum in question. To a certain extent, the code explains why most workers do not question their situation. It dictates that all debts must be paid, and acts as a symbolic and effective means of dominating and imprisoning workers in the workplace. This feeling of moral obligation is therefore part of the structure that makes modern-day slavery possible. (ILO, 2009b, 64)

Thus, even with excessive deductions, unreasonable charges, loans with very high interest rates, and questionable accounting, workers still internalise debt as their own particular problem that they need to solve. The use of debt to discipline labour, then, is not only an important indirect tool of control, but it is also something that can have a profound psychological impact. In extreme cases, debt is transferred across generations and debt-bondage can effectively be inherited. This is commonplace among bonded labourers in India and in 1976 the 'Bonded Labour Abolition Act of India' was passed in order to allow families to walk away from the debts of deceased relatives. Tellingly, the Act is still not widely used and many workers in debt-bondage have inherited their status. This underlines the point that laws often only go so far with respect to protecting vulnerable and precarious workers.

Debt-bondage appears particularly common in low-wage pre-capitalist labour markets across the developing world (Reid and Brewster, 1983). However, in-work poverty and indebtedness is something that is also evident in advanced capitalist economies, and beyond traditional 'peonage' systems (LeBaron, 2014; Shildrick et al, 2012). In my own research, for example, I found evidence of employers systematically underpaying already vulnerable workers:

"That boss was very, very stingy. When I worked ten hours, he would note it down as six or seven hours. Always a few hours less. He drove us there at 7 am. It took two hours to get there. We worked from 9 am to 6 pm, sometimes finished work at 10 pm, and got home at 2 am. He always calculated two hours less. We calculated the hours we worked, every day, but they never followed our records. They always paid less. Every week when the payday came, we had to argue with the boss. Arguing all the time." (male, 42y, Chinese)

"Then the war began. Men started to go mad. I thought that we will have to call the police. People were very annoyed and unhappy. They worked ten days (for 12 hours per day) and received £11. I understand we had to pay for the caravan and for travel, ok £60 for the week, but we had to receive the rest of the money. No one got all their money." (female, 59y, Latvian)

"I did not work there for long. We travelled to work an hour and a half one way and for an hour and a half back. We were starting to work at 6 am, so we were getting up at 3 am. We were earning around £2 per week! From our salary they deducted money for accommodation. After deductions we received £2 per week. Two of us were sharing a tiny room. We paid £65 per week each. This still goes on over there. New people are still arriving and are exploited." (female, 50y, Lithuanian)

"I felt fear all the time. I know some people are happy when they receive their wages but for me it was the worst day. At the morning, when I was checking the account, I was so nervous thinking how much this time is missing. What this time is wrong with my pay. I knew for 100% that something's going to be wrong." (female, 26y, Polish)

These workers above were not contractually obliged to their employer but they were in desperate need of payment when their employer decided to hold back wages.

For many workers, irrespective of whether they were paid the correct wages, poverty and indebtedness were the norm:

"My husband was off work for three weeks. Our rent is £65 a week, after all deductions we received £1.66 a week (for those three weeks)." (female, 38y, Lithuanian)

"I was working but ending up without any money at all. Because by the time I've paid my petrol, by the time I've paid my bills, by the time I've paid my food, all the money was gone!" (female, 31y, Polish)

"We all have ended up in debt. I have arrived on 5 January, but my first salary I have received a few days before my name day on 25 March. All this time I have survived on £119. I have borrowed twice a little bit of money to top up my phone, so I could call home…We have been buying in the shop the cheapest food…just to survive…We calculated that we were spending £2–£3 per week, this is how we lived. I was too ashamed to go back home. I could have ring my husband to ask him for money, but I did not want to. I was very ashamed…If they would told me that there is work only for two weeks, I would not have come. They told that we will be earning a lot of money…more than £200 after all taxes." (female, 56y, Latvian)

"I did not have enough money to live on, not talking about that I needed to send money home to support my children. It happened so that even after working for a month I still owed money to my employer. It was such a hard work. We were without money…They would give us money, but we had to return it with a percentage on top of it. I could not just leave the employer as I owed him money. I did not have a choice. I owed him money. I did not have my passport and without English language knowledge, where could I go to complain?…We were paid in envelopes, we had a lot of deductions for the caravan, for transport, to pay our debt and percentage on top of it and some other unexplained deductions, so we had nearly nothing left. I was not able to save any money for a year…We did not have regular work." (female, 42y, Latvian)

"We paid £55 for accommodation. We did not have a separate room. In addition, we paid for gas. In a winter we sometimes worked only one day per week, so we could not pay rent. [X] recorded our debt and it was taken out from our future wages. So we had to plan very carefully, but some people lived in debt on a constant basis." (male, 38y, Latvian)

The traditional systems of debt-bondage (peonage) across the developing world continue to give employers a hold over workers. At the same time, some, arguably more advanced, labour markets in the developed world also have a notable debt component to them. These relate to both worker indebtedness and more general citizen indebtedness (growing consumer credit, rising rent, increased mortgage costs, university fees and so on). This may not equate directly with debt-bondage, but once again workers' precarious financial circumstances are part of an overall system of control. The control is indirect in so far as employers are not forcing people to work and often do not actually own their workers' debts. What is occurring, however, is a wider disempowerment so that workers choose employment, of any type, over destitution. Moreover, the evidence shows that workers continue working even when wages paid to them are below the level they should be: indicative of extreme precarity. Debt, it seems, is a very effective tool to control labour (and is often used irrespective of whether labour actually needs to be controlled). The key issue for most in examining debt-bondage has been demonstrating the link between a worker's indebtedness and the actions of an employer or LMI. The wider question is whether systemic indebtedness, wherever it comes from, is in any way analogous to more traditional forms of debt-bondage? This is important given how many workers now experience severe debt of various kinds that is often not owned directly by an employer (see for example Killick, 2011).

Norms, expectations and workplace cultures

Over half a century ago, Wright Mills (1951) identified the role of psychology and manipulation in the new management of workers (well beyond the technical and task-based prescriptive methodologies of Taylorism) (see Chapter Four). At one level, Wright Mills was correct. The shift he detected has had profound implications in terms of how capital directly controls new forms of post-industrial labour, and insights into human behaviour have now been used for quite some time (Baritz, 1960) to affect workers. However, what was only loosely anticipated in the 1950s and 1960s was the way in which capital would require more of a personal investment more of the time from labour. By this I mean that there are sets of norms and expectations around jobs that extend beyond the bare component tasks associated with a particular job. These norms and expectations have become part of the workplace culture such that they now help to mould work/workers into particular types of performance/performers. These performances/performers are dependent upon soft skills alongside technical expertise and require considerable personal investment.

In short, knowledge of human psychology and human resource management, among other disciplines, has enabled new forms of direct workplace control to be 'imposed from above'. It has also, however, enabled more subtle and sophisticated forms of workplace controls to emerge 'from within'. To this end, capital recognised that in many jobs and workplaces it is better to try to create contexts where workers want to be 'good' and 'better', and want to 'play the game', than to dictate the rules of the game by diktat. As a result, a dominant aim since the 1960s has been to create worker consensus with respect to capital's objectives; and this consensus has been premised on workers' ability and willingness to self-regulate behaviour in line with the particular workplace culture (norms and expectations) being established.

A major component of this culturally-orientated workplace control infrastructure is the requirement on workers to be enthusiastic, energetic and 'sincere' irrespective of whether or not they are actually experiencing these positive sentiments. A classic early text, indicative of what was to follow, is Carnegie's ([1936] 2010) *How to Win Friends and Influence People*. The power of positive thinking is unequivocally demonstrated by this book, and it became a mantra for those aiming high. Positive thinking also, however, became a tool to cleanse what might otherwise have been seen from the outside as rather negative forms of employment. This was particularly evident in service work (Hochschild, 1983) where skilled emotional self-management quickly became an expected part of the job, irrespective of how one was actually feeling.

The investment of the self and one's identity in employment, especially customer-facing work, is now so widely accepted as to have become taken-for-granted. The 'managed heart' that Hochschild (1983) dissected back in the early 1980s is something that most of us now have experience of. It is a strategy of indirect workplace control that is certainly more positive than Taylorism, though it does require a greater depth of worker investment. Why this is important is because this commitment to particular sets of norms and expectations, that are enduringly positive, can actually close off space for alternative forms of work and employment. As a consequence, resistance, complaints and so on are positioned as illegitimate and deviant *vis à vis* the hegemonic positive workplace cultures that have become established. Moreover, within the 'smile or die' workplace (Ehrenreich, 2009) positive thinking has become a 'mass delusion' (p 13) such that restructuring, job losses, job downgrading, work intensification, and so on, are at best left unchallenged and at worst embraced in a way that management's positive 'doublespeak' language suggests they should be.

One of the problems of management through positive thinking and positive language, enduring even when negative events occur, is that perspective can be lost and that what one feels is not the same as what one is told he/she should feel. Moreover, this disconnect must be managed from view in order for workers to be seen to be performing successfully. These two acts – of disconnect and of self-surveillance – can actually mean that workers lose the will, ability and even the language, to challenge capital. Even more than this, workers often actually embrace their own emotional management/mismanagement in order to make work bearable. In such instances, the boundaries between public and private self, and between work and social life, merge and workplace controls, even though indirect, spill over into a range of non-work environments. This process is by definition a positive one, and for many workers it is actually a positive (that is, preferable to many other forms of control).

Nevertheless, there are clearly potential problems in constructing workplace cultures in order to produce/reproduce workers who actively want to be 'good' and 'better' whatever the circumstances. Most obviously, if performance is adjudged to be sub-standard then workers buying into positive workplace cultures are likely to internalise this as a personal failing. The norms and expectations of work, very simply, are unlikely to allow sub-standard workers the space or language to externalise their ascribed failings and frailties. Blame is, therefore, fixed on workers and within the positive workplace *milieu* any resistance to this is largely closed off as being unreasonable, excessive and very much out of place.

To paraphrase Burawoy (1979) the worker/workplace control agenda has shifted, particularly in advanced capitalist economies and in service work, towards the problem of 'manufacturing consent' and away from direct technical control from above. A large tranche of this shift has focused on the establishment of workplace expectations and norms that create positive workplace cultures that are not at all conducive to contestation. In extremis these cultures actually generate worker buy-in with respect to things such as increased workload and lay-offs. As Hodson (2001, 39) notes: 'When used manipulatively to undermine autonomous worker goals, employee involvement might heighten management control, increase work intensity, and, ultimately, undermine instead of increase worker dignity'. Put another way, workers can be co-opted, usually incrementally, into increasing levels of control over them, and possibly their own exploitation. The apparently democratic and flat management structures calling for worker self-determination can sometimes be less about capital relinquishing control and more about devolving responsibility and culpability onto workers.

In the positive workplace, which will usually have a less visible hierarchical structure (until challenged), there is not only a tendency to ensure worker buy-in and responsibility for a given project. There is also the need to ensure that workers respond collectively and consistently to the cultural norms and expectations, while not themselves establishing an independent collective identity from below. Dundon (2002, 240–1) notes for example how: 'Management actively sought socially to construct a workplace culture that would engender loyalty' but to a 'non-union corporate identity'. The construction of corporate loyalty is yet another example of indirect workplace control and helps explain, among other things, why workers buy into long hours, unpaid overtime, a non-union workplace and so on. Alongside this, workers are increasingly individualised at an everyday level and are expected to compete against peers for accolades, praise and simply sometimes just to maintain basic performance standards. As Green (2001, 76) notes, the age of the hard-driving supervisor has been replaced in many workplaces by individualised worker-to-worker competition.

Evidence of the effects of workplace culture (a positive ethos, flatter hierarchies, corporate loyalty, peer-to-peer competition and so on) comes in the form of workers' time commitment. As Hodson (2001, 144) observes:

> Since the 1970s the annual hours worked by full-time workers in the US has increased by 140 [hours] – an average of 3.5 weeks. Much of this increase in hours has been among professional workers. Many contemporary professional workers appear to be developing a pattern of 'self-exploitation' in which self-supervision results in greater work effort than even close management supervision.

Thus, despite the apparent labour saving of the ICT revolution, workers in advanced capitalist economies appear to be working harder than ever. The role of indirect control in this, especially the construction of particular workplace cultures, is undoubtedly significant.

Bunting (2005) talks, for instance, of 'willing slaves' among the white-collar class and charts the trend towards self-exploitation with workers putting in both more hours and working more intensely while at work. This trend is eroding individuals' work–life balance and in many instances leading to burnout among white collar workers (Bunting, 2005, xx). The issue, however, is that if workers actively want to perform 'better', and if employers are better able to cultivate this drive, then where is the harm?

A specific example of this 'self-exploitation' dilemma can occur when migrants move from peripheral to core economies (Scott, 2013a). In this situation, the working conditions that migrants are willing to accept often differ from the conditions native workers are willing to accept. Workers, in short, can bring with them different norms and expectations with respect to what is acceptable and unacceptable employer behaviour. Thus, in my UK research, I found that (native) labour market stakeholders often felt workplaces to be exploitative but that some of those (migrants) working in them did not:

> "What we see every day is that people do not understand that the way they're treated in the UK is unacceptable to our society…Or they believe the way they're treated in the UK, whether it's right or wrong, is infinitely better than the treatment they get in their home country. So they don't come forward because they're actually content with their lot." (Migrant Helpline representative)

> "These people, as I've said, you know, these victims don't necessarily consider themselves to be victims, so what you're doing, in effect, is taking their home off them, taking their employment off them, taking their salary off them, taking away their investment and taking away support for family back home and then you want to ask them for a statement at the end of all that." (UKHTC representative)[23]

> "They're being treated like the lowest of the low and really being ripped off…but they are in a position where they're better off than where they've come from…better off that they can survive here, and 'survive' is probably the right word, but they can still manage to send some money back to the families back home. So it shows you the gap from where they are and where we are." (Unite representative)

As Anderson (2010, 301) observes: 'Global inequalities mean that some migrants may be prepared to take on jobs at wages and conditions that many (UK) nationals will not consider'. Migration, in other words, can draw people together with different views as to what is and is not exploitative. It is a process that demonstrates how cultural norms and expectations shape workers' own sense of justice and injustice with respect to employment. What is accepted by one worker may actually be exploitative and harmful to another because of what they see as legitimate and normal workplace practice.

The pressure on employers to source 'good' workers may well lead them to peripheral economies to find 'more grateful' employees. The question is whether this strategy is ultimately beneficial, and to whom? Certainly, many labour market stakeholders I spoke to were concerned that uncontrolled immigration could change workplace culture with the mass influx of low-wage workers facilitating a deterioration in working conditions:

> "So English working-class drivers were dismissed and replaced by cheaper foreign labour and that caused a lot of bad blood. There was one company, within a year they had replaced 50% of their drivers with foreigners." (Churches Together)

> "What I find on the workshop floor level is that it's 'agency labour, well are they going to take our jobs' and 'migrant agency labour, oh my goodness well they're going to be prepared to do it for nothing, aren't they!'" (GLA)

> "The main thing is agency workers are being used to drive the race to the bottom regarding wages and terms and conditions. It's the purposeful creation of a two-tier workforce. Now a company will say, 'Well, we can use this amount of agency, we're only paying the minimum wage and so on, but what we also need to do is take the terms and conditions of our full-time employees down to the agency level.' And if they can do that, and they are trying to do it in certain places that I'm working, it's happening, we've got to stop that." (Unite)

It is clear that immigration has an impact on the workplace in a number of key respects and facilitates both direct and indirect employer control (see Box 5.2). The dilemma is over the extent to which employers should be allowed to source the 'best' workers from across the world, and the degree to which other would-be workers have a right to feel aggrieved with any associated changes in workplace regimes.

Box 5.2: Immigration and workplace norms, expectations and cultures

There is a widely observed 'good migrant' stereotype (see MacKenzie and Forde, 2009; Findlay et al, 2013; Scott, 2013b; Thompson et al, 2013) in low-wage labour markets of core economies. This stereotype is best understood in relation to the way in which immigration provides employers in the developed world with more control over their workers and 'regulates' labour markets (Cohen, 1987; Peck, 1996; Bauder, 2006). There are six main dimensions to this control:

1. Economic Need: Low-wage immigrants moving from peripheral to core economies are generally needier than citizens already living in core economies and, thus, circumstances mean that they are more willing to accept, or compelled to accept, the least desirable jobs (Castles and Kosack, 1973, 6).

2. Legal Status: The citizenship status of migrants (see Chapter 6) means that they often enjoy fewer rights than the indigenous population. Lack of welfare entitlements or an inability to change employer, for example, often makes them more willing workers, as does the ongoing threat of deportation (Anderson, 2010; Dwyer et al, 2011; Ruhs, 2015).

3. Transnational Wage: Immigrants bring with them a 'dual frame of reference' (Waldinger and Lichter, 2003) that means they are able to extract more value from low-wage work in core economies by transferring some of the income from this work to their home country. This underpins a more optimistic attitude towards low-wage labour than would otherwise be the case.

4. Labour Supply: Migration into low-wage labour markets often leads to a strategic over-supply of workers (Mitchell, 1996, 84–5; Martin, 2003, 31). Control is facilitated by the fact that there are more workers competing for work than would otherwise be the case with employers benefitting from 'highly visible pools of surplus labour' (Edwards, 1979, 127).

5. Human Capital: Labour migration, even into low-wage labour markets, can increase the level of human capital available to employers (Borjas, 1987; Chiswick, 2000). A rise in the quality as well as quantity of labour therefore results and low-wage employers benefit from this (see for example Scott, 2013a; 2013b; 2015a).

6. Class Fragmentation: Migration brings with it a racial, religious, ethnic, national and cultural diversity that helps to 'split' (Bonacich, 1972; Castles and Kosack, 1973) the working-class and reduce the potential for collective action.

Disciplining by proxy

Aside from employers creating particular workplace cultures in order to maximise labour power, it is also true that at certain moments this positive ethos will be challenged. This challenge is seen by employers as both a threat and as an opportunity. It is an opportunity because how an employer deals with deviance can actually help to control workers who do not themselves resist or challenge authority. This process I call 'disciplining by proxy'. It occurs when workers see what is possible (in terms of employers' ability to control) and, therefore, shy away from any future conflict as a result of the example that has been made of others. It may also occur in a positive sense: when certain workers are rewarded for their behaviour and serve as examples for others wishing to gain similar praise. Essentially, then, disciplining by proxy is about both positive and negative examples and how a minority of workers can shape the behaviour of the majority of workers for good and bad.

Academics, for instance, may appear to be free to critique society but, in reality, research deemed by managers, funders and so on as critical, controversial or politically sensitive is often avoided (Harvey, 1974). In addition, there is huge pressure to demonstrate research value in an immediate monetary sense and this can make social scientists 'servants of power' (Baritz, 1960). The academic, as with most workers, is aware of his/her vulnerability and the fact that stepping out of line might actually lead to discipline that in turn could be used as an example to others. A famous instance of this is documented in McIntosh (2001) where a controversial and politicised research agenda lead to eventual academic and professional sanctions and isolation. Radicalism was the label applied to a particular form of research in order to discredit both the research and researcher and to eventually limit the nature of work being carried out in the name of the university. Without getting into a debate about academic freedom, if there ever was such a thing, the above demonstrates how even in apparently critical and independent professional fields one is part of a larger system and that criticism has its limits. Stepping over the line for workers does lead to sanctioning and this in turn tends to send a message to others.

In other workplace environments, union activism, whistleblowing, organising and so on may be seen as just as problematic with employers wanting to make examples of those who, like McIntosh (2001), may be deemed to be 'rocking the boat'. This is entirely understandable behaviour on the part of employers. The issue is about the line between workers' independence and where this line impinges upon business success and reputation. Thus, in the past we had the following response to workers asserting rights: 'As with serf risings in Europe, slave rising in the colonies were usually brutally suppressed, and followed by savage punishments and harsh retribution, notably executions, in order to deter fresh upheavals' (Black, 2011, 136). Today we are largely free of serfdom and slavery but this does not mean that workers can criticise their employer without reprisal and retribution. It means that they can criticise to a certain degree, but if this is deemed excessive then disciplining will occur and that this, as in the past, will deter others.

Whistleblowing and union involvement are arguably the two main instances where employers seek to make an example of 'deviant' workers. In the case of whistleblowing, and despite laws apparently encouraging it, Lennane (2012, 252) concludes that: 'the organisational response to whistleblowing is not new. The traditional treatment of mutineers has always been similarly very savage, as a challenge to authority that can never be allowed, whatever the provocation.' Whistleblowing, the evidence shows, does not lead to a happy outcome for the exhaling workers:

> The organisation's response to the whistleblower is very powerful and follows a recognisable pattern. It is crushing in its intensity, as the organisation can use as many staff as it takes, for as long as it takes, to wear the lone whistleblower down. There is almost always some kind of disciplinary action, often on 'unrelated' matters, up to and including dismissal. (The employer's ability to take action on allegedly unrelated matters is a major barrier to effective whistleblower protection legislation.) In the study, 20% were dismissed and 14% were demoted; 14% were transferred (to another town, not just within the department); 43% were pressured to resign; and 9% had their position abolished (Lennane, 2012, 250).

One of the most famous whistleblowers of recent times with respect to work-based harm is Alan Wainwright. He drew the UK government's attention to the blacklisting of union–active construction workers in 2006 when he publicised (on a website) details of how the now defunct Consultancy Association (see Chapter Eight) operated and the names of the 3,000+ blacklisted construction workers on the organisation's secretive files (Evans, 2009). In theory, UK whistleblowers are protected by the Public Interest Disclosure Act 1998. However, following his whistleblowing Alan Wainwright lost his job, relationship, savings and home and was himself blacklisted.[24]

Although perhaps not aware of the harm many whistleblowers experience in seeking to expose employment malpractice, the workers in my own study were acutely aware that people had been disciplined, often quite severely, for criticising their employer or manager:

> "Some rebelled, but they were quickly got rid of. There were situations like that on the first farm, people rebelled... the piece-rate was too low and some of them did not want to go to work, the whole team rebelled. They were then dismissed and drove away from the farm." (male, 56y, Polish)

> "They treated us like dogs...I was dismissed because I did not like that treatment. I was standing up for my rights. I was brave to say what I was thinking, so in the end they get rid of me. By doing so, they set an example to other pickers, what will happen if you complain." (male, 31y, Belarusian)

> "There was a woman that tried to argue with them, but with no luck, and afterwards she did not get work for two or three weeks. Everyone else worked, except her. She argued, so she did not get work. That is why we did not want to argue with them. This is how it was...We could not complain, otherwise we would be sitting without work for weeks on end. We did not earn much, but not working at all, would put us further in debts." (male, 27y, Latvian)

It is difficult to gauge exactly how much disciplining by proxy actually works to limit employee dissent. Certainly, though, employers can make it implicitly and explicitly clear, through the way they treat certain forms of behaviour, that such behaviour 'crosses the line'. The problem for the would-be offender is knowing where that invisible line actually is, and so many workers choose to simply remain silent even when they have legitimate grievances or when they are concerned about potential harm to themselves or others.

Management by bureaucracy

A final way in which workers are indirectly controlled while at work is through the use of bureaucratic systems and structures. Fevre et al (2012, 153), for example, note that: 'the target culture of achieving more output with fewer resources appeared a central feature of the working lives of many employees interviewed. Irrational and punitive management manifested itself in many different ways and had an impact on managers as much as it affected non-management grades.' The 'irrational and punitive management' is not just about direct control via targets and associated monitoring and surveillance (as reviewed in Chapter Four). It is also about the use of bureaucratic systems and structures to keep workers indirectly in check. This might include having to re-apply for one's job, undergoing periods of prolonged parole/probation (note the language), seeing working roles and workplace structures continually restructure and so on.

The 'white noise' of change and bureaucracy can be a frightening sound to many workers and its volume may rise partly by default, but also partly by design. In terms of the latter, Skogstad et al (2007, 64–6) are highly critical of what they see as the modern problem of continual organisational change:

> A variety of organizational changes, as well as the number of such changes, may have severe consequences on interpersonal relations in organizations...there is reason to believe that organizational changes may result in interpersonal conflicts between superiors and subordinates, as well as between co-workers.

Rapidly or continually changing workplace systems and structures clearly have a detrimental effect on inter-personal working relationships (Baillien and De Witte, 2009; Roscigno et al, 2009). The fact that organisational change is so common, despite this evidence, says something about the way in which the white noise of change and bureaucracy is often used to control workers for particular ends. Managers and supervisors need not even set targets, the very systems they are part of can actually control workers by design, and lead to compliance for fear of bureaucratic 'misadventure'.

At its simplest this misadventure might ultimately manifest itself in a poor employer reference. This is one of the ultimate forms of indirect bureaucratic control. As Ironside and Seifert note: 'You are only free to quit in the same sense as you are free to leave a room when a person with a gun says that you are free to leave but that if you do they will shoot you. The misuse of 'free' should not disguise the material choices available' (cited in Duffy and Sperry, 2012, 175).

Conclusion

Understanding labour exploitation and work-based harm requires one to examine the question of why workers work as hard as they do. In many cases the answer to this can be found in direct forms of control, namely: targets, monitoring and surveillance; job insecurity; bullying and mobbing; and excessive hours. However, this chapter has shown how direct controls only take us so far in understanding the contemporary work ethic. In many of today's systems of capitalist accumulation it is difficult to locate sources of power as these are purposefully veiled from view and thus not exposed to potential protest and contestation. This means that systems of control are also often fragmented, convoluted and even apparently non-hierarchical. The resultant arm's-length management of workers is designed to distance and divide cause (capital's search for greater profitability and power) from effect (potential worker exploitation and harm). For workers, this means that controls may often be felt long before they are seen and that the true source of their control may often be impossible to determine.

Aware of the above, this chapter has added an additional level of complexity to our understanding of workplace-based controls by underlining the need to look at the ways in which 'good' and 'better' workers may be produced and reproduced via indirect means. From arm's-length employment occurring through LMIs, to the debt-based systems driving people to work, through to the moulding of staff via workplace cultures, the disciplining of workers by proxy (fear), and management by bureaucracy, there are myriad ways in which behaviour at work is shaped without capital 'getting its hand dirty'.

Crucially, we know that LMIs, indebtedness, certain expectations and norms, fear and bureaucratic overload, can all on their own harm workers. What we are now witnessing, however, is the use of these indirect controls in combination and allied with the direct controls reviewed in Chapter Four. This does not imply that workplace controls are by definition harmful. The issue is the combination of these controls and the intensity and longevity of their use. More broadly, there is also the question of what one loses when one gains control of others in the ways outlined above; and whether the quest for 'good' and 'better' workers may be more fruitfully achieved by looking beyond labour as 'a problem'. The social harm perspective would not advocate an absence of workplace control, but it does call for more of a critical approach to some of the solutions used by capital to maximise returns on investment in labour. Associated with this are questions around how 'good' and 'better' workers are defined and how much work now impinges upon active family, social and communal lives.

The black eye

She was the strongest of women; mother of two, waitress,
won everyone's respect with her skills with the drunks in the bar.

She filled in the extra hours when others left the apron on the counter and
asked the manager to go to hell. Was there when people were hospitalized,
attended funerals, fled the authorities.

She was divorced and struggled with pick ups, exchanges, day shift, night shift,
overtime and restraining orders.

When she came to work with a black eye and the manager got to see
her battered face, he said that she should not bring her problems to work.

He could not have her working when she looked like that and if it happened
again
she was not welcome back.

SIX

Exogenous controls

Reduced ontological security

Beyond the individual employment relationship, and beyond the workplace, there are numerous controls moulding people's behaviour as workers and would-be workers. Most obviously, we have seen over recent years workers' basic (ontological) security retreat and an associated change in the role of work in relation to one's core sense of identity, self and wellbeing.

The arguments of Sennett (1998), Bauman (1998), Beck (1992; 2000) and others, are important here. Ontological security (Giddens, 1991) is something that arises from continuity, stability and order in one's life. During the 1950s, 1960s and early 1970s there was a strong sense in which work provided this ontological security, at least in the developed world, and thus acted as an anchor for wider society. With the onset of neoliberalism and associated flexible forms of capitalism, continuity and stability in employment became undermined. Fewer workers now seem to be able to expect commitment and loyalty in their work contract and, as a result, are also unable to derive ontological security from their employment. Put another way, from the 1970s, something happened with respect to the employer–employee covenant and this change occurred at a structural level. It has affected almost all workers.

Numerous academics have sought to capture the changing nature of work and the way in which employment, at all levels, seems to be providing less and less security. Ulrich Beck (2000, 3) has argued, for instance, that: 'One future trend is clear. For a majority of people, even in the apparently prosperous middle layers, their basic existence and lifeworld will be marked by endemic insecurity.' This endemic insecurity means that work can no longer provide most people with a stable basis to plan over the medium to long term. It also means that workers are much more reticent, and even unable, to commit to their employer and so traditional career-path identities related to elongated achievement in and through work have been eroded (Sennett, 1998). In short, the employer now seems to care less about the employee and the employee has had to respond to this new reality of indifference and alienation.

Bauman (1998, 27) characterises the situation as follows: 'A steady, durable and continuous, logically coherent and tightly-structured working career is no longer a widely available option. Only in relatively rare cases can a permanent identity be defined, let alone secured, through the job performed.' Not only, then, has 'the 'job for life' disappeared' (Beck, 2000, 2) but the patchwork of jobs that now make up an individual's careers have changed the ways and means through which one's identity and sense of self is secured. Consumption rather than production is the sphere through which now uncertain (work) identities are grounded and, corresponding to this, individualism has flourished.

This loss of the anchoring of identity in the productive sphere of work has four apparent benefits for capital. First, the risks of the market are more efficiently and effectively transferred onto labour. Second, the 'endemic insecurity' that Beck talks of is apparently conducive to productivity gains, because as people feel more at risk they are likely to fight harder to simply hold on to what they have. Third, any collective resistance to capital is likely to be eroded by the lack of ontological security associated with neoliberal employment regimes. Fourth, consumer culture is likely to be bolstered by the fact that people become less able to ground their identity in the productive sphere. Thus, through the transfer of risk onto workers, greater productivity, lower collective resistance and greater consumerism, a new world of work has been established for all but the most privileged of employees. This world of work no longer provides the space or the time for meaningful productive identities, and associated loyalties, to emerge. Individuals are, therefore, forced to look at their employment in a highly instrumentalist and short-term manner. This has also shaped personal relationships at work. At the same time, and as we saw in the previous chapter, via the rise of a 'positive thinking culture', employees are often expected to embrace these changes.

Some have questioned the basis of this 'age of insecurity' thesis. They point out either that insecurity has always been with us, or, that the loss of work-based identity is not as severe as theorised. Fevre (2007, 517), for instance, concludes that: 'Data from the countries which social theorists had in mind when they elaborated the idea of a new age of employment insecurity do not support their theories.' Others, point towards greater insecurity among some types of workers in some sectors, but generally a more variegated picture than the grand theories allow for (Hollister, 2011). Few, however, argue that the relationship between work and ontological security is moving in a positive direction.

One area where there has been apparent consensus over recent years has been at the lower end of the labour market. Standing (2011, 37), for instance, makes a classic distinction between a privileged 'salariat' and an insecure 'precariat'. This echoes early 'segmented/dual' labour market theories around there being a 'primary' and a 'secondary' labour force (Piore, 1979; Goos and Manning, 2007). The idea of insecurity welling up at the bottom of the labour market and the concentration of precarity and related presence of a precariat has now been widely discussed (see Waite, 2009 for a review). The arguments are convincing, though where they fall short is through their principal focus being on a specific group/class of workers (the precariat) rather than on retrograde employment processes *per se* (rising informalisation, greater control, exploitation and harm).

There is evidence, for example, that employment insecurity – whether one is part of the precariat or not – affects one's physical and psychological health (Ferrie, 2001; Virtanen et al, 2005; Lewchuk et al, 2008). A classic study of white-collar civil service workers (Ferrie et al, 1995; Ferrie et al, 2005), for instance, found links between falling job security (associated with neoliberal restructuring) and ill-health. Follow-up studies have supported this link, and underline the importance of not always getting embroiled in fragmentary class-based analyses (that is, simply looking at the precariat) when examining 'trouble at work' (Fevre et al, 2012).

One of the problems in examining both the 'age of insecurity' thesis and the relationship between general work insecurity and exploitation/harm is that the available data is limited. Most evidence, therefore, concentrates on particular case studies and so international comparisons are difficult. The best international data we have comes from the OECD. The organisation ranks countries according to the regulations they have governing temporary forms of employment. From this ranking it is clear that across the developed world an Anglo-Saxon (neoliberal) work regime is in the ascendancy. The emphasis is basically on enabling temporary forms of employment, with minimal state intervention.

Countries such as Canada, the US, the UK, New Zealand and Australia all score very lowly, for example, in terms of regulations on temporary employment (see Table 6.1). These same countries also have, relative to other developed world economies, low union densities and/or limited worker-union rights (see Table 6.2). In contrast, social democratic and northern corporatist countries tend to have higher degrees of intervention/regulation and greater union activity (see Tables 8.3 and 8.7). The state, then, can be a key element in enabling the flexible career (low regulation, low union densities, limited worker–union rights) to flourish. I will look in more depth at the varied role of the state in enabling and preventing work-based harm in Chapter Eight.

Table 6.1: OECD regulations on temporary forms of employment, 2013

Country	Regulations on temporary forms of employment (Scale: 0 low–6 high)
OECD un-weighted average	2.08
Canada	0.21
USA	0.33
UK	0.54
New Zealand	0.92
Australia	1.04

Source: OECD Employment Database, http://www.oecd.org/employment/emp/employmentdatabase-labourmarketpoliciesandinstitutions.htm

Table 6.2: Union activity in Anglo-Saxon (neoliberal) work regimes

Country	OECD Union Density (2011, as per cent of employees)	ITUC (2014) Worker–Union Rights Country Ranking (Scale: 1 best–5 worst)
Australia	18.5	3
Canada	27.1	3
New Zealand	20.8	2
UK	25.6	3
USA	11.3	4

Source: ITUC (2014); OECD Employment Database, http://www.oecd.org/employment/emp/employmentdatabase-labourmarketpoliciesandinstitutions.htm

Entrenched inequality

Slaves had security of sorts in their employment but were certainly not free. Thus, one should not equate security with freedom and insecurity with unfreedom. For some, freedom from a monolithic career may well be liberating. For others, a sense of being able to commit to, and show loyalty towards, a job and an employer, over a prolonged period of time, may be an essential platform for wellbeing. There is, therefore, no 'one-size fits all' approach to addressing work-based harm. Nevertheless, a second dimension to exogenous worker controls demonstrates that generalisations are sometimes possible. To elucidate, freedom from the type of debt and poverty captured in Chapter Five does provide workers, in whatever state of security/insecurity, with greater insulation from excessive and oppressive employer control.

From a social harm perspective, this means that the overall socio-economic structure of a country, and the relationship between countries, can be key to understanding why workers might accept exploitative conditions. Very simply, when inequality is high within and between countries there are likely to be groups of workers, often the majority, who must accept the working conditions set for them with limited scope for discussion or contestation. Put another way, the prevailing socio-economic structures within and between countries place workers, to different degrees, in danger of experiencing either absolute or relative poverty. It is this absolute and relative poverty that most work to try to escape, if not always, then at least at times. The desire to work, therefore, is linked to the desire to escape destitution (absolute poverty) and marginalisation and isolation (relative poverty). Systems that insulate most workers from these two threats are likely, then, to be more successful in empowering workers to act (to discuss, to contest, to change) should exploitation or harm arise. Systems that expose workers to these threats, in contrast, are likely to produce and reproduce more deference.

Most acknowledge that there is a link between economic need and exploitation and harm. The ILO, for instance, accepts this but argues that economic circumstances alone are not commensurate with coercion, stating that forced labour does: 'not cover conditions of pure economic necessity, as when a worker feels unable to leave a job because of the real or perceived absence of employment alternatives' (ILO, 2005a, 5). The ILO is aware of the problem of poverty, debt and associated socio-economic inequality in shaping work experiences but is clear that these factors, on their own (unless there is direct employer-driven debt bondage), cannot be used to define the worst forms of modern slavery.

Socio-economic circumstance can, according to some authors, be used beyond the workplace as a means of systemic labour control. LeBaron (2014), for instance, argues that mass indebtedness is part of a strategy to shift power from labour to capital. That is, that debt-bondage is not just something affecting relatively primitive workplaces, but is hard-wired into the contemporary system of capitalist accumulation *en masse*. Beyond the arguments of LeBaron, it does appear that personal debt is increasing and that this may, at least in part, act as an exogenous control over labour by tying citizens more strictly into the wage-labour system (Soederberg, 2013; Walker et al, 2015). It is, for example, harder to contest employment conditions if one has a large mortgage or student debt to pay.

Alongside personal debt, inequality among workers also appears to have grown over recent decades (Cingano, 2014; OECD, 2011a). Cingano (2014, 8) summarises the situation for OECD countries as follows:

> Over the 20 to 25 years leading up to the global economic crisis, average real disposable household incomes increased in all OECD countries, on average by 1.6% annually. However, in three quarters of OECD countries household incomes of the top 10% grew faster than those of the poorest 10%, resulting in widening income inequality. Differences in the pace of income growth across household groups in the pre-crisis period were particularly pronounced in most of the English-speaking countries.

Table 6.3 draws on the latest OECD data to compare income inequality between the 1980s and 2010s and it is clear, based on the Gini coefficients, that there has been a widespread rise in inequality over this period across the developed world.

The Gini coefficient ranges between 0 (in the case of perfect equality) and 1 (in the case of perfect inequality) and most countries in Table 6.3 moved closer to 1 over the 1980s, 1990s and 2000s. In short, countries became more unequal. The US, for instance, saw the Gini coefficient rise from 0.336 in 1983 to 0.389 in 2012 and rises were not just confined to liberal and neoliberal states. The social democratic states of Denmark, Finland, Norway and Sweden all also saw inequality rise.

This trend indicates that the balance of power between labour and capital has shifted (towards capital) and one can expect, from this shift, a greater systemic ability for capital to exercise control over labour. Thus, the arguments around 'secondary and primary labour' (Piore, 1979), 'lousy and lovely jobs' (Goos and Manning, 2007) and a 'salariat and precariat' (Standing, 2011) that were visited in the previous section appear to hold. Not only, therefore, do we have an age of insecurity in employment, but we also have debt and inequality affecting the power balance between labour and capital at a systemic and structural level. Additionally, addressing this rising inequality is one of the key solutions to tackling labour exploitation and work-based harm (see Chapter Eight).

Table 6.3: Income inequality ('Gini Coefficient') in OECD countries, 1980s–2000s

Country	1980s	2010s	Change
Canada	0.292 (1986)	0.316 (2011)	+0.024
Denmark	0.224 (1986)	0.253 (2011)	+0.029
Finland	0.209 (1986)	0.265 (2011)	+0.056
Germany	0.251 (1985)	0.293 (2011)	+0.042
Greece	0.352 (1986)	0.335 (2011)	-0.017
Italy	0.291 (1984)	0.321 (2011)	+0.031
Japan	0.304 (1985)	0.336 (2009)	+0.032
Luxembourg	0.247 (1986)	0.276 (2011)	+0.029
Mexico	0.452 (1984)	0.482 (2012)	+0.030
Netherlands	0.272 (1985)	0.278 (2012)	+0.060
New Zealand	0.271 (1985)	0.323 (2011)	+0.052
Norway	0.222 (1986)	0.250 (2011)	+0.028
Sweden	0.198 (1983)	0.273 (2011)	+0.075
Turkey	0.434 (1987)	0.412 (2011)	-0.022
United Kingdom	0.309 (1985)	0.344 (2011)	+0.035
United States	0.336 (1983)	0.389 (2012)	+0.053

Source: http://stats.oecd.org/Index.aspx?DataSetCode=IDD

Political–legal constraints

A lack of state involvement, as workers appear to be losing more control over their employment at the hands of neoliberal capitalism, has been very much apparent in the arguments made so far. However, there are instances where the state intervenes to produce and reproduce 'good' workers. The next two sections of this chapter will consider the active role of the state in this respect. As far as this section is concerned, states can play a key role in determining the rights workers have within and outside the labour market. This occurs both through the construction of different levels of 'citizenship' for different types of worker, and, through the legal classification of 'employee', 'worker' or 'contractor' for different forms of labour.

The former (citizenship) most commonly varies according to whether one is a migrant or native and/or a member of a minority or majority group. Invariably, migrants are given fewer rights than natives, at least initially, and in some countries native minority groups are also given fewer rights than native majority groups. (Note that in some cases ruling minority elites enjoy more rights than the majority population.) The most disadvantaged of all, however, are those who are deemed 'illegal' by the state and thus forced to exist without even basic citizenship rights such as the Rohingya profiled in Box 6.1.

Box 6.1: Denial of citizenship and the Rohingya people

In May 2015 widespread media attention focused on the Muslim 'Rohingya' minority/migrant community in Buddhist Burma. The Rohingya have been subject to widespread forced labour and forced segregation in Burma, something documented in the late 1990s and again in the 2010s (Arakan Project, 2012; ILO, 1998b). The Burmese nationality law of 1982 denies the Rohingya citizenship and they have recently, and as a result, become one of the most persecuted indigenous minorities in the world according to the UN. On top of this, the Rohingya are now both internally displaced (into ghetto-camps) and internationally displaced. In terms of the latter, even after escaping their non-citizen status in Burma, the Rohingya have still ended up stateless. Thousands have now died both through persecution within Burma and while escaping this persecution. The May 2015 media coverage concerned Rohingya boat people driven out of Burma through exploitation and persecution but denied entry into Thailand, Indonesia and Malaysia and, as a result, stranded (some dying) in the Andaman Sea with no food or water and dependent upon people traffickers for survival. The Rohingya case clearly demonstrates the importance of citizenship and the relationship between statelessness and exploitation and harm that characterises the lives of many of the worlds minority/migrant groups.

Anderson (2010, 312) argues that:

> As well as a tap regulating the flow of workers to a state, immigration controls might be more usefully conceived as a mould constructing certain types of workers through selection of legal entrants, the requiring and enforcing of certain types of employment relations, and the creation of institutionalised uncertainty.

The idea that states, through various political–legal means and mechanisms, can 'mould' people into particular types of citizen/ worker is extremely important. This is because the moulds states use tend to restrict migrant and minority rights and entitlements. Some have argued that such restrictions generate forms of 'unfree' labour (Miles, 1987) and, related to this, that migrants/minorities are 'denizens' (Hammar, 1990) rather than genuine citizens.

Citizenship can affect migrants'/minorities' access to welfare, political rights, workplace rights and the time that they are able to remain within a country (Anderson, 2010; Dwyer et al, 2011; Ruhs, 2015). In terms of workplace rights, particular 'guestworker' style migration policies often limit migrants' ability to choose and move jobs and this can make them a more 'captive' and therefore lucrative form of labour. Ruhs (2015, 3), for instance, notes the link between citizenship status and the productivity and cost of labour: 'whether or not migrants enjoy the right to free choice of employment and other employment-related rights in the receiving country's labour market is likely to affect their productivity and earnings'. This is true for both low-wage and skilled migrant labour and has a long history (Clark, 2016).

In order to limit migrant/minority workers' exploitation as a result of their partial or absent citizenship status various ILO and UN instruments have been drafted. The 1975 ILO Migrant Workers (Supplementary Provisions) Convention (Number 143), for instance, protects all migrant workers irrespective of status. Article 9 (1) states the following:

> The migrant worker shall, in cases in which these laws and regulations have not been respected and in which his position cannot be regularised, enjoy equality of treatment for himself and his family in respect of rights arising out of past employment as regards remuneration, social security and other benefits.

Building on the work of the ILO, and aware of the growing issue of irregular migrant labour, the UN adopted the 'Convention on the Protection of the Rights of all Migrant Workers and their Families' in 1990. This took a decade of negotiations and is the most comprehensive international standard there is dealing with migrant workers. As with ILO Convention Number 143, the UN Convention also gives irregular migrants certain core rights (see Box 6.2).

Currently, and despite the ILO and UN conventions, individual nation-states appear reluctant to ratify and/or implement global human rights codes. Ruhs (2015, 1) summarises the situation as follows: 'The most cursory review of the rights of migrant workers around the world confirms that the majority of them, and especially those working in low-waged jobs, enjoy few of the rights stipulated in international conventions.' The result is that different tiers of citizenship exist within different countries, with migrants/minorities often denied rights that native/majority groups enjoy.

Box 6.2: UN 'Convention on the Protection of the Rights of all Migrant Workers and their Families 1990'

Evidence of equal rights for regular and irregular migrants:

- the right to life (Article 9);
- the right to be free from forced labour (Article 11);
- the right to equality with nationals before courts and tribunals (Article 18);
- the right not to have identity documents confiscated (Article 21);
- the right to equal treatment with regard to remuneration, other conditions and terms of employment, and social security (Articles 25 and 27); and
- the right to join and take part in meetings and activities of trades unions (Article 26).

Source: Ruhs (2012, 1280)

The division of workers into different political–legal categories is perhaps at its crudest when one compares legal with so-called illegal immigrant workers. Some states, for instance, experience strong economic pressures towards expansive immigration, ostensibly seek to limit this immigration, but at the same time ultimately preside over the large-scale influx of 'illegal' workers. Holmes (2013, 13) explains the rationale behind this apparently chaotic state of affairs:

> Systems of labour migration involve economic forces inviting and even requiring the cheap labour of migrants at the same time that political forces ban migrants from entering the country. Such systems must include a set of political and legal mechanisms that presuppose that the migrant is without citizenship rights and has only limited power in the state of employment. The reproduction of a system of migrant labour hinges on the inability of the migrants, as individuals or as a group, to influence the institutions that subordinate them to the other fractions of the labour force and to the employer.

Thus, in some contexts the moulding of 'good' workers involves the denial of citizenship rights to migrants and their almost complete subordination. Being 'illegal' comes at a price, that the migrant worker bears and that the host country employer benefits from, with the state often choosing, albeit tacitly, to side with the employer.

In the US, particularly in agriculture (Holmes, 2013) and the day-labour economy (Theodore, 2007; Visser, 2016), there is now a well-established 'need' for 'illegal' migrant workers and an undoubted economic rationale behind this. Moreover, there is the paradox that such workers are economically lucrative and in demand while at the same time experiencing social, cultural and legal closure. It is almost as if countries are embarrassed by their ability to exploit the riches of migrant labour by virtue of rendering this labour, but not its exploitation, illegal.

Alongside the moulding of workers through a lack of citizenship, there is also the more active work carried out by states to produce different tiers of citizenship. This strategy has received most critical attention with respect to low-wage labour migration into the Middle East and, specifically, the operation of the 'kafala' system. With its origins dating back to the 1950s, and used in countries including Bahrain, Kuwait, Oman, Qatar, Saudi Arabia, the UAE, Jordan and the Lebanon, the kafala system is a term used loosely to describe types of migration regimes targeted at attracting temporary rather than permanent migrants. The system is expressly designed to distinguish in a legal sense between temporary labour migrants and permanent domestic citizens and in this sense is very similar to the 'guestworker' systems of the developed world (Baldwin-Edwards, 2011, 37). Where the kafala system differs, however, is the strict requirement for a 'kafeel' (an employer/sponsor) in order for a labour migrant to enter and exit a given host country with the sponsored migrant also not allowed to 'abscond' from his/her kafeel. As Khan and Harroff-Tavel note (2011, 294) this means that: 'under the kafala, the employer assumes full economic and legal responsibility for the employee and thereby holds considerable power over him or her'. Some go further and equate kafala migration with out and out slavery (see Cooper, 2013).

The kafala system has underpinned mass migration to Arab states over the past half-century (see Tables 6.4 and 6.5). In the UAE, Qatar, Kuwait and Bahrain, for example, immigrants account for over half of the population. Moreover, in some states (such as Qatar, Saudi Arabia, Oman and Bahrain) less than one-third of nationals are actually in employment with migrants relied upon to do the bulk of the work. In terms of origins, Table 6.6 shows how migrants from Asia dominate in the Arab kafala countries. In fact, in Oman, UAE and Bahrain over 80% of migrants come from Asia.

Effectively the state benefits from the kafala system by virtue of it ensuring that levels of migration are aligned to the economy and do not negatively affect (and in fact usually improve) native workers' career prospects and affluence. This is because migrants will only remain legally resident under a kafala system while they are being sponsored and they are excluded from full and free labour market access by virtue of this sponsorship. Similarly, employers benefit from the kafala system because it creates a disempowered and relatively cheap group of workers, in plentiful supply, who are unlikely, and in most cases unable, to complain, protest or abscond. Moreover, migrants who do leave their kafeel generally become illegal and this can make them even more appealing to unscrupulous employers (Baldwin-Edwards, 2011, 38–41).

Table 6.4: Migration levels in selected Arab kafala countries, 2013

Country	Migrants as % of total population	Number of migrants (million)
UAE	83.7	7.8
Qatar	73.8	1.6
Kuwait	60.2	2.0
Bahrain	54.7	0.7
Jordan	40.2	2.9
Saudi Arabia	31.4	9.0
Oman	30.6	1.1

Source: UN (2013)

Table 6.5: Percentage of nationals and expatriates in employment in selected Arab kafala countries, 2007–08

Country	Nationals	Expatriates
Qatar	7.5	92.5
Saudi Arabia	13.3	86.7
Oman	22.3	77.3
Bahrain	26.4	73.6

Source: ILO (2009c, 6)

Table 6.6: Proportion of labour force from Asia in selected Arab kafala countries, 2005

Country	Asian migrants as % of workforce
Oman	92
UAE	87
Bahrain	80
Kuwait	65
Saudi Arabia	59
Qatar	46

Source: ILO (2009c)

In theoretical terms the kafala system, by dividing workers according to a hierarchy of citizenship, creates a 'segmented' or 'dual' labour market (Piore, 1979). Migrants are invariably used to fill the 'secondary' labour market vacancies and in the Arab world this has meant construction (for male migrants) and domestic worker jobs (for female migrants) in particular. More generally there is a clear public sector (indigenous workers) versus private sector (migrant workers) divide (Baldwin-Edwards, 2011, 15) and it is also clear that wages of indigenous and migrant workers are highly unequal. In Bahrain, for instance, the average migrant monthly wage was 168 Bahraini Dinar in 2007 compared to 507 Bahraini Dinar for native workers (ILO, 2009c, 4).

Qatar is a particularly interesting case with respect to the kafala system. It is the world's richest country with a per capita GDP of US$102,100.[25] An estimated 93% of the country's workforce are, however, migrants (see Table 6.5).[26] The country has been widely criticised for the treatment of its lower wage migrants (mainly from India, Pakistan, Nepal, Bangladesh and the Philippines) under the kafala system (Amnesty International, 2013; HRW, 2012). In the face of this criticism, Qatar has engaged with a range of international organisations and rights groups (something less evident in other Arab states) and 'appears' willing to reform the kafala system: in 2012 the end of employer sponsorship was announced (HRW, 2012: 33), though this termination was again announced in 2014 (Black et al, 2014).

Five specific objections appear to have dominated the international outcry against the kafala system in Qatar, though not all are related explicitly to this system (Amnesty International, 2013).[27] First, is the 'no objection certificate' or the requirement of workers to secure their employer's permission before changing jobs. Second, is the 'exit permit' workers must acquire from their employer before leaving the

141

country (only Qatar and Saudi Arabia of the Arab Gulf states require workers to obtain exit visas from the kafeel before they can leave the country). Third, is the barring of certain migrant workers (domestic maids) from protections enshrined within Qatari labour law.[28] Fourth, is the fact that only Qatari citizens are entitled to engage in union activity. Fifth, is the fact that despite having quite significant worker protections in place, it is rare in practice for migrants to step forward and use the law against employers.

Given the international outcry, reforming the kafala sponsorship system has become, ostensibly at least, a priority in many Arab states. Leading the way in this regard has been Bahrain, where the end of the kafala system was announced in 2009 (Kuwait followed in 2010).[29] In its place workers are now sponsored by the state 'Labour Market Regulation Authority' and are able to move jobs without their employer's consent provided that they give three months' notice. Qatar is heading in a similar direction to Bahrain but there is a danger in equating the formal end of the kafala system to real progress in terms of addressing the huge power imbalance that exists between the state/ employers and migrant workers.

In Qatar, for example, authorities jailed and deported 90 Nepali migrant construction workers in 2009 because they went on strike after their employer cut their wages from 1000 riyals (US$275) to 650 riyals (US$180) (HRW, 2012). Despite the imminent ending of the kafala system then, migrant workers still do not enjoy freedom of association or collective bargaining rights. Moreover, the right to freedom of movement created by the ending of the kafala system is also not as strong as one might expect; with ample evidence that employers are willing to hold back wages, use debt bondage, and confiscate passports in order to tie migrant workers to their job above and beyond the formal sponsorship tie-in (Amnesty International, 2013; HRW, 2012). The inaction of the state to tackle these abuses, despite laws that empower them to do so, is another reason not to be complacent in the wake of the apparently enlightened decision to end the kafala system.

Whether in Bahrain, Kuwait, Qatar or in other Arab states, the writing appears to be on the wall for the kafala sponsorship system. However, migrant workers – despite being in the majority in many countries – are still treated as 'denizens' and do not enjoy the same rights or entitlements as full citizens. This is the result of the continued pact between the state and business that requires a certain type of productive and compliant, yet temporary and expendable, migrant worker. Despite ostensible commitment to reform the sponsorship system, there is still no desire to see migrant workers as equals or to treat them as such, and while this remains, the legacy of the kafala system is likely to linger on.

As a final point, it is worth stressing that many believe that there is a malaise in government with respect to migrant worker exploitation in kafala countries (Cooper, 2013). Moreover, even where the exploitation of migrant workers has been exposed, and deemed to be morally wrong, abuse has tended to be linked to the individual minutiae of the employer–employee relationship (the 'bad-egg' employer discourse) rather than on the structurally embedded power imbalances of the kafala system and its replacements (Pande, 2013). In other words, indignation from within the Arab world towards employer behaviour, in the rare instances where it occurs, has not connected this behaviour to the wider social, political, economic, legal and cultural structures that have sustained and legitimated the kafala system. Blame has been fixed on what is most easily identified and least threatening. This tendency to personalise the causes of exploitation rather than to criticise the broader structural environs within which exploitation is allowed to germinate is a feature also shared with the western world.

Aside from the kafala systems in the Middle East, there are a range of other migration schemes that give migrants limited rights. Migrant agricultural workers across the developed world, for instance, can obtain special working visas (see Scott, 2015a for a review). In many cases these tend to tie them to a given employer, or at best make free mobility difficult given the criteria of the agricultural visas. As the following quotations from employers, relating to the erstwhile UK Seasonal Agricultural Workers Scheme (SAWS), demonstrate:

> "Under SAWS it was regimented and uniform, and you could come and work at this company for six months, or go and work at that company for six months. The issue now is they're free to do whatever they want. So that's where the negativity and the pressure's coming from…I think if we could give people permits, not to put them on a leash, that's the wrong way to do it, but you know, incentivised them…If you've got a bit of control over it, you know, I'm not saying we've got to have a bloody prisoner of war camp here, but let's have a bit of control…That's what we got from the Russians and Ukrainians. They came over here, they knew they'd got a job, they knew they'd earn lots of money, they knew they had to go back home before their visa ran out. So they'd do everything by the book." (Human Resource Manager, Lettuce Grower and Processor).

"SAWS is really the best controlled form of immigration that the government has ever come up with! It comes back to what we were saying about those people who come on SAWS, we offer all our seasonal staff six-month contracts. I could, you know, go away and come back with figures to show that every single SAWS worker that we employ is much more effective, earns much more money because they're much better at the job, they're much more committed than any other EU or UK member of staff, and they stay for six months…SAWS, they don't leave, they just do not leave and that security of knowing that when you get those peaks during July and August, you know you can at least rely on that backbone of 40 staff. If we take SAWS away, we don't have that reliable workforce…they've seen the commitment's there, they're enthusiastic, they want the job more than anything. You could argue it's 'cos they have no alternative, they're here on a SAWS permit to work for us for that (six-month) period…It's a controlled form of immigration, it works, it suits the industry, there's never been any problems with it. As long as you have freedom of movement in the EU, which you will always have, you won't get the consistency (of SAWS)." (Human Resource Manager, Tomato, Cucumber and Chili Grower)

Beyond the role of migration policies in moulding and controlling workers, states also affect labour–capital relations by the classifications and distinctions they make between various legal categories of 'employee', 'worker', 'self-employed' and 'contractor'. In the UK, for example, a key distinction is between worker, self-employed and employee. The government outlines the distinctions as follows:

'Employees' are people who work for an employer under the terms of a contract of employment. 'Workers' are people who work for an employer whether or not under a contract of employment. Workers without employment contracts include temporary agency workers, casual workers and some freelance workers but not genuinely self-employed people. Under UK labour law therefore all employees are workers but not all workers are employees, and the genuinely self-employed are not deemed to be 'workers' (House of Lords, 2007, Chapter Five)

The contentious distinction as far as UK unions have been concerned is between worker and employee, with the latter enjoying more rights than the former (see Table 6.7). This is especially contentious in an era when labour market flexibility is being championed and labour costs are being re-examined by employers with the move from employee to worker potentially offering both flexibility and cost-saving. The UK's union confederation, the TUC, has called on governments to treat all workers (that is, workers and employees) equally but this call has been rejected (House of Lords, 2007).

Table 6.7: Worker exemptions in the UK

Worker entitled to:	Worker usually not entitled to:
• Equality of opportunities (non-discrimination) • National minimum wage • Health and safety • Working time entitlements such as paid annual leave, daily and weekly rest breaks • Protection against unlawful deductions from wages • Right to be a member of a trade union	• Dismissal procedure • Redundancy pay • Notice • Maternity leave • Parental leave • Grievance procedure

Source: https://www.gov.uk/employment-status/worker

Other than the employee–worker legal distinction in the UK, there have been challenges across the EU in relation to workers' designation as 'self-employed'. The issue is with what has been called 'bogus self-employment' and it has been raised across Europe in relation to both blue-collar (for example, construction) and white-collar (for example, aviation and journalism) workers. Bogus self-employment occurs when workers are expected to declare themselves as self-employed but then to also commit to working for a given company, who entirely control their pay and working conditions. The self-employed status is used because it allows employers to make tax savings and to employ workers without meeting obligations around holiday pay, sick pay and pensions. In construction, for example, workers are often asked to sign contracts with a third-party payroll company and to then work as self-employed on a construction site when in reality they have committed to an employer who does in fact dictate pay and working conditions. Essentially, then, the legal status of self-employed is being used by some employers to employ workers, but on reduced terms and conditions. As with the distinction between worker and employee, the boundary between being self-employed and not being self-employed appears to have been left open to interpretation.

In the US, a key legal distinction is between 'employee' and independent 'contractor'. Employee status is usually assigned if the employer controls the labour process, whereas contractor status is usually assigned if the employer only controls the outcome of the work being done. The distinction is also determined by the workers' ability to generate profit or loss and by the length of the working relationship. Whether one is an employee or a contractor has different tax and benefit implications. An employee, but not a contractor, will have the following: an employer withholding income, social security and medical taxes; an employer making contributions to these schemes; federal and state discrimination protection; subsequent entitlement to unemployment, medical and other welfare insurance benefits; fringe benefits such as pensions scheme membership. In short, employee status generally carries more cost to an employer than contractor status. As with the employee–worker and bogus self-employment examples above, however, the distinction between employee and contractor is often blurred.

Most recently, in 2015, the online taxi firm Uber was ruled against by the California Labour Commission for designating a driver as a contractor rather than an employee. Until this case, Uber designated all drivers using its service as contractors but the Labour Commission ruled that Uber was fundamentally involved at all stages of the labour process and was not simply providing a software platform to match supply and demand. The case was only a single action brought by an individual contesting her employment status. It serves to once again underline, however, the legal complexities between the different official worker classifications.

Not only, then, do workers often have different rights and entitlements according to their citizenship status. They can also have different rights and entitlements according to the legal category of labour (worker, employee, self-employed, contractor) they fall within. Alongside this, the picture is further confused by the types of contracts that are encouraged or permitted in different country contexts. The UK, for instance, now has a large number of workers on 'zero-hours' and 'short-hours' contracts. The size of the zero-hours workforce has grown most significantly: up from 100,000 in 2005 to 801,000 by the end of 2015.[30] In New Zealand, however, the state has recently (in 2016) passed legislation to outlaw zero-hours contracts. Thus, in different settings workers are rendered more or less insecure (flexible) by virtue of the often highly complex political–legal system that prevails.

As a final point, it is also worth noting that rights and entitlements at work can also vary according to occupation and industry. The classic examples here are the *au pair*, domestic work and agricultural sectors, which often have fewer protections than other areas of the labour market.

In the UK, for instance, an *au pair* is not classed as a worker or an employee and so is not entitled to the national minimum/living wage or to paid holidays. Instead, he/she is treated as a member of the family and is entitled only to 'pocket money', with government guidance stating £70–£85 per week to be fair remuneration.[31] Similarly, migrant domestic workers in the UK have had particular restrictions placed on their labour market participation and rights that bear similarities to the tied status of kafala workers discussed above.

The UK visa arrangements for overseas domestic workers (ODWs) have generated considerable debate (Mantouvalou, 2013; Idowu Salih, 2015). The question is whether domestic work and ODWs should be treated any differently by the state to other sectors and other workers? Following concern over the exploitation of ODWs, who were at the time tied to an employer for a specific period of time (similar to the kafala system discussed above), the UK government (after lobbying from unions and NGOs), introduced renewable visas which allowed ODWs to change employers. Ten years later, however, the UK government announced that it was considering changing this system to give migrant domestic workers a time-limited non-renewable visa under which they could not change employers. As part of this change, they would also not be recognised as workers but rather as domestic 'assistants' and consequently would not receive certain benefits or safeguards under law. Unions and NGOs mobilised against this policy exceptionalism towards ODWs, as they had done in 1998, and in June 2008 the government announced that the current visa system would be retained. In 2012, however, and despite further union and NGO protest, a new visa system for ODWs did eventually come into force.

For ODWs in private households, these changes set a maximum stay of six months and removed various rights and entitlements including the right to a visa renewal, to permanent settlement, to change employer and to sponsor dependents. For ODWs in diplomatic households the period of stay is five years or the duration of the employer's posting (whichever is shorter). There is no right to change employer or to permanent settlement. ODWs do retain a statutory right to use an employment tribunal, but because they cannot change employer or remain in the UK after they stop working for their employer this right to a grievance process is largely theoretical. The 1998 progressive changes to the ODW visa, followed by the 2008 announcements of new restrictions, and the 2012 partial implementation of these, demonstrates the considerable debate in the UK over whether there should be migration and employment policy exceptionalism with respect to domestic work and ODWs. The UK law in 1998 eroded this exceptionalism but in 2008 and 2012 it was re-established confirming domestic work and domestic workers' special place at the UK policy table.

In the US context, political–legal 'exceptionalism' has tended to be greatest with respect to farm workers. Most obviously, the sector has benefited from temporary visas, first via the *bracero* (1940s–1960s) and then via the H-2A[32] programmes. These schemes have restricted workers' rights while in the US and brought with them the ever-present threat of deportation (Clark, 2016). They have, to quote Anderson (2010), been used to 'mould' certain types of (deferent) low-wage workers. In addition, US agricultural employers have also benefited from a ready pool of irregular labour and lax immigration enforcement. In California, for example, around 50% of crop workers are estimated to be clandestine.[33]

Not only is US agricultural employment regulated by specialist visa programmes and by the tacit acceptance of irregular workers, the political–legal exceptionalism is also underscored by federal labour legislation:

- Farm workers were excluded from the National Labour Relations Act (1935) which protects workers who are acting collectively to form unions.
- The Fair Labor Standards Act (FLSA) initially excluded farmworkers from the minimum wage. The minimum wage provisions that now exist still do not apply to smaller farms (those that employ fewer than seven workers in a calendar quarter) and agricultural workers remain excluded from the FLSA's overtime pay provisions.
- The Migrant and Seasonal Agricultural Worker Protection Act (MSAPA) is now the principal federal employment law for farmworkers. In itself it demonstrates exceptionalism. It also provides rights and protections to farm workers but not at the same level as those guarantees available to other workers via federal law. For instance, the MSAPA does not give farmworkers the right to join a union or the right to collective bargaining.

Political–legal exceptionalism in the US with respect to farm workers, and particularly migrant farm workers, is deep rooted (Martin,

2002). The question for sectors such as agriculture, domestic work and *au pairing*, is whether this exceptionalism is/was ever justifiable? Put another way, should certain areas of the economy be entitled to political–legal privileges that result in workers being subject to greater control and/or fewer rights than elsewhere?

Socio-cultural controls

In Chapter Five we saw how workplace cultures can be used by employers to produce and reproduce 'good' workers. The question for this chapter is whether social and cultural *milieus* beyond the workplace can be, and have been, used to produce and reproduce 'good' workers? Certainly, it is in a state's and an organised business's interest to influence workers, to some degree, outside of the immediate workplace. In many contexts, this is of mutual benefit: such as through vocational training and education. However, questions have been raised about the degree to which society and culture should be orientated towards the needs of the business and/or the state and the impact that this orientation might have both on societies/cultures and upon notions of individual liberty and freedom.

The most prominent high-profile academic debate in this respect has been centred upon libertarian paternalism and the idea that people can and should be 'nudged' towards certain decisions within a particular 'choice architecture' (Sunstein and Thaler, 2008). The argument goes that society can and should be steered and that individuals when given particular (constrained) choices can be allowed to make the 'right' (however defined) decisions that are 'best for all' (however defined) concerned. Libertarian paternalism has been particularly applied in relation to individuals making health choices, pensions investment decisions and environmental behaviour. In all three examples, immediate short-term benefits (for example, of unhealthy food, of more disposable income, of greater car use) may be better delayed for longer-term sets of benefits (for example, of longevity, of financial security, of limiting climate change).

The idea of nudging people within a choice architecture takes ideas from a range of disciplines (though especially behavioural economics and psychology). Advocates argue that the right or better decision, even if achieved through constricted choice, is ultimately preferable to the alternatives, namely: individuals making poor decisions and/ or individuals being pushed into particular decisions without any real choice. Many, however, are concerned about this apparently benevolent and benign art where both the individual and wider societies gain

(Hausman and Welch, 2010; Selinger and Whyte, 2011; Goodwin, 2012).

Perhaps the biggest issue with social steering, aside from whether it actually works, revolves around the related questions of who initiates the steering, how it occurs, and who benefits most from it? Many believe that the state and related financial interests are most likely to be those initiating the steering and benefiting from it, and that steering is simply another way in which the mass public is manipulated and controlled in the interests of capital. Even if this were true, some backers would counter that what is in the interests of capital is also in the interests of the public at large. More problematically, however, is the question of how nudging occurs and whether an individual's free will is constrained, controlled or manipulated in order to achieve the required outcomes?

The issue of manipulation and control through hegemonic means is not something to be taken lightly. It involves detailed knowledge of individual and group psychology, and physiology, in order to trigger certain forms of behaviour. McIntosh identifies certain 'hypnotic' (2001, 106) tools and techniques, or 'white man's black magic' (2001, 107), as examples of the ways in which mass human control is now possible. The examples are too numerous to mention, though most clearly there are the sciences of marketing and of the media that have very discernible impacts upon consumer behaviour at an everyday, and often sub-conscious, level.

Despite the reservations about free will being compromised, the idea of nudging people through a choice architecture so that they make the 'right' and the 'better' decisions has taken hold at the heart of governments. In the UK, for example, the government established the 'Nudge Unit' (Behavioural Insight Team) within the Cabinet Office, though it was then moved outside government, to advance the insights from Sunstein and Thaler (2008); who themselves have been prominent in US policy-making circles (Brown, 2012; Gill and Gill, 2012).

Largely, the explicit use of social steering by states has been confined to particular types of issues around health, wellbeing, sustainability and the environment. The link between nudging and human behaviour in the fields of consumption and production (work) has largely been avoided or left to others. What is interesting, though, is that the libertarian paternalism movement does potentially have a lot to say in relation to the social and cultural construction of 'good' and 'better' workers (and 'good' and 'better' consumers).

Workfare is one of the few areas of state policy where ideas from libertarian paternalism have been directly used on citizens (Standing, 2011). Since 2014, for example, the long-term unemployed in the

UK have been 'helped' into employment via various, albeit restricted, options. A constrained choice architecture is open to them in the sense that the unemployed now either accept unpaid employment in return for benefits or they experience various sanctions, which ultimately could mean the loss of all benefits if the wrong choices are made. Policy, then, has become more hardline but the controls associated with workfare have been packaged within a choice architecture that is designed to nudge workers towards a particular outcome. In the case of workfare, the unemployed are being asked to choose to labour for free and to then receive unemployment compensation as their reward for making the right choice. This may be seen as a form of decision-making empowerment by some. Others, though, see it as a form of additional control.

Historically what is interesting is that social and cultural steering has been used for centuries in relation to the mass production of 'good' workers. Well before Sunstein and Thaler's book (2008) certain religious doctrines, most notably the Calvinist branch of Protestantism (Weber, 1930), were central in establishing the work ethic via the link between individual endeavour at work and delayed gratification in heaven (or delayed retribution in hell). As Weber (1930) notes, Protestantism lead to the: 'formation of a moral outlook enhancing labour discipline within the lower and middle levels of capitalist economic organisation' (p xiii). Thus, labour was faithful, even when pay and conditions were poor, because this was 'highly pleasing to god' (121).

As society moved from religious to secular, and as work became more white-collar and service-based, Ehrenreich (2009) argues that the protestant work ethic has been replaced by positive thinking as the doctrine driving the proletariat in their work (90–6). Ehrenreich (2009, 90) summarises the control parallels as follows: 'The most striking continuity between the old religion and the new positive thinking lies in the common insistence on work – the constant internal work of self-monitoring.' Put another way, certain social and cultural structures have been used historically – whether the Protestant work ethic or positive thinking – to enable workers to choose to be good and to help in the production and reproduction of better workers. It is somewhat surprising, therefore, that the ideas from the 'nudge', 'steering' and 'choice architecture' revolution of the late 2000s have only engaged in a very limited way (ostensibly at least) with the world of work.

Beyond the specific example of libertarian paternalism, it is clear that in a broad sense the social and cultural realms can be used to underpin, legitimate and draw consensus around highly unequal sets of power relations. Control by one person/group over another person/group can be achieved, maintained, and even rendered natural by and through the social and cultural worlds we inhabit. This is something that the French sociologist Pierre Bourdieu underlines through his concept of 'symbolic violence' and the idea that the 'dominating' and 'dominated' co-exist in large part by the production and reproduction of taken for granted and apparently natural and subtle social and cultural structures and inequalities (Bourdieu, 1997; 2001; Holmes, 2013).

From a work perspective, the power asymmetries between labour and capital, and between different segments of labour, are maintained by the very fact that the control of workers is not just exogenous to the workplace but it is also rooted at the level of perception and thus largely hidden from the conscious mind. Socio-cultural control beyond the workplace, then, is not simply about manipulation and nudging people into certain forms of behaviour (for example, to be more productive workers) it is also about people accepting, and even embracing, rather than contesting, the inequalities that structure their everyday disempowerment. To this extent, socio-cultural control beyond the workplace is, for some, the fundamental building block to all other forms of control.

Human enhancements

The final section of the chapter will consider the ways in which technology can/could be used by both labour and capital to enhance human behaviour in order to produce and reproduce 'good' and 'better' workers beyond the immediate workplace. Human enhancement may be achieved, theoretically at least, in four main ways:

1. Biological Enhancement: selection and use of preferred genetic make-up in a population.
2. Recruitment Enhancement: better matching of people's innate capability, through various screening techniques, to particular job types.
3. Medical Enhancement: intervening through chemicals and surgery to make people more employable.
4. Behavioural Enhancement: shaping cognitive functions through cerebral intervention.

The four types of human enhancements noted above are no longer just theoretical, they are becoming very active possibilities. As yet, however, there has been very little discussion regarding the relationship between human enhancement and control with respect to the world of work (though see Academy of Medical Sciences, 2012)

The first time human enhancement was formally linked to the idea of producing and reproducing 'good' and 'better' workers, and achieving a stronger economy, was by the US military in 2008:

> One spokesperson for the US Military, which is actively exploring the potential of human enhancement technology, said: 'The world contains approximately 4.2 billion people over the age of twenty. Even a small enhancement of cognitive capacity in these individuals would probably have an impact on the world economy rivaling that of the internet.' (cited in Savulescu and Bostrom, 2009, 20)

The big worry is that human enhancement possibilities will become commercially available and that their use will become stratified according to wealth and income. Moreover, there is a worry that workers will be targeted by the technological advancements being made to the extent that there will be pressure for mass human enhancement of different sorts and at different levels of society.

The Academy of Medical Sciences (2012) has been one of the few organisations to raise ethical questions with respect to the relationship between human enhancement and work. Its report argues, for instance, that human enhancement may be a double-edged sword:

> Enhancement could benefit employee efficiency and even work–life balance, but there is a risk that it will be seen as a solution to increasingly challenging working conditions, which could have implications for employee wellbeing. (Academy of Medical Sciences, 2012, 6)

It goes on to note that employees might actually feel compelled in some instances to undergo enhancement for fear of being deemed ineffective, inefficient and surplus to requirements (Academy of Medical Sciences, 2012, 53).

One of the problems with human enhancement technology is that if it becomes commercially viable, and provides employers with a competitive edge, then there could be an 'enhancement race' (Academy of Medical Sciences, 2012, 39). Thus, both workers and employers may eventually succumb to pressures for greater performance in order to survive. The danger of this 'enhancement race' is that one's natural identity and sense of self may become compromised, especially when multiple forms of enhancement are carried out (Academy of Medical Sciences, 2012, 47). There is also the danger that an enhanced 'elite' eventually emerge with vastly superior cognitive capacities and human capital.

Many of those at the cutting edge of human enhancement science believe that substantially more progress is likely to be made and that this is inevitable despite the ethical concerns. Savulescu and Bostrom (2009, 18), for instance, argue that:

> Human enhancement has moved from the realm of science fiction to that of practical ethics. There are now effective physical, cognitive, mood, cosmetic, and sexual enhancers – drugs and interventions that can enhance at least some aspects of some capacities in at least some individuals some of the time. The rapid advances currently taking place in the biomedical sciences and related technological areas make it clear that a lot more will become possible over the coming years and decades.

Thus, the positive potential of human enhancement appears to have largely trumped the ethical concerns over social stratification and the related techno-scientific potential to generate 'good' and 'better' workers and therefore competitive advantage.

In terms of specific examples for the four forms of human enhancement listed above, progress is still quite limited as far as employment is concerned:

- Biological enhancement would effectively involve the selection or splicing of favourable genes to create better workers, which in the extreme might involve the cloning of the 'ideal worker'. This might sound like the scenario from a dystopian science fiction novel, but we have known that cloning is possible since 1962 when Professor Sir John Gurdon (Cambridge University) managed to show that the genetic information from a cell inside a frog's intestines contained all the information needed to clone that frog.
- Recruitment enhancement would involve the screening of individuals in order to match them with suitable jobs that they are naturally equipped to perform. Psychological testing already occurs in certain professions. However, we also know that other traits could be tested for using DNA screening and also that particular areas of the brain are associated with particular skills. The size of the hippocampus, for example, is key to spatial awareness

(Maguire and Mullally, 2013) and appears to be enlarged in many taxi drivers. This demonstrated both on the job learning, and also the potential, in theory at least, to select according to physiology as well as psychology.

- Medical enhancement would occur when workers use chemicals or surgery to make themselves more employable. The classic examples here are the use of Botox and plastic surgery in public facing roles, the use of tiredness antidotes such as caffeine and Pro-Plus for night-workers and those with multiple jobs, and the use of performance enhancers by elite athletes.

- Behavioural enhancement would occur when non-chemical and non-surgical interventions directly 'improve' cognitive functions. Traditional overt techniques in this field include hypnosis and talking therapies such as counselling. As with biological enhancement, though, there are dystopian visions on the horizon. It is now possible, for example, to alter cerebral functions remotely through sound and laser waves (see for example Bath et al, 2014). There is also a related branch of electro-magnetic science that has been in operation since the 1950s which had by the 1970s found that: 'the spoken word of a hypnotist may also be conveyed by modulated electromagnetic energy directly into the subconscious parts of the human brain that is, without employing any technical devices for receiving or transcoding the messages and without the person exposed to such influence having a chance to control the information input consciously' (Schapitz, 1974 in Becker and Selden,. 1998). Thus, there may be scope in future for both the conscious and sub-conscious production of 'good' and 'better' workers.

The above is just a snap-shot of the potential for human enhancement. Much of this enhancement is likely to be positive, but the use of the term 'enhancement' should not imply that all progress is successful or inexorably positive. There is also certainly room for concern with respect to the potential armoury of worker controls in this field and the relative lack of ethical discussions around this. In addition, there is the spectre of an enhancement 'arms race' driven by employer and employee competition; and possibly even by the emergence of artificial intelligence technologies as machines vie to out-compete human beings.

Conclusion

When considering the link between work and social harm it would be naïve to restrict analysis to the workplace and to the direct (Chapter Four) and indirect (Chapter Five) controls within it. 'Good' and 'better' workers are clearly produced and reproduced beyond the workplace and it is to exogenous controls that this chapter has turned. Issues of insecurity, inequality, variable citizenship, social steering and human enhancement were all visited in order to demonstrate how people, outside of the workplace, may be conditioned to perform appropriately when at work. A social harm perspective would argue that these exogenous controls are often problematic and that we should be aiming for greater ontological security, greater equality, the equalisation of citizenship rights, reduced work-related social steering, and an ethical stance towards human enhancement that respect diversity and dignity.

Put another way, outside of the workplace the aim should not be to achieve ever-greater control over labour. It should be to allow humans the space and time to flourish. This requires not only the relinquishing of certain forms of control but it also requires the active encouragement of a life-world that sees work as a step towards fulfilment rather than the end point. The degree to which state and corporate interests would view such liberation as a threat to the production and reproduction of 'good' and 'better' workers is open to debate. What is clear is that when individuals are empowered (rather than simply controlled) outside of work they are more likely to be able to defend themselves (and others) from exploitation and harm. The argument here is not a zero-sum game, it is not about the absence of exogenous controls, rather it is about choosing the right types of controls and tying ethical and moral discussions and justifications to these choices.

'Sitting down, you can do on your own time'

When the queue thins out and
you in the murmur of the restaurant
can distinguish voices,
the display stand is polished,
tables wiped
everything ready for the next rush

when the dulled sound of unslept hours and
the weight of tired muscles press behind the eyes

when you take the three steps up into the kitchen after
seven hours on the go,
searching for a cardboard box and
just need a little rest

you sag down,
feeling the carton's elasticity,
resting *your* legs

then suddenly, she stands there
above you

telling with only a glance
how interchangeable you are

you get up
correct the smile and
go down to the counter
again

SEVEN

Navigating the edges of acceptability

This chapter focuses on the nebulous boundary between acceptable and unacceptable (that is, exploitative) work-based control. Along this boundary one must ask a number of questions in order to attempt to gain some definitional clarity. There are at least five key questions: 1) Is there evidence of workers consenting to exploitative or harmful employment, and does this consent matter?; 2) Is there evidence of 'decent quality' employment?; 3) Is there evidence of harm?; 4) Is there evidence of knowledge, intent or motives underpinning exploitation and harm?; 5) Is there evidence of exemptions, rendering exploitation and harm acceptable, and how are these justified?

Evidence of worker consent?

A focus on the labour exploitation continuum (as outlined in Chapter Two) moves one away from coerced labour to focus on various forms of work-based control (as reviewed in Chapters Four, Five and Six). This shift calls into question the idea that the presence of worker consent is enough to make exploitation and harm acceptable. As Barrientos et al (2013, 1039) argue:

> The idea that labour may be 'voluntarily' offered at the point of entry does not therefore mean that the labour relation is 'free', as understood in the conventional sense: straightforward notions of consent, choice or 'voluntariness' are poor guides to understanding the processes by which workers enter into severely exploitative arrangements.

The key task, given the above, is to therefore investigate the nature of consent and the blurring of the voluntary/involuntary divide. This is central both to understanding when control becomes excessive and oppressive and to understanding why workers apparently accept, and even knowingly enter, exploitative and harmful relationships.

The ILO, via its definition of forced labour (see Chapter Two), acknowledges that ambiguity exists even in relation to the idea of 'force'. Force is not just about one being coerced at the point of entry into a particular set of working conditions but involves 'the menace of any penalty' (ILO Convention Number 29, 1930) and the involuntary offer of labour that may result from this. Thus, the line between free and unfree labour is blurred by the ILO, even in relation to the relatively tightly defined criminal–legal concept of forced labour. The question, of what constitutes a 'menace' and a 'penalty' is answered via the now well-established ILO forced labour indicators (see Box 2.2). These begin to problematise issues around worker control rather than just privileging the issue of coercion.

As Anderson and Rogaly (2005, 40) note, it is: 'in practice very difficult to distinguish between a free and consensual and an unfree and coerced employment relationship'. One key dimension to this complexity is the way in which the holds that employers have over workers appear to be getting more sophisticated and are now: 'usually invisible (and) the forms of coercion more subtle' (Belser and de Cock, 2009, 179). Not only then is the boundary between voluntary and involuntary labour a blurred one, but the means that make work involuntary are now often very difficult to detect. As a result, and as Strauss (2012, 140) notes, there is currently therefore: 'no international agreement on what constitutes freedom of choice and great difficulty in determining the reality of consent'.

To illustrate the complexity, there are at least five ways in which workers may end up in exploitative and harmful situations but ostensibly of their own volition and with relatively limited evidence of force as conventionally conceived:

1. Deception: Commonly, especially among migrants, promises are made in relation to the provision of quality jobs and accommodation. These promises often also persuade workers to pay up-front fees, leading on to indebtedness in many cases. The work and housing that is eventually provided, if indeed any is provided at all, is then frequently below the expected/promised level. In essence employees voluntarily enter an employment situation to then find that they are exploited through deception. As Skrivánková (2010, 7) explains: 'A common misunderstanding is that those in forced labour had to be forced to work. However, in reality, people often freely agreed to take up work and only once they started working discovered that they were deceived about the conditions or the nature of the work.' In a recent UK study, deception came out as the most significant of all forced labour indicators (Scott et al, 2012, 29).

2. Self-Exploitation: This is often the case with migrants who may be better off financially in a host country than in their home country, and are therefore willing to accept sub-standard pay and conditions (Craig et al, 2007, 17). As Plant (2009, xi) observes people may: 'subject themselves through rational choice to conditions that most people used to the enjoyment of labour standards and rights would consider inhumane'. This poses a difficult moral question in the sense that if workers are willing and knowledgeable participants in labour markets that exploit them should outside actors intervene to help them?

3. Psychological Pressure: Exploitation may be accepted by individuals experiencing psychological controls that are excessive and oppressive. These might be explicit threats or more implicit control mechanisms. The ILO, for example, recognises that: 'Alleged forms of abuse may be extremely subtle, involving psychological pressures and threats rather than overt physical restraint and violence' (ILO, 2009d, iii). An example of this is cited by Andrees and Belser (2009, 102): 'Threats can be effective by using a person's sense of shame – such as in the case of a woman forced into prostitution or a man humiliated in front of others' (see, for example, Lewis, 2004).

4. Economic Necessity: Workers may accept exploitative work due to a lack of alternatives and in order to avoid destitution. This is especially likely for irregular migrants or those migrants with limited citizenship rights who do not qualify for welfare support (Dwyer et al, 2011). The ILO, however, rules out economic necessity as part of forced labour, stating that: 'Forced labour cannot be equated simply with low wages or poor working conditions. Nor does it cover situations of pure economic necessity, as when a worker feels unable to leave a job because of the real or perceived absence of employment alternatives' (ILO, 2005a, 5). The ILO accepts economic necessity does lead to exploitation but states that forced labour is something substantively more severe than this involving, in addition, the 'menace of a penalty'.

5. Agency: There is a common misconception that workers who are subject to exploitation, especially slavery and forced labour, must lack individual agency and free will. This is not the case: 'workers — however disempowered — have agency' (Mitchell, 2011, 584). Studies of exploited and disempowered workers across the world demonstrate this paradox (Scott, 1985; Rogaly, 2009). The key point is that workers' choices are severely constrained and limited in exploitative situations, but some agency will almost always be discernible (Strauss, 2012, 144).

One should not, therefore, when focusing on exploitation and harm fetishise the idea of coercion. The ILO's notion of forced labour (around the menace of penalty) illustrates this as do the five examples listed above. Moreover, the very focus of this book – on control – is designed to underline the fact that ostensibly free workers can experience a blurring of the boundary between free and forced labour and between coercion and consent.

Exploitative or 'decent quality' work?

In 1998 the ILO produced the 'Declaration on Fundamental Principles and Rights at Work' (Box 2.4). A year later the ILO announced the 'Decent Work' agenda (see for example Lerche, 2012). These two developments were designed to identify what acceptable employment should look like. The decent work agenda, in particular, helps us to define labour exploitation by what it is not. The Director General of the ILO at the time (Juan Somavia) defined decent work in his address to the 87th International Labour Conference in 1999 as:

> productive work in which rights are protected, which generates an adequate income with adequate social protection. It also means sufficient work in the sense that all should have access to income earning opportunities. It marks the high road to economic and social development, a road in which employment, income and social protection can be achieved without compromising workers' rights and sound standards.

The idea of promoting a 'high road' to employment has caught on less than the idea of preventing the worst forms of exploitation (that is, chattel slavery, modern slavery, forced labour, human trafficking, child labour). It is important, however, to establish what 'decent work' involves in order to problematise what is not included in the definition. Thus, while one might choose to particularly problematise chattel slavery, modern slavery, forced labour, human trafficking and child labour, this does not mean that everything else is by definition decent work. Therefore, knowing what decent work is, is an important part of defining the boundary between exploitative and non-exploitative employment.

One of the key elements of the decent work agenda is an income that allows individuals to have a good life. Beyond this, workplaces should: allow individuals to be able to develop themselves equally well; provide a safe environment; outlaw forced and child labour; and prevent discrimination. Trade union and state activity in work, via social protection and social dialogue, is also seen as a key part of ensuring decent work and protecting those who might otherwise be marginalised (sick, elderly, pregnant women). Although the decent work agenda emphasises adherence to the ILO's core conventions (see Table 7.1), it also goes beyond these.

Table 7.1: ILO core conventions as part of the 'decent work' agenda

Domain	ILO Convention Number
Freedom of association and the right to collective bargaining	• Convention Number 87 – Freedom of Association and Protection of the Right to Organize, 1948 • Convention Number 98 – Right to Organize and Collective Bargaining, 1949
Elimination of forced labour	• Convention Number 29 – Forced Labour, 1930 • Convention Number 105 – Abolition of Forced Labour, 1957
Abolition of child labour	• Convention Number 138 – Minimum Age, 1973 • Convention Number 182 – Worse Forms of Child Labour, 1999
Elimination of employment discrimination	• Convention Number 100 – Equal Remuneration 1951 • Convention Number 111 – Discrimination (Employment and Occupation), 1958

The breadth of the decent work agenda and its implications, in terms of problematising significant swathes of employment not defined as 'decent', undoubtedly contributed to its limited global success and impact. Reflecting this point, Likic-Brboric and Schierup (2015), in their review of the ILO's decent work agenda, argue that there is a stubborn 'implementation problem'. Nevertheless, the framework is useful because it moves us beyond baseline definitions (see Chapter Two) by defining what exploitative and harmful employment is not. Put another way, it is an essential 'aspirational' complement to the much larger body of 'cautionary' work focused on the very worst forms of worker abuse.

Similarly, within the EU, there has been interest (though also rather muted) in defining 'quality' in employment and once again, by definition, problematising work falling outside this benchmark. In 2014 (EUROFOUND, 2014), and based on data from the fifth European Working Conditions Survey (EWCS), job quality across the EU was assessed. The conceptual framework employed (EUROFOUND,

2014, 7) emphasises four key domains in defining and measuring job quality: quality of employment; perceived job insecurity; perceived employability; and, intrinsic job characteristics (see Table 7.2). As with the ILO's decent work agenda, the EU-wide 'job quality' framework is designed to establish what should be part of acceptable employment. It is also able to measure this and compare country performances.

Table 7.2: Defining and measuring job quality

Domain	Sub-domain	Indicator
Quality of Employment	Employment Conditions	• Contract security • Income and rights • Working time • Employability
	Employment Relations	• Employee representation • Employee empowerment
Perceived Job Insecurity		• To lose current job in next 6 months
Perceived Employability		• To find a job with a similar salary
Intrinsic Job Characteristics	Working Conditions	• Environmental, Ergonomic, Social relationships at work • Support • Emotional demands • Work speed
	Job Content	• Autonomy • Skill • Discretion • Control

Source: EUROFOUND (2014, 7)

The ILO's 'Decent Work' and EUROFOUND's 'Job Quality' frameworks have both had rather limited success (Burchell et al, 2014; Di Ruggiero et al, 2014; Sehnbruch et al, 2015). It appears to be easier to build international consensus at the very bottom of the labour market 'below the baseline' (see Chapter Two). This may be because it is here where one's priorities should lie: in the sense that those interested in tackling work-based control, exploitation and harm should initially focus on the worst cases. It is also true that grey areas are, by their very nature, more difficult to build moral consensus around. Furthermore, it is in the interests of capitalism not to open up the 'Pandora's box' that is the labour exploitation continuum and be challenged by the implications of this.

Evidence of harm?

A further dimension to the definition of exploitative control is the presence of work-based harm. At its extreme, and as we saw in Chapter Two, harm is associated with worker fatality. However, there is a great deal more to work-based harm than death. Workers regularly experience physical and psychological ill-health as a result of exploitative controls imposed upon them, and this in turn can affect the wider social–communal realm. Work-based harm can also bring public costs, mainly through health and welfare expenditure.

Research into work-based harm has tended to look at four specific aspects. First, there is the issue of work-based health and safety with Slapper and Tombs' critical work on fatality standing out (Slapper, 1999; Tombs, 1999; 2007; 2008; Tombs and Whyte, 2010). Second, there is a much larger literature on the relationship between job insecurity and ill-health (Heaney et al, 1994; Quinlan et al, 2001; Benach and Muntaner, 2007; Clark et al, 2007). Third, there is an equally significant literature on the health effects associated with discrimination at work, for example through bullying (Lewis, 2004; Hansen et al, 2006), mobbing (Leymann, 1990; Leymann and Gustafsson, 1996) and through the isolation of whistleblowers (Lennane, 1993; 2012). Fourth, numerous studies highlight the link between work length and/or intensity and poor health (Virtanen et al, 2009, 2011; Carter et al, 2013). Thus there is an extensive, albeit fragmented, literature detailing the various ways in which particular working contexts and relationships may be harmful.

One of the interesting developments with respect to work-based harm, that to some extent reflects the transition from a blue- to a white-collar proletariat in the developed world, is that the original conception of harm as involving physical hazards (slips, trips, falls, injuries and death) has changed. A key symbolic piece of legislation in this respect was Sweden's Work Environment Act 1978 (Gallie, 2003; 2007) that broadened 'health' at work to include psychological as well as physical health. As a result, many countries now ensure that workers are protected beyond conventional physical 'health and safety' (slips, trips, falls, injuries and death) regulations. There is also a related recognition in health research that there are socio-psychological determinants of health and that what goes on in the workplace may be indirectly harmful to worker's physical health. The classic example here is the way in which stress can affect an individual's health outcomes (Ganster and Rosen, 2013).

In studying and seeking to define labour exploitation one must be aware, however, that work-based harm does not always result. In other words, it is useful to use the presence of harm as an indicator of exploitation but it should only be an indicator. Most obviously, the potential for work-based harm will vary between individuals. Resilience will depend upon factors such as: one's personal circumstances; psychological make-up; previous benchmark experiences; relationships with peers and managers; and, level of pay and other rewards. What is harmful for one exploited worker might not be particularly harmful for another exploited worker.

In my own research into exploited migrant workers in the UK food industry I found that the evidence of work-based harm was largely psychological:

> "I had enough, I could not take it any longer. I felt depressed, apathetic, I had problems with concentration, I stopped believing in myself, in what I was good at for 30 years. I was afraid even to come to work. I believe this all has happened because of my employer, because I didn't want to work for free, I didn't want to be his slave anymore and work so many hours overtime. So I found myself like I said before. I went to see my GP who advised me to change my work and he sent me for a sick note for a month. My employer absolutely laughed at this and ignored this completely… When I came back to work again I had to go back to my GP because I didn't feel any better; my depression actually got worse. I was afraid to go back to work after how I was treated by that employer. I was feeling that I won't cope. This employer actually destroyed my 30 years of experience, my professionalism." (female, 58y, Polish)

> "I was hating the alarm clock. When it was ringing in the morning and I knew I had to go back there, I felt like the sky was falling on me, but I had to go as I had no other choice. I needed money I needed work…I didn't care any more, I was at the point when you'd rather kill me than go back there…I lost weight, I was a poor being, my shoulders fallen, sad all the time, tense and day-by-day you are being treated like the least nothing on earth." (female, 30y, Romanian)

"At the time, I felt so miserable. I thought that I was the most unfortunate person. The situation seemed to me to be so hopeless. I thought that I got into hell and sold my soul and arms to dishonest people. I felt like a slave or cattle. It is hard to describe how I felt. You have to experience it in order to understand how people might feel in these circumstances." (female, 42y, Latvian)

It is interesting that much of the focus on harm from a governmental perspective, where it exists, tends to be on the reduction of physical hazards in the workplace to prevent slips, trips, falls, injuries and death. This is the conventional approach to health and safety at work. It ignores, however, the fact that for most exploited workers psychological health is where damage is done, which in turn can have an impact on physical health. Harm can also erode the societal–communal realms (see Polanyi, 1944) not to mention generate considerable public costs, mainly in terms of health and welfare expenditure.

Evidence of knowledge, intent or motives?

When exploitation or harm is evident a key definitional question is one of knowledge and intent. Specifically, did the person/organisation, directly or indirectly responsible, know what they were doing and did they know that what they were doing was wrong? Indifference, in this respect, is also no defence (Pemberton, 2015) as it implies knowledge of what was occurring and a failure to act. Another key definitional question revolves around motives and whether an individual/organisation has any motivation to exploit or cause harm? The presence of motives, alongside knowledge and intent, are key to determining culpability and also key, in complex employment relationships, to ensuring that all those responsible for exploitation and harm are identified.

Classically, one might distinguish between an unknowing and a knowing exploiter. In terms of the former, controls are often used without the intention to exploit or harm. It is also the case that knowledge of what constitutes exploitation and harm is often patchy and there is room for ambiguity in definitions. In addition, controls are often only exploitative or harmful when used in combination and, even then, they will have different impacts depending upon the particular worker concerned. Controls may also become normalised within the labour–capital relationship and so taken-for-granted and accepted by the perpetrator (and possibly wider society). It is clear, then, that in various ways employers may exploit or harm workers but without full knowledge of the consequences of their actions.

For the knowing agent, a distinction must be made between those who exploit or harm out of choice and those who do so out of necessity. It is the former that is morally problematic, while the latter should cause one to look deeper into the means and mechanisms underpinning an individual's/organisation's use of excessive and oppressive control.

Those actively choosing to exploit and harm may be motivated in a number of ways. Most obviously, there will be financial and status incentives associated with professional advancement through excessive and oppressive control. Some abusers may also have particular psychological traits (vanity, sadism, jealousy, racism and so on) that underpin their willingness to exploit and harm others. In addition, there will be those who exploit and harm for 'altruistic' reasons, claiming that this is a small part of a much wider project that is ultimately beneficial. Finally, there are those who believe in a natural social order whereby it is logical, legitimate, and even essential, to control others for the greater good. In the case of the latter, exploitation and harm may be deemed a price worth paying for the preservation of hierarchical authority. Essentially, then, even for those who knowingly exploit and harm, and do so out of choice rather than constraint, such behaviour can still be justified and rationalised.

The task for readers in light of the above, when exploitation or harm is present, is to assess knowledge, intent and motives and to answer the following four questions:

- Did the individual/organisation know that what they were doing was exploitative?
- Did the individual/organisation appreciate that what they were doing could cause harm?
- Did the individual/organisation have any alternatives open to them to avoid exploitation and harm? Why were these not taken?
- If the individual/organisation actively chose to exploit and harm, even in the light of alternatives, what were the justifications for this course of action?

As far as understanding the fourth question, the ILO, via the Abolition of Forced Labour Convention Number 105 (1957), has identified five motives behind forced labour. It is used as:

1. a means of political coercion or education or as punishment for holding or expressing political views;
2. a means of mobilising and using labour for purposes of economic development;
3. a means of labour discipline;
4. a punishment for having participated in strikes;
5. a means of racial, social, national or religious discrimination.

These five scenarios, according to the ILO, explain the presence of extreme forms of labour exploitation. Though it is worth noting that they appear to relate more to state-based harm than to harm caused by private economic actors. In the private economy, where most forced labour is now located (see Table 2.6), many would argue that it is the uneven nature of capital–labour relations that effectively make the excessive and oppressive control of workers possible and that labour must accept this unevenness or suffer severe consequences: 'Without the jobs capital offers, labor might starve. Being exploited, then, is usually better than the alternative. That is in fact why exploitation works. Exploitative exchanges are typically mutually advantageous. Both gain from the trade, but the gains are disproportionate. This is why these transactions are considered unfair' (Mayer, 2005, 318).

Evidence of legal exemptions?

Can exploitation and harm ever be justified? Some may condone it when there is no sign of *a priori* knowledge, intent or motives; though much depends on what the perpetrator does once aware of exploitation and harm, and whether this action is sufficient. Even when there is *a priori* knowledge, intent or motives, though, many argue that exploitative and harmful work is at times defensible.

Most obvious in this respect are the ILO's forced labour exemptions. The forced labour definition within Convention Number 29 (1930) excludes:

1. work imposed under compulsory military service;
2. normal civic obligations;
3. prison labour (if conviction by a court and public authority supervision);
4. work in emergency situations (war, calamity and so on);
5. minor community services.

In other words, people can be forced to perform particular duties under particular circumstances and this work is not to be deemed problematic.

The exemptions appear, at first glance, to be relatively understandable. However, there are areas of debate and contestation. Most notably, discussion has emerged around 'normal civic obligations' and 'prison labour'. In terms of the former, there is the 'workfare' debate over whether people should be required to work for free in return for subsistence level state benefits and the implications mass workfare might have for the wider labour market (Krinsky, 2008). In terms of the latter, many question the ways in which it is becoming lucrative to incarcerate people both for private prison providers and for those benefiting from virtually free prison labour (LeBaron, 2008; forthcoming).

Looking at the prison labour debate in more detail critical scholars point to a dominant 'prison–industrial complex' in neoliberal states (Newburn, 2002; Schlosser, 1998) underpinning a general trend towards increased imprisonment, even when crime rates are falling. This is an important trend because it underlines the point that incarceration is not inevitable but reflects prevailing social and political–economic structures. In a similar vein, Downes and Hansen (2006, 1) note that: 'countries that spend a greater proportion of GDP on welfare have lower imprisonment rates and that this relationship has become stronger over the last 15 years'. There are, then, temporal and spatial variations in imprisonment that do not simply reflect crime rates but reflect things such as the strength of the prison–industrial complex and the power of the welfare state.

Downes and Hansen (2006) crystallise this argument by comparing statistics on imprisonment and welfare (see Table 7.3). It is clear that in different countries there are different sets of factors underpinning imprisonment and that there are dramatic inter-country differences. In the US, for example, the absence of significant welfare intervention appears to be contributing to crime and imprisonment, as does the hardline approach of the state legislature, often in response to pressure both from the public and the prison–industrial complex. The question, given prison labour is widely used in the US, but given that the US imprisonment rate is so high, is whether this use is acceptable?

The US, according to the figures in Table 7.3, has around a ten times higher imprisonment rate than countries at a similar level of economic development. This also appears to be linked to the neoliberal nature of the welfare state, with imprisonment in social democratic countries much lower and welfare spending much higher. Is it right, then, given this rate is so high to profit from it via the use of prison labour? This question takes on added degrees of saliency when one considers the class and racial composition of incarnation. The black imprisonment rate is 2,207 per 100,000 in the US, for example, compared to the white imprisonment rate of 380.[34] Moreover, the various pieces of legislation needed to allow prison labour to be used have been passed following significant lobbying, most notably from the American Legislative Exchange Council (ALEC) (Elk and Sloan, 2011; Walshe, 2012). There has, in respect to ALEC, been a strong element of commercial interest in 'enabling' the US's unusually high prison population to work.

Table 7.3: Comparison of national imprisonment and welfare rates, 1998

Country	Imprisonment ranking	Imprisonment rate (per 100,000 of the adult population)	Percent of GDP spent on welfare
US	1	666	14.6
Denmark	15	63	29.8
Sweden	16	60	31.0
Finland	17	54	26.5
Japan	18	42	14.7

Source: Downes and Hansen (2006)

The US prison labour example is designed to problematise blanket forced labour exemptions. There may well be times when forced labour is justified but international comparisons show that it is important to always interrogate these exemptions. Most obviously, when the state is weak, there may be profits to be made out of incarceration and the associated use of free labour, and there is also associated pressure to keep welfare de-commodification to a minimum. This combination, in the US, means that the prison labour exemption of the ILO is widely used. It is also widely used on a particular group of largely black prisoners. Some would argue, in light of this, that resources should be directed towards tackling the causes of crime and imprisonment rather than profiteering from the outcomes via free (forced?) labour.

Beyond the ILO's forced labour exemptions there are also other times when workers are rendered exempt from particular employment laws that are designed to protect them from exploitation and harm. Most obviously, and as discussed in Chapter Six, there are particular political–legal structures that mean that certain categories of worker are created, with more or fewer rights and entitlements. The classic example usually cited here is the 'denizen' migrant (such as those within the kafala system) who only enjoys partial citizenship status; though there are also many different domestic classes of labour too (for example, worker, employee, self-employed and contractor).

Another grey area relates to the payment of the national minimum/ living wage (see Chapter Eight for a discussion of these). To elucidate, there are situations when states, businesses and wider society deem it to be legally and morally acceptable, and in some cases desirable, for workers to be paid under established legal wage benchmarks. These situations are outlined in Box 7.1.

Box 7.1: Work situations when a minimum pay level is deemed immaterial

The following low-wage or no-wage scenarios are all permitted or tolerated by nation-states:

1. Volunteers: Most states encourage people to volunteer. An example of an international volunteer scheme for migrant agricultural workers is the 'World Wide Opportunities on Organic Farms' (WWOOF) programme. This states that 'Volunteers do not pay to stay with hosts and hosts do not pay volunteers for their help (generally 25–30 hours a week)'.[1] In other words, free labour is provided in exchange for board and lodging. A similar situation exists for live-in *au pairs* in some countries. In the UK, for instance, *au pairs* are entitled to 'pocket money' only.[2] There are many other volunteer programmes like these and they can provide would-be workers with the skills (including language skills) and work experience necessary to ultimately get paid work.

2. Unemployed: In certain states the unemployed must work for free, or below the minimum wage, in order to receive their unemployment benefit (often termed 'workfare').

3. Interns: Many internships are unpaid but are viewed as a vital stepping-stone into paid professional employment for young people in particular. This is especially true in certain industries (such as politics, fashion and the media). Unpaid internships have, though, come under considerable criticism particularly around the way in which only those who are already wealthy can afford to embark on them, and how they thus hamper social mobility. A number of campaigning groups exist calling for interns to be paid for the work that they do.[3]

4. Apprentices: Apprenticeship schemes usually pay well below agreed minimum wage rates. In the UK, for example, the adult minimum (now living) wage is £7.20 per hour (April 2016) versus £3.30 for an apprentice, and the use of apprenticeships by firms has grown dramatically since the 1990s (House of Commons, 2015, p 6).

---

5. Informal Workers: it has been estimated that the majority (1.8 billion) of the world's three billion workers are employed within the informal economy (Jütting and Laiglesia, 2009) and that the informal economy is growing even in developed countries (Portes et al, 1989; Schneider et al, 2010). Those working in the informal economy, which states often tolerate, cannot be guaranteed a minimum wage by law or collective agreement.

Notes: [1] See www.wwoof.org.uk/how_it_works.[2] See www.gov.uk/au-pairs-employment-law/au-pairs.[3] In the UK see www.internaware.org/about_us and www.rightsforinterns.org.uk/.

The question is whether states/citizens should tolerate and even promote situations where workers are not paid a minimum wage and where there are apparently legitimate exemptions to established norms, laws and standards? Certainly there are arguments for this – mainly around getting valuable work experience – but there are also many counter-arguments pointing towards exploitation.

Conclusion

Most trouble at/through work occurs 'above the baseline' in the exploitation grey area between illegal employer activity and decent work. It is impossible, however, to unequivocally define this grey area. Rather, the aim of the critical social harm scholar is to better understand its morphology. In outlining the exploitation continuum (Chapter Two), and then identifying potentially problematic forms of worker control (Chapters Four to Six), the book partially met this aim. However, a number of critical questions were opened up in the process that this chapter has sought to address.

Most obviously, one needs to consider the divide between involuntary and voluntary labour when studying and defining exploitation. My argument here has been that we should not fetishise coercion as the key to defining exploitative and harmful control, and that workers may be victims as well as apparent free agents. I then argued that definitions of exploitation can be helped by scholars not simply focusing on the problems but, instead, establishing the types of positive working relationships (decent quality work) that should be promoted and championed.

The grey area, above the baseline between illegality and decent work, is also usually associated with various harms but this does not mean that the presence of such harm is a necessary feature of the exploitation continuum. In other words, one may be exploited without being directly harmed: though the latter is usually a good indication of the former. Indeed, when workers suffer in a physical and/or psychological sense at/through work, alarm bells should ring more than they do at present, not only because this damages the individual concerned but also because it harms families and wider communities.

As a final foray into the edges of acceptable versus unacceptable work I looked at questions of moral responsibility and culpability. Specifically, I emphasised the need to consider knowledge, intent and motives when apportioning blame and when defining the scale and scope of the problem. I also asked whether exploitation can ever be justified and, related to this, whether certain groups of workers can ever be treated 'exceptionally'.

Overall, then, this chapter was intended to illuminate, and help one to navigate, the edges of acceptability with respect to work-based exploitation and harm. It has opened up critical debates around: consent versus coercion; the value in defining decent work; the relationship between exploitation and various harms; and the notion that some forms of exploitation might be easier to explain, rationalise and justify than others. In all areas there remains a need for much greater scholarly input from those interested in debating and delineating the problem of work-based control, exploitation and harm.

Terrified animals

It is not that we are alone,
us together, we can not be
alone

the simplest logic is the most difficult
how one and one can be three
how much stronger one gets if one stands up
how we see that together we can help ourselves
through each other

we must dare to teach ourselves how we belong together
that we have built a city here along side other cities,
in a country along side other countries
that we are thoughts next to thoughts

we are terrified animals
we are smart animals

when we look out into a pitch-black universe
we do not think "impossible"
we build a ship

we must see the people around us,
learn to count to three

we have to build a ship

EIGHT

Preventing exploitation and harm

Documenting or preventing exploitation and harm?

There has been a huge and recent interest among academics in issues such as human trafficking, modern slavery, child labour and forced labour. This has occurred 'over a timeframe that has seen the continued ascent of neoliberal globalisation and worsening conditions and relative rewards for the majority of workers worldwide' (Coe, 2013, 279). In other words, there is a danger that this book, and others like it, simply end up documenting growing problems rather than challenging and ultimately preventing them. Aware of this danger, the penultimate chapter outlines the different types of solutions to the problems of labour exploitation and work-based harm.

The more common and favoured type of solution revolves around the establishment of legal baselines through national and international conventions, codes and laws. In many countries these are then used as the basis for labour inspection and enforcement regimes. Although a central component in the fight against exploitation and harm, this baseline approach only takes us so far. Most obviously, it is clear that there is a 'justice gap' between paper-based *de jure* protection and the levels of exploitation and harm actually experienced by workers on the ground.

To address this justice gap, and consistent with the social harm agenda, we must also look beyond criminology for solutions. Most obviously, it is clear that the form of capitalism in operation at a given time and in a given space can dramatically shape workers' lived experiences. For instance, the modification of capitalism away from a neoliberal and toward a social democratic regime is generally associated with a reduction in work-based exploitation and harm (Pemberton, 2015). At present, however, the direction of travel appears to be the other way: towards neoliberal capitalist regimes that are associated with greater levels of exploitation and harm.

Other than looking at changing the nature of capitalism, one can also look to the power (im)balance between labour and capital as a cause of, and solution to, labour exploitation and work-based harm. Specifically, the role of trade unions, the level of income inequality between workers, and the ability of workers to peacefully protest, are all markers of labour–capital relations. While at present union powers appear to be on the wane, inequality between workers is growing, and worker protests are often limited, these markers nonetheless represent a third type of solution.

Baselines: transnational governance

The most visible forms of 'baseline' worker protection have emerged at a global level via the International Labour Organization (ILO). Most notably, the 1998 ILO *Declaration on Fundamental Principles and Rights at Work* outlines four basic rights (see Box 2.4). The ILO has also established a series of minimum global standards for individual nation-states to sign up to, and the main Conventions pertinent to combating work-based harm are outlined in Box 8.1.

Conventions are established by the ILO based via a tri-partite structure – involving employer, government and worker representation – and must then be ratified by individual nation-states.[35] This global labour governance approach, however, has been criticised. Principally, academics have been concerned that the ILO's need to forge consensus, based on its tri-partite structure, means that the organisation's role has been one of establishing indicative safety-nets that may either not have any concrete practical impact, or, do not actually deal with the causes underpinning the need for safety-nets in the first place (Lerche, 2007; Rogaly, 2008b; Phillips and Mieres, 2015). In short, the ILO is 'fire-fighting' when it should really be tackling the causes of the fires. Moreover, even when fire-fighting the ILO can only provide guidance to those actually on the ground and this guidance is often ignored (Appelbaum and Lichtenstein, 2016).

These criticisms are more valid than they are fair in the sense that the ILO is actually fulfilling its role and remit and it is difficult to imagine: 1) nation-states actually agreeing on a global critique of the capitalist system (to address the causes of exploitation and harm); and 2) nation-states agreeing on a global system of labour market regulation (to ensure that Conventions are actually implemented on the ground). There is, of course, another issue with the global governance of labour approach of the ILO in that it seeks to establish minimum baselines for labour when in fact there are exploitative and harmful forms of worker control above the minimum baselines.

Put another way, a twin-track approach to the control–harm dynamic is required whereby there is an acceptance of basic global baselines but, at the same time, surpassing these baselines does not inevitably lead to the conclusion that 'decent work' has been achieved. Instead, exploitation is a slippery and amorphous phenomenon and simply meeting basic standards does not mean that workers are safe from harm. On the contrary, some may actually use basic global baselines to gauge what it is possible to get away with. This is a problem the ILO is aware of but it is perhaps asking too much for the organisation to work above its baseline conventions given how, globally, there are still so many workers falling through these safety-nets.

The debate, then, is whether one should simply focus on worst-case scenarios from a global social policy perspective (that is, baselines) or whether there is also space for a broader parallel approach. The latter would take into account local context and recognise that even when minimum standards are met that there may still be problems (exploitation and harm) and that these problems may be growing but may be denied legitimacy by the primacy so often afforded to worst-case scenarios.

Box 8.1: ILO labour baselines

- Forced Labour Convention, 1930 (Convention Number 29)
- Labour Inspection Convention, 1947 (Convention Number 81)
- Freedom of Association and Protection of the Right to Organise Convention, 1948 (Convention Number 87)
- Migration for Employment Convention, 1949 (Convention Number 97)
- Right to Organise and Collective Bargaining Convention, 1949 (Convention Number 98)
- Equal Remuneration Convention, 1951 (Convention Number 100)
- Abolition of Forced Labour Convention, 1957 (Convention Number 105)
- Discrimination (Employment and Occupation) Convention, 1958 (Convention Number 111)
- Minimum Age Convention, 1973 (Convention Number 138)
- Migrant Workers (Supplementary Provisions) Convention, 1975 (Convention Number 143)
- Private Employment Agencies Convention, 1997 (Convention Number 181)
- Worst Forms of Child Labour Convention, 1999 (Convention Number 182)
- Decent Work for Domestic Workers Convention, 2011 (Convention Number 189)

The UN more generally, of which the ILO is a part, has also helped to establish universal labour baselines. The first concerted global attempt in this respect came via the League of Nations (the precursor to the United Nations), which passed the 'Slavery Convention' in 1926. This defined slavery and outlawed it among member states.[36] Following on from this, the 1948 United Nations 'Universal Declaration of Human Rights' outlawed slavery and a number of other questionable employment practices. Notable provisions include the assertions that everyone has the right to: life, liberty and security of person (article 3); protection from slavery or servitude (article 4); protection from mistreatment (article 5); freedom of movement and to leave any country and to return to their country (article 13); just and favourable conditions of work (article 23); and the right to rest and leisure including reasonable limitation of working hours and periodic holidays with pay (article 24). Many subsequent national and transnational legal frameworks have built upon the 1926 Slavery Convention and the more expansive Universal Declaration of Human Rights that followed (such as the 1950 European Convention on Human Rights – see below).

At a regional level, both the Council of Europe and the European Union have been championed for protecting worker rights. The EU has also, however, been criticised for undermining worker rights and allowing a 'race to the bottom' based on 'social dumping'. Dealing first with the positive side to European cooperation, the Council of Europe established in 1950 the 'European Convention on Human Rights' (based on the 1948 United Nations Universal Declaration of Human Rights) which led to the establishment of the European Court of Human Rights. The Convention, among other things, includes the rights: to be free from servitude (Article 4); to association, for example, via a trade union (Article 11); to be free from discrimination (Article 14). The European Court of Human Rights has acted to enforce the 1950 Convention and in so doing has protected many workers from exploitation and harm.[37]

At the EU level, many believe the organisation has tempered a neoliberal deregulation agenda that would otherwise have dominated (if it does not already). This was the view, for instance, of the unions in the UK in the run up to the 2016 referendum when the UK voted to leave the EU (TUC, 2016). The main 'wins' for workers at an EU level appear to have been achieved via the 'Charter of Fundamental Rights of the European Union' (see Box 8.2) and the following Directives:

- Working Time Directive – this stipulates a 48-hour maximum working week (that includes on call periods), a daily rest period, a weekly rest period, breaks during a shift and the statutory right to paid annual leave.
- Agency Worker Directive – this gives agency workers the same rights as permanent employees.
- Transfer of Undertakings (TUPE) Directive – this protects working conditions when a company for which a person is working is sold or taken over.
- Employment Equality Directive – this means employers cannot discriminate due to the age, sexual orientation, religion or disability of a worker.
- Racial Equality Directive – this means employers cannot discriminate due to the race or ethnicity of a worker.
- Equal Treatment Directive – this means employers cannot discriminate due to the gender of a worker.

Nevertheless, the EU has recently come under criticism for presiding over some downward convergence in working conditions or what has been termed a 'race to the bottom' due to 'social dumping'.

Box 8.2: Charter of Fundamental Rights of the European Union

The Charter of Fundamental Rights of the European Union, which became legally effective after the Treaty of Lisbon in 2009, gives EU citizens a number of basic rights many of which relate to working conditions. If these rights are impinged upon then EU citizens can use the European Court of Justice to enforce their Charter rights. Relevant Articles as far as labour exploitation is concerned (see FRA, 2015) include:

- human dignity (Article 1)
- prohibition of slavery and forced labour (Article 5)
- freedom to choose an occupation and right to engage in work (Article 15)
- non-discrimination (Article 21)
- workers' right to information and consultation within the undertaking (Article 27)
- right of access to placement services (Article 29)
- protection in the event of unjustified dismissal (Article 30)
- fair and just working conditions (Article 31)
- prohibition of child labour and protection of young people at work (Article 32)
- social security and social assistance (Article 34)
- consumer protection (Article 38)
- and right to an effective remedy and to a fair trial (Article 47).

Two recent cases stand out where the EU has appeared to allow working conditions to deteriorate. First, there is the corporate manipulation of the EU's 1996 Posted Workers Directive as exemplified by the case of the transnational recruitment company 'Atlanco-Rimec'.[38] Atlanco-Rimec is a truly European business: it is based in Ireland (Dublin); registered in Jersey (where accounts can remain private); and its Director (Michael O'Shea) lives in Switzerland. Furthermore, Atlanco-Rimec recently made the headlines for posting workers from Poland to France, and registering the Polish workers, for the purposes of their social insurance contributions, in Cyprus. The company has effectively been using the confusion around the posting of workers within the EU, and specifically the 1996 EU Posted Workers Directive, as a basis for supplying labour at a cheaper rate than other firms are able to.

It operates by supplying workers from a low-wage economy (for example, Poland) to a relatively higher wage economy (for example, France) and registering these workers in an EU country where the social insurance contributions are lowest (for example, Cyprus) while masking the financial implications of this (for example, by registering in Jersey). This business model not only means that workers see increasing competition and downward pressure on pay and conditions, but that when they require social insurance it is paid at a very low rate and often insufficient to live off in the country they are working in or come from. Moreover, when workers show any dissent the company has a database to record this and effectively blacklist them, much like the Consultancy Association (see below) in the UK once did.[39]

The case of Atlanco-Rimec and the Posted Workers Directive shows that not all EU measures to protect workers from a downward competitive spiral work out in practice (see also Mesini, 2014). Most obviously, laws are either not fully implemented by Member States, are ambiguous and left open to interpretation, or allow different national contexts to be played off against each other. As Lillie (2016, 61) notes in a paper that also refers to the Atlanco-Rimec case: 'Regulatory regimes, and firms' ability to successfully strategise between them, are a competitive parameter favouring less restrictive and cheaper regulatory environments. The regulation of posting creates windows of opportunity for labour-cost competition by defining posted workers as partially outside the regulatory scope of the receiving country.' Some benefit from this – such as the Atlanco-Rimec Director – who is now worth an estimated €65 million – but for most workers affected there is simply a growing sense of powerlessness, alienation and frustration. Moreover, the fact that getting someone to work can involve at least six nation-states (Ireland, UK, Switzerland, Poland, France, Cyprus) may well be a sign of the cosmopolitan age we live in: it may also be a sign, however, of the ways in which neoliberal globalisation can manipulate different national and transnational governance and welfare structures to cheapen (and even exploit and harm) labour.

Related to the issues raised by the Atlanco-Rimec case there are the 'Viking' and 'Laval' cases that were brought to the European Court of Justice (ECJ).[40] These revolve around the right of workers to take industrial action when experiencing what is known as 'social dumping'. In the case of 'Viking' – a Finnish passenger ferry operator – its route between Finland and Estonia became unprofitable and so the company decided to re-flag its ship to another country to reduce costs. This was specifically to allow collective agreements reached in Finland to be sidestepped and thus facilitate job cuts and the lowering of employment terms and conditions for the workers that remained. In the case of 'Laval' – a Latvian construction company – the company won a Swedish contract to build a school and decided to post Latvian workers to Sweden for this project. The Swedish unions wanted Laval to sign collective agreements covering pay, holidays and other terms and conditions to avoid a lowering of employment standards but Laval declined. In both the Viking and Laval cases the unions took industrial action to contest the deterioration in pay and working conditions.

The union action in both Finland and Sweden ultimately led to cases at the ECJ which made its decision in 2007 (Davies, 2008). The ECJ upheld the basic right of workers to take industrial action. However, this was qualified, and the right does not now apply as unequivocally as it did in the past. In particular, the ECJ stressed that employers have a right under European law to establish in other EU countries and that workers have a right under European law to live and work in other EU countries. Thus, the ECJ decided, strike action – because it compromises these rights – must be 'justified' and 'proportionate'. In other words, unions' (and workers') ability to contest transnational capital when it engages in 'social dumping' has now been partially restricted by the EU via the ECJ.

Baselines: national legal frameworks

National laws and policies to tackle exploitation and harm vary (see, for example, Clark, 2013). The Walk Free Foundation (2016), for instance, has attempted to rate countries according to their ability and willingness to combat modern slavery. The Foundation has scored governments based on 98 good practice indicators. These take into account factors such as national laws and levels of victim support.

Table 8.1 lists the countries taking most action and Table 8.2 lists the countries taking least action to address modern slavery. There is, to some extent, a developed–developing world divide.

Table 8.1: Countries taking most action to combat modern slavery

Most action	Most action by GDP
• The Netherlands	• Philippines
• United States of America	• Georgia
• United Kingdom	• Brazil
• Sweden	• Jamaica
• Australia	• Croatia
• Portugal	• Montenegro
• Croatia	• Macedonia
• Spain	• Moldova
• Belgium	• Albania
• Norway	• Serbia

Source: Walk Free Foundation (2016)

Table 8.2: Countries taking least action to combat modern slavery

Least action	Least action by GDP
• North Korea	• Qatar
• Iran	• Singapore
• Eritrea	• Kuwait
• Equatorial Guinea	• Brunei
• Hong Kong	• Hong Kong
• Central African Republic	• Saudi Arabia
• Papua New Guinea	• Bahrain
• Guinea	• Oman
• Democratic Republic of the Congo	• Japan
• South Sudan	• South Korea

Source: Walk Free Foundation (2016)

It is also clear that even countries taking most action on the Walk Free Foundation global index have contradictions. In the UK, by way of an example, there have been a large number of recent Acts designed to protect employees against work-based harm, including: the Public Interest Disclosure Act 1998 (Whistleblowing); the Asylum and Immigration Act 2004 (trafficking for labour exploitation); the Corporate Manslaughter and Corporate Homicide Act 2007 (fatalities); the Coroners and Justice Act 2009 (Forced Labour); and the Modern Slavery Act 2015. In all cases, however, the prosecution and conviction rates have been low. The Corporate Manslaughter and Corporate Homicide Act 2007, for instance, had 12 convictions up to 2015, while the Asylum and Immigration Act 2004 had 22 trafficking for labour exploitation convictions in the period 2005-2011 (House of Commons, 2014a), and up until 2012 only 15 forced labour cases had been brought to the prosecution stage (HM Government, 2012, 32).

It has been widely observed that legal approaches to combating work-based exploitation and harm are, on their own, largely ineffective (Hillyard et al, 2004; Dorling et al, 2008; Pemberton, 2015). They cover a very small number of victims (see for example Clark, 2013, 10–11) and, by virtue of this, can deny space and legitimacy for the vast majority of victims of work-based exploitation and harm. As a result, the scale of the social policy problem is often minimised (Slapper and Tombs, 1999; Tombs, 2007).

Tombs (2008, 61) argues, for instance, that: 'there is institutionalised condoning of widespread violence in terms of offences against health and safety law and an acceptance that much of this offending is and will remain beyond the scope of the law'. This relates to the fact that, historically, corporate crime rarely gets identified and defined, never mind punished (Clinard and Yeager, 1980). As Tombs notes this is because: 'a tough regulatory climate tends to be antagonistic towards the interests of firms operating within a capitalist economy' (Tombs, 2008, 47).

The turn towards strong legal protections for workers, then, is often more theoretical than anything else. There will always be a small number of headline cases under acts targeting things such as whistleblower victimisation, trafficking for labour exploitation, corporate manslaughter, forced labour and modern slavery. Beyond these headline cases, however, most workers experiencing exploitation and harm will find the legal system closed off (FRA, 2015). As Ewing et al (2016, 59) conclude with respect to the UK:

> The current approach to employment regulation is unsustainable. There is too much law, informed by an ostensible belief that every problem must have a legal solution (or none at all). Although voluminous in content and covering a wide range of issues, legislation – as a means of regulation – can only set minimum standards with which every employer can comply, large or small, productive or chaotic. Very often regulation is barely a step above deregulation or non-regulation, and very often those who most need the protection of the law are either deliberately excluded, denied access by sham employment arrangements contrived by their employers, or simply give up in the face of cost and complexity.

One of the main reasons there is a justice gap between *de jure* and *de facto* worker protections is that the legal system simply does not have the means or capacity to deal with the problems of exploitation and harm. Alongside this, there has been a very strong and concerted focus on individual rights and empowering people to enforce these via particular formal laws. This approach, however, works in theory but not in practice because individuals lack the power and resources to challenge employers and corporations. There is also a significant imbalance between labour (worker) and capital (employer) and a worker on their own is unlikely to be in a position to overcome this should he/she experience exploitation or harm.

The norm in many countries, especially where union density and/or labour inspection activity is low, is for workers to police their own rights supported by the criminal–legal system. In this respect: 'The evidence points to the accumulation of frustration, anger and resentment underlying attempts to achieve justice, and the usual pattern of failure' (Pollert, 2006, 37). Workers are empowered on paper but in actual fact they remain powerless and, while the state appears to be performing a safeguarding role, it is in effect perpetuating a light-touch approach to combating exploitation and work-based harm. Moreover, nothing is done to check the growing individualisation and anti-union ethos of the modern workplace and, in fact, the laws being put in place may actually mask the retrograde neoliberal retrenchments affecting increasingly isolated workers at an everyday level (Brown et al, 2000; Hepple and Morris, 2002; Pollert, 2005; 2007; 2010; Holgate et al, 2011; Tailby et al, 2011).

The truth is that complaints against employers' exploitative and harmful practices are unlikely to surface on their own whatever legal protections are in place on paper. Furthermore, they are particularly unlikely to surface when workers feel insecure or fearful, when they are outside of a collective/union context, and when there are migrants involved. As Pollert (2010, 81) notes: 'the fundamental problem (is) the individualisation of employment relations and the weakness of the isolated worker'. Few workers, for example, would want to take on management with all the resources they have to hand and the ability they have to close ranks and isolate the already individualised worker. Few would also want to be involved in the lengthy legal process and the psychological trauma of this. Bureaucracy, to some, represents the insurmountable barrier between *de jure* and *de facto* workplace rights and its existence allows for stringent laws safeguarding workers in the knowledge that these laws will rarely be called upon because the system is impenetrable (Martin, 2003; Martin and Rifkin, 2004, 223).

In addition, taking on an employer often has a detrimental health impact and can cause further harm. We know this from whistleblowing cases, for example, where reporting wrongdoing in the workplace is often unsuccessful and can lead to long-lasting stress and even reprisals (Lennane, 1993, 667; De Maria, 2006, 646; Pemberton et al, 2012).

Among the exploited workers I interviewed for the Joseph Rowntree Foundation *Experiences of Forced Labour* project (Scott et al, 2012) it was common for a fatalistic attitude to emerge:

> "We come here to work, to make a living. It's about survival. Sometimes I come across difficulties and feel bullied and suppressed, but I put up with it, and it will pass. Feeling bullied or suppressed is normal and unavoidable...You have to put up with it. There are no alternatives." (male, 50y, Chinese)

> "I was happy that I had a job and wages at the end of the week and I didn't argue. That's it. And if you go and talk with people, they never say anything against their employer." (male, 54y, Polish)

None of the 62 interviewees had gone through any form of grievance procedure never mind investigating the actual legal protections in place that could have prevented their exploitation. The general consensus was, however reluctantly and fearfully, to accept the work on offer and not to complain.

What value, then, is there in passing legislation to criminalise certain forms of exploitation if individuals are so unwilling/unable to take cases to court? Most obviously, offences serve to underline actions that are not acceptable, and in so doing, reduce the likelihood of these actions occurring in the first place so that the legal system is not actually required. This is the very basis of the argument around a need for basic standards, safety-nets and baselines. These can be established at a global and nation-state level and, although they may rarely be used by workers, they act as a key deterrent.

More cynically, however, new laws show that the state is doing something that is ostensibly good when in fact it may actually be doing very little, or may be contributing to exploitation and harm and even rendering this acceptable. Thus, when states intervene to purportedly protect the most vulnerable there is a sub-text behind such intervention that requires deciphering. To elucidate, states may want to be seen to be acting to tackle what they variously refer to as 'modern slavery', 'human trafficking', 'forced labour' and 'child labour' and will loudly seek to combat such abuse. At the same time, however, efforts will be directed towards a problem that is residually defined. There is, in short, no genuine desire to tackle the broader exploitation continuum: just a desire to tackle the very worst labour market abuses. This allows states to win moral capital, while also ensuring intervention is kept to a minimal and capital is left largely untroubled.

Recent events in the UK illustrate this point over symbolic rather than substantive policy with respect to work-based exploitation and harm. On 1 April 2013 the UK's Legal Aid system was fundamentally reformed. The Legal Aid, Sentencing and Punishment of Offenders Act 2012 came into force. Its main purpose was to reduce the Legal Aid bill and it specifically meant that Legal Aid was no longer available for employment law cases except those involving a contravention of the Equality Act 2010 (that is, discrimination) and those involving victims of human trafficking. In short, the government was saying to workers that they would no longer, unless they could represent themselves or had sufficient private funds, be entitled to legal support to pursue a case against an employer. This decision is significant. In the tax year 2011/12 20,203 Legal Aid cases were focused on employment disputes (Ministry of Justice, 2013). Thus, the April 2013 restrictions have effectively reduced the powers of redress to thousands of workers per annum.

The UK government rationalised its decision to cut employment Legal Aid as follows: 'We consider that, given the need to prioritise resources, employment matters are of a lower importance than cases involving life, liberty or homelessness' (Ministry of Justice, 2011, 25). It went on to acknowledge that 'some employees find facing their employer, who may be legally represented, daunting' (p 129) but argued instead that people can 'use alternative, less adversarial means of resolving their problems' (p 4). Related to this, the government has promoted the use of ACAS (the Advisory, Conciliation and Arbitration Service) outlining a 'vision for an employment dispute resolution system that promotes the use of early dispute resolution as a means of dealing with workplace problems' (BIS, 2011). Indeed, from April 2014 (via the Enterprise and Regulatory Reform Act 2013) any worker wanting to make an Employment Tribunal claim must first go through the ACAS Early Conciliation service.

What these measures effectively do is to remove the vast majority of employment disputes, and the vast majority of work-based exploitation and harm cases, from the independent legal arena in the UK. In the process they downgrade instances of exploitation and harm and move them into the remit of an agency (ACAS) that is funded by the UK government, and specifically the Department for Business, Innovation and Skills (that has been traditionally pro-business and very much anti-regulation). This may lead to quicker and cheaper dispute resolution but it also sends a message to labour and to capital that exploitation and harm are not serious legal issues in the UK anymore.

Reviewing the impact of some of the post-2013 changes in the Employment Tribunal system, the House of Commons Justice Committee noted the following trend:

> The introduction of issue fees and hearing fees for claimants in employment tribunals led to an undisputed and precipitate drop in the number of cases brought, approaching 70%. The number of single cases brought declined by about 67% to around 4,500 per quarter from October 2013 to June 2015; and the number of multiple cases declined by 72%, from 1,500 per quarter in the year leading to June 2013 to around 400 per quarter since October 2013. (House of Commons, 2016b, 25)

On paper, then, and in isolation, the statistics might imply that work-based grievances in the UK are on the wane and that employment relations are improving. However, the reality is that the UK government has simply made the pursuit of justice much more costly than it was in the past and so there are now many fewer cases being brought to employment tribunals. Put simply, 'the regime of employment tribunal fees has had a significant adverse impact on access to justice for meritorious claims' (House of Commons, 2016b, 27).

In parallel with the UK government's lighter-touch approach to workplace exploitation (located within BIS/ACAS) there has been the development of a strong anti-slavery agenda (located within the Home Office). This has crystallised most recently in the Modern Slavery Act 2015 (Home Office, 2013). Even before this, however, there was the Coroners and Justice Act 2009 which created a stand-alone offence of forced labour for the first time in the UK.

On the one hand, then, the government is championing a de-regulation agenda – evidenced by the removal of legal aid and imposition of employment tribunal fees – while on the other hand it is also seeking to bring in more severe punishments for a very small number of employers engaged in extreme forms of exploitation and harm. The message is a moral one (slavery will not be tolerated) and a pro-business one (that the vast majority of employees will be less empowered to bring cases against employers and/or these cases will be less formal). It demonstrates the need for caution before celebrating very visible, yet possibly symbolic and strategic (even cynical?) attempts to criminalise exploitation and harm. It also demonstrates a need for an awareness of what else is going on in government and the fact that contradictory policies and hidden agendas may be being pursued contemporaneously.

Box 8.3 illustrates the point that government agendas might not actually reflect the reality on the ground for most workers. The UK unions, for example, appear to be particularly concerned with the criminal–legal turn with respect to framing contemporary labour exploitation. Unite, the largest UK union, felt that 'the forced labour title is unfortunate as it sounds over the top to most people', while for the TUC 'forced labour is not a term that is used very much in relation to enforcement of UK employment rights', and the GMB union thought the term to be 'archaic'. These views show that language is politics when it comes to workplace relations and, interestingly, the forced labour (and modern slavery) nomenclature is seen to involve a politics that might actually restrict debate and frame the problem in a restrictive and residual way.

Box 8.3: Evidence from the front-line with respect to forced labour in the UK

- "The most sensationalist, extreme end of forced labour we all know is there, but we all know there is a far greater mass of practice, which is very grey and, you know, we don't know whether it is or is not forced labour." (EHRC representative)
- "Is there a lot of illegal working practice out there? You know the evidence doesn't come through. Whether that means that the channels are wrong or it isn't there...it's very difficult to establish." (PWRH representative)
- "My staff have been trained on (forced labour) but I have to say I was talking to one of my colleagues who's been here since 2002 and I said 'Have you ever seen anything like that?' and she said [that] no that we'd never actually seen anything that could have constituted this. I'm not saying it doesn't exist, I'm saying that in our investigations, it's not something that's coming to the fore." (EASI representative)
- "I've never met any forced labour since I've started at HSE and also never heard actually of someone here being forced to come to the country...it's not something I deal with here on a regular basis." (HSE representative)

Source: Geddes et al (2013)

Baselines: labour inspection regimes

Globally, the ILO Labour Inspection Convention 1950 (Number 81) has had 145 ratifications out of 185 ILO member states. This means that, in theory at least, most of the countries in the world have agreed upon the need for labour inspection and have been agreed upon this for quite some time.[41] The problem, as we have already seen, is that there is a gap between signing up to the principle of labour inspection and its actual operationalisation in practice and: 'In most of the countries the number of labour inspectors is seen as inadequate in relation to the extent of their responsibilities, the increasing number of enterprises and workers, and the increasing complexity of the labour market' (SYNDEX, 2012, 18). Or as the ILO put it, there has been a tendency to focus on, and arguably overplay, legal baselines and 'to overlook the valuable and complementary role of labour inspectors' (ILO, 2010b).

Thus, many countries of the world have signed up to transnational legal baselines and, as part of this, have established their own national laws to combat certain forms of labour exploitation and work-based harm. However, there has been more reluctance to proactively check compliance, and enforce against, these legal baselines via labour inspection regimes. Globally, we have what are conventionally termed liberal or neoliberal regulatory regimes, characterised by low labour inspection activity and also by low union density. In the US, for instance, while the number of workplaces covered by federal workplace regulations actually increased by 112% over the period 1975–2005, the number of investigators declined by 14% (Bernhardt and McGrath, 2005). Despite the growing regulation, then, employers in reality face little chance of being investigated and view regulation as a minor second-order concern (Weil, 2009, 420).

Similarly, despite the growing prominence of discourses around forced labour and modern slavery in the UK – via the Coroners and Justice Act 2009 and Modern Slavery Act 2015 respectively – the resources devoted to inspecting 'illegal' workers (for benefit fraud, immigration non-compliance) is vastly greater than the resource directed towards inspecting 'illegal' employers for exploitative and harmful practice (Metcalf, 2008, 499; TUC, 2008). Illustrative of this, the UK National Minimum Wage inspection team (based at Her Majesty's Revenue and Customs) had only 93 compliance officers in 2009 and the Gangmasters Licensing Authority (regulating labour market intermediaries in the food production industry only) had only 25 inspectors. In contrast, the number of UKBA (UK Border Agency) staff for the same period was put at around 7,500 (Anderson, 2010,

307). It seems, then, that labour inspection may only be a priority in neoliberal states when there is a parallel immigration control agenda (see Box 8.4). Put simply, neoliberal regulatory regimes are strong on the rhetoric of enforcement but weak on actual employer inspection as it is seen as a burden to business. Moreover, they appear more likely to problematise workers than employers.

Box 8.4: The uneasy relationship between labour inspection and immigration control

A number of countries have sought to 'double-up' when inspecting employers and have mixed their labour inspection and immigration policy agendas. For instance, the UK's new Gangmasters and Labour Abuse Authority was established via the 2016 Immigration Act rather than by distinct employment regulation. Similarly, in the Netherlands, at least half of labour inspection visits are carried out with the 'Aliens Police' (Clark, 2013, 36–7). Both the ILO and OECD have highlighted problems with merging the labour inspection and immigration policy agendas, not least that it compromises worker trust, and have argued that labour inspection works best when immigration issues are kept separate (FLEX, 2016, 4).

Social democratic, and to a lesser extent northern European corporatist, regulatory regimes are more likely to have genuine labour inspection resources directed towards worker welfare. Moreover, in many cases this resource will actually go further and be less called upon because either the problems of exploitation and work-based harm are more contained and/or union density is high. Examples of relatively well-resourced labour inspectorates include the inspectorate of the *Ministerie van Sociale Zaken en Werkgelegenheid* (known as the SZW) in the Netherlands and the *Arbeidstilsynet* in Norway.

The SZW had a staff of 1,114 in 2012 and was formed in January of that year out of the merger of the Labour Inspectorate, the Work and Income Inspectorate, and the Social and Intelligence Investigation Service. The SZW is based in the Ministry of Social Affairs and Employment and, crucially, is one of the few inspectorates to explicitly focus on the relatively nebulous concept of exploitation, defined as:

- being forced to do work that is dangerous or harmful to your health;
- not being allowed to keep your passport or travel documents;
- having to pay off a heavy debt to your employer;
- getting little or no payment for the work you do;
- being mistreated, blackmailed or threatened;

- your employer threatens to report that you are in the Netherlands illegally;
- being unable to go where you like outside working time;
- not being able to see a doctor or go to hospital if you are ill.

The SZW also has departments devoted to: labour market fraud, working conditions, hazards, investigations, work and income, analysis and monitoring, and information and support. What makes SZW stand out is not only its staff base and its willingness to adopt the nomenclature of exploitation but also its location within a labour ministry and its integrated structure where issues like exploitation and workplace hazards are dealt with in the same organisation.

The Norwegian *Arbeidstilsynet*, or Labour Inspection Authority, shares many of the advantages of the SZW. It is located within the Ministry of Labour and acts by: issuing written warnings; issuing fines; initiating shutdowns; and, finally, initiating police investigations. In this sense, the *Arbeidstilsynet* is the first port of call for issues of labour exploitation across the Norwegian economy and the organisation has a staff of 600 across seven regional and 16 local offices.

As Table 8.3 demonstrates, the proportion of labour inspectors to workers in both the Netherlands and Norway is much higher than in the UK. Not only this, but a social democratic country like Norway also has a strong tradition of egalitarianism, low inequality and high union density rates which means that the size of the exploitation and harm problem is likely to be lower in the first place.

Table 8.3: Labour inspection regimes in the UK, Netherlands and Norway

Country	Harm reduction regime	Labour inspectorate	Working population (World Bank 2014)	Labour inspectorate staff	Labour inspectorate staff per million workers
UK	Liberal	EASI, GLA, NMW, HSE	30.1m	1358	41
Netherlands	Northern Corporatist	SZW	9.0m	1114	124
Norway	Social Democratic	Arbeidstilsynet	2.7m	600	222

Source: FLEX (2016); https://www.inspectieszw.nl/english/publications/; http://www.arbeidstilsynet.no/artikkel.html?tid=79289

One might be forgiven for assuming, from the above, that there are a small number of 'best-practice' social democratic and northern corporatist countries with strong worker and workplace checks, alongside a large rump of countries with little positive to say about labour inspection. This might be true as a generalisation, but there are also clear examples of best-practice across different regulatory regimes. A celebrated example in this respect comes from Brazil and its use of a 'dirty company' list (ILO, 2009b, 79–113). In 1992, the government of Brazil denied that forced labour existed in the country. The situation changed from 1995 and a number of initiatives then developed. One of these was the creation of the Special Mobile Inspection Group under the Ministry of Labour and the associated emergence of the government's 'dirty list' of firms using forced labour. This list is regularly updated, and the 'name and shame' policy has been widely praised. The list is available on the Ministry of Labour's website. Alongside the inspectorate and dirty-list, Brazil has also developed an associated media campaign to mobilise public opinion against forced labour. In other words, from a position of denial, Brazil has chosen to tackle head-on what was, and still is, a fairly sizeable problem of extreme labour exploitation. Furthermore, it has done this via a policy of public transparency designed to shame employers into raising standards that is contingent upon both labour inspection and the use of the media. Such a multi-dimensional and integrated approach demonstrates that ideal-type divisions between social democratic and neoliberal regulatory regimes are not always straightforward.

Varieties of capitalism: harm reduction regimes

Lasslett (2010, 11) has argued that: 'a discipline based on social harm would aim to approximate with greater clarity how (capitalist) processes, flows and relations produce particular forms of harm' (see also, Pemberton, 2015, Chapter Three). This is an important recognition because, outside the social harm agenda, there has been a tendency to focus on what Pemberton calls 'individual biographies' (Pemberton, 2015, 24). This is essentially referring to two things. First, that a criminal act must have an identifiable individual perpetrator behind it with a set of associated motives. Second, that an individual victim often has particular personal characteristics and traits rendering him/her vulnerable to the criminal perpetrator.

Lines of investigation into exploitation and harm, especially as far as legal baselines are concerned, have tended to be heavily informed by this logic. Marxist scholars, in contrast, would argue that outcomes like exploitation and harm cannot be discussed without reference to capitalist structures. Some argue that exploitation *per se* is hard-wired into, and an essential feature of, capitalist accumulation (Pemberton, 2015, 36). Beyond this, Marxists also point to specific instances of what they term 'unfree labour' as both a feature of particular forms of agrarian capitalism and as part of a modern process of deproletarianisation within advanced capitalist economies (Brass, 2014). Thus, in both general (exploitation) and specific (unfree labour) senses, labour relations that can cause work-based harm are linked by Marxists to particular features and forms of capitalism.

It is not, however, Marxist to suggest that outcomes such as exploitation and harm can in some ways be connected to capitalism. However, those suggesting this may well be accused of being Marxist as a form of reprimand. One of the important distinctions to be made in this respect is around whether one is arguing that exploitation and harm can only be solved through a radical transformation of the economic system or whether capitalism can be retained but modified to reduce these problems. It is the latter perspective that I am interested in within this section.

Pemberton (2015, 60–5) outlines the different forms of state–capitalist relations (Esping-Anderson, 1990; Gallie, 2003; 2007) and how these have a bearing upon 'harm reduction regimes' of individual nation-states. These regimes are outlined in Tables 8.4 and 8.5, and, as we have already seen above, the northern corporatist and social democratic regimes tend to be associated with higher degrees of labour market regulation and associated labour inspection. The regimes are derived from the mode of production, welfare, criminal justice, regulation and social solidarity criteria of individual nation-states. They suggest, albeit in a crude sense, relationships between variations of capitalism and social harm. The big divide in this respect is between neoliberal and liberal regimes, on the one hand, and northern corporatist and social democratic regimes on the other. Some of the statistics available to compare harm reduction regimes as far as work-based differences are concerned have already been outlined in the Introduction (Tables 2.11 and 2.12).[42]

Table 8.4: Harm reduction regimes

	Nature of Regulation
Neoliberal	Voluntarism or self-regulation. Minimal legal enforcement. Minimal resources for regulatory agencies.
Liberal[1]	
Corporatist	Tri-partite system (interest group, corporate, state). Moderate legal enforcement. Moderate resources for regulatory agencies.
Meso-Corporatist	Corporate-state relations. Minimal legal enforcement. Minimal resources for regulatory agencies.
Social Democratic	Tri-partite system (interest group, corporate, state). High legal enforcement. High level of resources for regulatory agencies.

Source: Pemberton (2015, p 63)

Note: [1] Although there is a distinction between liberal and neoliberal regimes as an *outcome* (see Pemberton, 2015), this text largely refers to the *process* of neoliberalism as affecting a variety of harm reduction regimes. This is consistent with the extant literature.

Table 8.5: Harm reduction regimes – exemplar countries

	Exemplar Countries
Neoliberal	Chile, Russia, Mexico, Turkey
Liberal	UK, US, Canada, Australia, Ireland, New Zealand
Corporatist	*Northern*: Germany, Belgium, Netherlands, France *Southern*: Italy, Spain, Portugal, Greece *Post-Socialist*: Poland, Czech Republic, Hungary, Estonia, Slovak Republic, Slovenia
Meso-Corporatist	Japan, Korea
Social Democratic	Sweden, Finland, Denmark, Norway

Source: Pemberton (2015, pp 60–5)

It is important not to assume that harm reduction regimes are static and there has been a tendency over recent years for corporatist and social democratic countries to move towards their more liberal and neoliberal neighbours. To be sure, differences still make regime characterisation valid, but especially as far as labour markets are concerned distinctions have been blurring. Recently, the case of France's 2016 Labour Bill illustrates the pressures towards more neoliberal governance with respect to working conditions. The 2016 French Labour Bill is essentially about the weakening of collective bargaining and the desire of French businesses to increase flexibility in the labour market by making it easier to reduce pay, easier to lay off workers, and easier to extend working time beyond the 35-hour week. The Labour Bill has been widely resisted in France with protests and strikes in Spring/Summer 2016 led by the CGT (General Confederation of Labour) union. The government did, however, force the Bill through the lower house of Parliament without a vote, using emergency measures.

The French example is interesting because the labour reforms were led by a Socialist government and opposed by the majority of the public. Business, though, was very much in favour of these reforms but rather than make the business case, the Socialist government has mainly argued that the stubborn unemployment rate in France (especially youth unemployment) would be addressed by the Labour Bill's ability to reduce labour market red-tape and increase flexibility. More generally, and related to this argument, there is often a taken-for-granted assumption that labour market regulation of the corporatist or social democratic kind poses a threat to jobs whereas neoliberal labour market policies provide more opportunities for employment. The data, however, does not support this assertion, with employment rates in many social democratic and northern corporatist countries exceeding those of their liberal neighbours (see Table 8.6).

Table 8.6: Employment rates (2015) for Social Democratic, Northern Corporatist and Liberal countries

Country	Employment rate (%)	Harm reduction regime
Sweden	75.5	Social Democratic
Norway	74.8	Social Democratic
New Zealand	74.3	Liberal
Netherlands	74.2	Northern Corporatist
Germany	74.0	Northern Corporatist
Denmark	73.5	Social Democratic
UK	72.7	Liberal
Canada	72.5	Liberal
Australia	72.2	Liberal
US	68.7	Liberal
Finland	68.6	Social Democratic
France	63.8	Northern Corporatist
Ireland	63.3	Liberal
Belgium	61.8	Northern Corporatist

Source: http://stats.oecd.org

Varieties of capitalism: corporate structures

As well as there being different national varieties of capitalism, large corporations operate at a supra-national level. This means that, as far as exploitation and harm is concerned, one should look at supply-chain constellations and structures. Put simply, the way in which corporate supply chains are organised and governed can be critical to understanding why exploitation and harm occurs where it does. The 'global production network' (GPN) and 'global value chains' (GVC) perspectives (Barrientos et al, 2011a; 2011b; McGrath, 2013; Gereffi, 2014; Stringer et al, 2014; Phillips and Mieres, 2015) have been the most prominent in this respect and a great deal of recent attention has been directed towards linking exploitation in one area of a supply chain with what goes in an, often ostensibly independent, segment elsewhere. The basic argument in terms of exploitation and harm in supply chains is that power and responsibility is fragmented throughout GPNs/GVCs but that pressure tends to cascade downwards towards workers at the producer-end of the network (Gereffi and Korzeniewicz, 1994). This cascading of pressure, allied with the fragmentation of power and responsibility, makes it very difficult to use conventional criminal–legal approaches to tackle exploitation and harm.

This explains why, since the late 1990s, a whole host of multi-stakeholder CSR initiatives have emerged, ostensibly independent of big business, designed to improve working conditions, principally in the developing world. These initiatives draw together a range of actors (NGOs, businesses, unions, workers, activists, government bodies) and their activities have been wide and varied (Box 8.5). They have, at their core, attempted to modify capitalism to prevent the worst forms of labour abuse.

Two of the most commonly used benchmarks for CSR activity have emerged out of these multi-stakeholder initiatives. They are:

1. The Social Accountability International SA8000 Standard (established in 1997)
2. The Ethical Trading Initiative Base Code (established in 1998)

These standards and codes draw on baselines established by the ILO and UN (see above) to guide individuals and organisations seeking to assess a business's social and ethical performance. Undoubtedly, organisations such as Social Accountability International (New-York based) and the Ethical Trading Initiative (London-based) have played a pivotal role in helping to prevent exploitation and harm. They have done this by a consensus among the core corporations of global capitalism that what goes on in the supply chains they preside over, usually in peripheral economies, is their responsibility. The ETI model (see Box 8.6) has received particular praise.

Perhaps the most widely covered sector as far as multi-stakeholder CSR initiatives are concerned is the garment/apparel industry. Among other groups, there are the Clean Clothes Campaign, the Fair Wear Foundation, Labour Behind the Label and the Worker Rights Consortium that are all explicitly focused on the garment/apparel industry (see Box 8.5). In addition, there are more general multi-stakeholder initiatives, such as the Ethical Trading Initiative, the Fair Labour Association and Social Accountability International that have also had a positive impact on this specific industry.

Overall, then, there has been a sea-change as far as business attitudes, procedures and policies are concerned since the late 1990s with the proliferation of multi-stakeholder initiatives partly reflecting and partly driving this. Views on the ultimate power of CSR to combat exploitation and harm remain, however, somewhat mixed. Advocates point towards reductions in extreme forms of labour abuse (such as slavery and child labour) and a rise in the incomes of the world's workers (with levels of absolute poverty declining). Critics, though, question whether the CSR agenda goes far enough beyond minimum standards baselines and, related to this, whether it is simply a 'measure of public relations for maintaining good images of brands without actually changing anything on the shop floor' (Weber et al, 2015, 259). There are also related technical concerns over how CSR information is collected, who pays for this, and the actual reach of CSR into decentralised supply chains (Blowfield and Frynas, 2005; Banerjee, 2008; Devinney, 2009; Mezzadri, 2014).

Most notably, the data provided to auditors, who are usually paid from within the supply chain being audited, often comes either from management or from workers within the workplace, and therefore under pressure from management. This can provide false results and mask the real problems. An example of this, already discussed in Chapter Two, is the Apple–Foxconn industrial complex. Following an apparent cluster of worker suicides Apple invited the Fair Labor Association (FLA) to conduct independent, third-party audits of the Foxconn factory conditions in 2012. The FLA reported in 2012 and followed this up in 2013 with a positive progress report (FLA, 2013). Campaigning organisations (see SACOM, 2011; China Labor Watch, 2012) were sceptical, however, given that the FLA was actually paid to investigate Foxconn by Apple, who gain from the conditions in the

Foxconn factory. Despite the issues, a world without the late-1990s proliferation of multi-stakeholder CSR initiatives, and associated voluntary self-regulation, would certainly be a harsher one for many workers. It is possible, it seems, to modify capitalism from within; but the critical question is whether this modification is principally serving the interests of labour or whether it is fundamentally about the needs and priorities of capital and specifically the needs and priorities of core corporations?

Box 8.5: Examples of multi-stakeholder CSR initiatives

The following exemplar initiatives have emerged over recent years, principally from within the developed world, to help advance the corporate social responsibility agenda and improve working conditions, principally in the developing world:

- Clean Clothes Campaign (www.cleanclothes.org/)
- Ethical Trading Initiative (www.ethicaltrade.org/)
- Fair Wear Foundation (www.fairwear.org/)
- Fair Labour Association (www.fairlabor.org/)
- Labour Behind the Label (http://labourbehindthelabel.org/)
- Social Accountability International (www.sa-intl.org/)
- Worker Rights Consortium (www.workersrights.org/)

Box 8.6: The Ethical Trading Initiative (ETI) model of self-regulation

The ETI Base Code was developed in 1998 by a tripartite alliance of corporate, trade union and NGO members. The ETI is funded by corporate membership and the UK government and is responsible for independently ensuring that the 1998 Base Code is complied with in global supply chains that serve the UK retail market. The fact that the base code emerged out of a tripartite consensus, and that the ETI is part business and part state funded, ensures a high degree of independence. Moreover, businesses are responsible for ensuring adherence to the tripartite Base Code throughout their supply chains. This basically means that there are clear universal standards which suppliers must meet and which corporations have a duty to monitor. There is less scope within such a system for charges of vested interest to be levied; though it is true that those corporations at the head of GPNs/GVCs are still the guardians of the system from which they ultimately benefit, albeit with close independent scrutiny.

The big debate, then, is whether the self-regulation of GPNs/ GVCs, as part of a broader CSR agenda, can solve the problems of labour exploitation and work-based harm? Certainly, the FLA model where Apple directly paid for an audit of its supplier Foxconn would appear flawed. Instead, there needs to be independent oversight, but the question is whether the ETI model (Box 8.6) actually goes far enough to replace the need for government inspection and/or union protection? Banerjee (2008, 52), for instance, in what has become a widely-cited article is cynical:

> Corporations do not have the ability to take over the role of governments in contributing to social welfare simply because their basic function (the rhetoric of triple bottom line aside) is inherently driven by economic need (and) despite its emancipatory rhetoric, discourses of corporate citizenship, corporate social responsibility, corporate sustainability (are) ideological movements that are intended to legitimise the power of large corporations.

Thus, it is entirely consistent for suppliers to be asked to trade ethically but also be required to reduce costs, with ethical conformity masking the harmful effects of cut-price mass production capitalism. Supply chain governance in this respect can simply become another tool of neoliberalism, rather than something genuinely transformative in the lives of workers. This explains why unions in particular are cynical with respect to the potential for self-regulation to critique and then transform capitalism so as to reduce exploitation and harm. The following is an extract from a longer conversation (Geddes et al, 2013) with the Unite union in the UK around the ultimate merits of relying on self-regulation within GPNs/GVCs:

> "The (problem) is the rampant casualisation within the manufacturing and construction sectors. And that's basically been built by sort of monopolism at the end of the product scale. So you take food...you've got the big four retailers... So you're talking about huge amounts of leverage for individual companies who all have fierce competition with each other. Then you end up with price squeeze...price squeeze on to producer, producer on to producer, you know. And you have agency workers, who would tend to be migrant workers now, brought in to undercut permanent workers: work longer hours for less, cover the overtime, all

that kind of thing. So it's always about 'Isn't it terrible that Fred got burnt with the bacon strimmer and didn't speak?' That's all lovely, but the reason Fred's there in the first place with the bacon strimmer on £4 an hour is because of [the supermarket], but nobody ever wants to mention [the supermarket] because it's all a bit...too many lawyers would get involved and sue them and stuff...People who look and investigate issues, they never get to the underlying issues...So let's not lose the focus on the reasons why the bad people are allowed to exist in the first place, you know. What breeds the environment and the cultural environment for them to exist? And for us it's just completely about the monopoly power of major retailers forcing down prices... The companies try and produce ethical reputational barriers really where they send out their ethical people to sign a code that in theory means they're all squeaky clean, but really means they haven't got to do anything, you know 'cos it's everybody else's fault but theirs! It would be unfair to say it's complete corporate washout, but by and large if you went to the ETI AGM nine-tenths of the people there are corporate ethical people who are there just to minimise reputational risk...No other motive at all. It's nothing to do with ethics, it's nothing to do with anything, it's just reputational risk." (Unite representative)

One of the problems with self-regulation, alluded to above, is that companies have been able to elongate and fragment chains of responsibility. This has centred upon the use of intermediaries in supplying labour into firms and particularly migrant labour. It has also centred on the sub-contracting of firms within global production networks and global value chains. In other words, there may be a few firms at the head of a given production system but there are likely to be myriad firms beneath. Not only this, but the labour entering the fragmented production system will not always be directly recruited or permanently employed. This corporate fragmentation and labour variability makes the job of preventing exploitation and harm very difficult. Moreover, fixing responsibility and blame is simply not achievable and a legal framing can appear naïve.

One important recent development designed to bring more clarity into labour relations within often highly complex and fragmented global value chains is corporate reporting. To elucidate, there has been concern that transnational corporations within the capitalist core economies need to do more to ensure that problems like modern slavery and human trafficking are not present within the supply chains which they oversee and ultimately govern. The state has recently intervened in both the US and UK, for example, to require large businesses to report on the efforts being undertaken to ensure that their supply chains are based on ethical trading relationships.

In the US, the 2010 Californian 'Transparency in Supply Chains' (TISC) Act (Senate Bill 657) came into force in 2012 and was the first major piece of legislation anywhere in the world requiring firms to report on their supply chain governance. TISC covers retailers and manufacturers with sales in California exceeding US$500,000 per annum and with a gross global turnover in excess of US$100 million. Its purpose is to ensure large transnational companies' corporate social responsibility infrastructure is fit for purpose and to make these companies more cautious and discriminatory when selecting suppliers. Information provided due to TISC must either be posted on companies' websites or provided in writing on request. The rationale for such transparency is that it helps consumers to make more informed purchasing decisions and ultimately, therefore, helps prevent modern slavery and human trafficking across supply chains. In the UK, similar transparency and corporate reporting is now required as a result of the Modern Slavery Act 2015, which has been widely praised by experts.[43]

On face value the US and UK transparency regulations appear to be extremely progressive: they put pressure on large firms to treat workers, mainly in the smaller firms that supply them, more ethically. However, some believe that this newfound role for the state in modifying capitalism is actually a relatively passive one, arguably more symbolic than substantive (New, 2015; Phillips, 2015). A number of criticisms stand out:

- The state is effectively requiring corporations to regulate themselves.
- The state is requiring corporations to regulate their suppliers in foreign territories over which it would not otherwise have jurisdiction.
- What counts as a corporation's supply chain is open to interpretation.
- Attention is being directed only to the worst forms of (criminal–legal) abuse within supply chains.
- Given the previous two points in particular, transparency can be achieved with relatively weak regulatory compliance.
- The logic of empowering consumers with more information to allow them to make informed decisions does not always work.

Put another way, transparency in supply chains may well be about the prevention of work-based exploitation and harm but it also allows companies to demonstrate compliance very visibly and, at the same time, gives them an even greater rationale for policing and controlling their suppliers. Essentially, then, there are a variety of logics behind the recent embrace of the corporate social responsibility agenda and some of these may well serve the interests of capital as much as, and possibly more than, they serve the interests of labour.

Given the above, more radical scholars have called on businesses to adopt alternative structures that tackle head-on unevenness in capital–labour relations, rather than to seek to address the consequences of this unevenness. Large (2010, Chapter Eight), for example, identifies two fundamental principles for an alternative form of capitalism: 1) that capital is viewed as a socially created commons rather than as a commodity to be conquered and owned; and 2) that labour, as a result of this alternative view of capital, is treated as more than a mere commodity to be exploited for surplus value. In view of these principles, Large talks about repositioning capital in order to achieve a 'common good' (2010, 146) and emphasises the potential for trusts, foundations, cooperatives, partnerships and so on, to transform the nature of capitalism in the interests of both the environment and workers (and the wider social and communal realms which they inhabit).

In short, there is a view among some that the actual contemporary corporate basis of the capitalist economy is the cause of the exploitation of land and labour and that reform is needed. This is not about a transition from capitalism to socialism or even communism, as some detractors would suggest, but about a modification of the rules and structures of the capitalist system so that harmful outcomes (to workers or to the environment) are, as far as possible, avoided. It is about a form of capitalism that is not based upon 'winner-takes-all' but is based around a notion of commons, where the system is hard-wired to guard against harm and is, ultimately, socially and environmentally sustainable.

Capitalist structures that are aligned to the common good and attempt to avoid rather than promote social or environmental harm are more prevalent than one might first expect, though no economies are defined by them *per se*. The Norwegian Government Pension Fund (also known as the Oil Fund) is one interesting example of how capitalism can be re-orientated towards longer-term and ethical goals. The fund was established in 1990 to safeguard the revenues from Norway's oil reserves. Crucially, it is focused on ensuring that these revenues benefit future generations of Norwegians rather than just those around at the time the oil is extracted and sold. The fund also has a Council on Ethics and an associated company exclusion list. This ensures that the fund does not invest in companies and activities defined as unethical. This includes those companies causing severe environmental harm, certain arms companies, tobacco companies, highly corrupt businesses and firms committing gross human rights abuses.

Another illuminating business model is provided by the UK's John Lewis partnership. The partnership structure means that the company is effectively employee-owned with workers entitled to an annual bonus determined by the profitability of the business in a given year. In addition, the partnership is structured so as to enable workers a say in decision-making through Branch Forums and then, higher up the chain of command, Partnership Councils and a Partnership Board. There are also in-house magazines that allow workers to air any concerns or grievances anonymously. The overall structure, therefore, is one of stakeholder governance where workers are brought into the control of the company and also share the benefits from the company's success.

If the Norwegian Oil Fund is about making capital more long-sighted, sustainable and ethical, then the John Lewis Partnership model is about breaking the divide between labour and capital to make capitalism more democratic and inclusive (see Box 8.7). These are all qualities that matter when one is considering the causes of exploitation and work-based harm and demonstrate that capitalism can be modified for the common good. The key challenge is about hard-wiring the lessons from structures such as the Oil Fund and the John Lewis Partnership across other businesses with less concern for social and environmental harm. It is also about developing harm reduction regimes at the level of the state that are conducive to more rather than less sustainable, ethical and democratic forms of capitalism. The social democratic regimes stand out in this respect.

Box 8.7: Increasing democracy in the workplace

There has been a lot of attention recently directed at the need to bring workers' voices into corporate and state decision-making to a much greater degree than is currently the case. These proposals build upon models like the John Lewis Partnership. Suggestions to modify corporate and state structures include:

- an onus on company directors to consider workers' as well as shareholders' interests in decision-making;
- boards to include workers' representatives;

> • workers to have a percentage vote at general meetings;
> • governments to have a Ministry of Labour to represent workers' interests at Cabinet.
>
> Crucially, those advocating the need for greater workplace democracy and an enhanced voice for workers in state and corporate decision-making structures usually see strong unions as an essential complementary element (Ewing et al, 2016). In other words, it is difficult to imagine isolated workers being able to confidently and effectively reflect workers' views without some form of underpinning collective support.

Capital–labour relations: trade unions

So far I have profiled two types of solutions to work-based exploitation and social harm. These have been focused on the establishment and enforcement of legal baselines and on the modification of the capitalist system and associated corporate structures. A final type of solution centres on the power (im)balance between capital and labour and the mechanisms that alter, affect and reflect this. Three of these mechanisms will now be discussed in turn: trade unions, worker inequality and peaceful worker protest.

The mention of trade unions can cause considerable alarm, with many instinctively against these employee organisations because of their connection to left-wing politics. This is true across both the developing and developed world. What is also true, however, is that worker collectivism does help to prevent the balance of power between labour and capital from shifting too far in favour of the latter. We know, for example, that where union density is high income inequality tends to be low (Weeks, 2005) and that the post-1970s decline in union membership explains a significant proportion of contemporary job insecurity and income inequality (Western and Rosenfeld, 2011). The evidence also suggests that union membership helps improve workers' as well as societal wellbeing (Keane et al, 2012; Dollard and Neser, 2013, 114). It also acts as a form of labour market regulation, preventing a 'race to the bottom' in terms of employment standards (Hjarnø, 2003). There is a lot to be celebrated, then, when workers are empowered, not least the fact that this can act to prevent exploitation and harm.

Traditionally, it has been in social democratic and northern European corporatist systems where union density rates have been greatest and where collective agreements and protections have been strong. The Nordic countries, in particular, offer workers a particular type of social contract (see Esping-Andersen, 1990; Gallie, 2003; 2007) of which union membership is a key part. Moreover, this contract appears to be beneficial in terms of physical and psychological health and guards against worker exploitation. It is also at the centre of systems designed to keep social inequality, and the harms associated with this, to a minimum.

Neoliberalism, however, has eroded union membership in advanced capitalist economies (Harvey, 2005; Holgate et al, 2011, 1081). The ideology has not only reduced people's propensity to value union membership, it has also underpinned the state's use of legislation to erode union power. The UK, for instance, saw nine acts of parliament in 13 years curtailing union power over the 1980s' and 1990s' Thatcher era (Pemberton, 2015, 50). Thus, the norm of union membership is either no more (in liberal and neoliberal regimes) or under threat (in corporatist and social democratic regimes). Table 8.7 outlines the changing union density rates between 1993 and 2011 based on OECD data and what is striking is how, by 2011, in most OECD countries union density rates were lower that 25%, with an average of 17%. Put another way, only around one in six workers are now union members in most advanced economies.

These are only the aggregate rates, though, and union density is even lower in the private sector, among SMEs and among migrants (Kersley et al, 2006, 119; Brown and Nash, 2008, 94; Barratt, 2009, 2). In the UK, for instance, the rate of unionisation among new migrants has been put at just 3% (TUC, 2007). Moreover, and at the other end of the spectrum, the only (mainly social democratic) countries with union density rates above 50% – Norway (53%), Belgium (55%), Denmark (66%), Finland (68%), Sweden (68%) and Iceland (84%) – saw rates fall between 1993 and 2011 (with the one exception of Belgium) and sometimes quite sharply.

The decline in union density has meant that collective bargaining has also eroded. Collective bargaining involves the negotiation of pay and working conditions between an employer and group of organised (normally via a union) employees. In the UK, for instance, 82% of workers were covered by collective agreements in 1980 but by 2012 this had declined to 23% overall, and 16% in the private sector (Ryan, 2013, 71). The decline has been seen by some as a cause of the increased precariousness of the working-class with collective bargaining viewed as a key solution to avoid work-based exploitation and harm (see for example Ewing et al, 2016). The picture of dramatically reduced collective bargaining power is not uniform, however, and is mainly

Table 8.7: Trade union density in OECD countries 1993–2011 as per cent of all employees

Country	1993[1]	2011[2]
Australia	37.2	18.5
Austria	43.2	27.9
Belgium	52.1	55.1
Canada	35.6	27.1
Chile	17.9	14.9
Czech Republic	51.5	13.9
Denmark	76.7	66.4
Estonia	40.8	6.8
Finland	80.7	68.4
France	9.3	7.7
Germany	31.8	18.0
Greece	35.4	22.6
Hungary	49.1	11.4
Iceland	86.5	84.0
Ireland	47.5	32.6
Italy	39.2	35.7
Japan	24.8	19.0
Korea	14.0	9.9
Luxembourg	44.4	33.9
Mexico	20.3	14.5
Netherlands	25.1	18.2
New Zealand	33.7	20.8
Norway	58.0	53.5
Poland	19.0	13.5
Portugal	26.1	19.5
Slovak Republic	64.2	17.0
Slovenia	58.0	23.1
Spain	17.7	17.2
Sweden	83.9	67.5
Switzerland	23.0	16.7
Turkey	19.6	5.4
United Kingdom	36.4	25.6
United States	15.1	11.3
OECD[3]	25.1	17.5

Source: www.oecd.org/els/emp/onlineoecdemploymentdatabase.htm#epl
Notes: [1] 1994 for the Czech Republic, Estonia and the Slovak Republic; 1995 for Hungary. [2] The last year for which data was available for all countries. [3] OECD is the weighted average of 31 countries (excluding Iceland, Israel and Slovenia).

a feature of liberal and neoliberal regimes. The EU average coverage rate for collective bargaining at present remains high at around 60% with a number of (mainly social democratic and corporatist) countries having rates in excess of 80% (Eurofound, 2015, 43).

Interestingly, where union density and collective bargaining decline, income inequality appears to grow (Ewing et al, 2016, 11). Related to this, there is a concern that the loss of the union norm is associated with a deproletarianisation at the lower echelons of the labour market and a growing asymmetry between the individualised worker and the employer. It is certainly the case that many disempowered workers are finding it hard to gather any collective momentum. It has been estimated, for example, that 40% of firms discourage employees from joining a union, with 25% victimising union activists (Heery, 2000, 3). This anti-union ethos among employers is pronounced in liberal and neoliberal regimes, and especially in the US (Cohen and Hurd, 1998). In fact, US union-busting tactics have also been commodified and exported to other countries such as the UK (Dundon, 2002; Logan, 2002; 2006). Often the contemporary culture is as follows: 'In many cases, management effectively substituted worker resistance with a climate of "fear". At Water Co., one worker commented: "Join the union and you get sacked, that's it"' (Dundon, 2002, 240).

The conditions for union members and activists vary globally as evidenced by the ITUC Global Rights Index (see Table 8.8). Though social democratic and northern corporatist states do stand out for their best practice, there is no easy developed/developing world divide, nor does the ITUC Global Rights Index always align neatly with the harm reduction regimes identified in Tables 8.4 and 8.5.

For example, Guatemala and the UK are two very different countries but both have been highlighted for strong anti-union measures. In Guatemala, for example, 53 trade unionists have been murdered over the past six years and unsurprisingly only 1.6% of workers are trade union members in the country (ITUC, 2013, 7, 20). The 'Maquila' industry (manufacturing in special economic zones) is particularly interesting in this respect. It is an industry where more than 51% of production is exported and it qualifies for significant government tax breaks designed to encourage an export economy. However, while these tax breaks specify that companies must comply with Guatemala's labour laws, this is often not the case and the government rarely, if ever, uses the threat of removing Maquila tax breaks to persuade businesses to comply with labour law. Instead, Maquila businesses – there are approximately 110,000 workers employed in the roughly 740 enterprises – are generally known for poor employment conditions.

Moreover, union activity is limited to just six unions and three collective agreements covering a mere 4,600 workers. In fact the ITUC has observed that: 'Efforts to organize are quickly and sometimes violently brought to an end through targeted or mass firings, death threats, blacklists, or simply closing the plant' (ITUC, 2013, 22). The fact that the Maquila goods are orientated towards export markets also appears to have little bearing upon the way union activity is dealt with in Guatemala.

Table 8.8: ITUC 'Global Rights Index', 2014

Countries with worst union-worker rights	Countries with best union-worker rights
Central African Republic	Barbados
Libya	Belgium
Palestine	Denmark
Somalia	Estonia
South Sudan	Finland
Sudan	France
Syria	Germany
Ukraine	Iceland
	Italy
	Lithuania
	Montenegro
	Netherlands
	Norway
	Slovakia
	South Africa
	Sweden
	Togo
	Uruguay

Source: ITUC (2014)

Similar anti-union measures have been observed in the UK construction industry. Following a 2009 investigation by the UK Information Commissioner's Office, it emerged that union activists in the construction industry were subject to surveillance and blacklisting via an organisation called The Consultancy Association (Smith and Chamberlain, 2015). The Consultancy Association was funded by major construction companies and allegedly supported by the Metropolitan Police (Taylor and Hurst, 2013). It began in 1993 and eventually blacklisted 3,212 UK workers but it was only 20 years later that, under considerable legal pressure, eight of the main construction firms involved in the blacklist (Balfour Beatty, Carillion, Costain, Kier,

Laing O'Rourke, Sir Robert McAlpine Ltd, Skanska UK and Vinci) finally apologised (Evans, 2013).[44]

The activities of The Consultancy Association were exposed following an Information Commission raid in 2009, initiated by a whistleblower (see Chapter Five) and subsequent media expose. This raid unearthed confidential files on 3,212 workers, files that contained details on their working lives and trade union activities. A Parliamentary inquiry into *Blacklisting in Employment* (House of Commons, 2014b) followed on from this and an interesting development from the 'sinister and odious practice' (House of Commons, 2014b, 4) of blacklisting has been the realisation that the state does have capacity for action. Specifically, the Welsh government, which spends approximately £4.3 billion per annum on procurement, of which around £1 billion is spent on construction, set out guidance in June 2013 aimed at tackling blacklisting through public procurement. This makes it clear that contractors should be excluded from tendering for public contracts if they have been involved in blacklisting unless they comply with certain 'self-cleaning' conditions. Moreover, in May 2016, 256 construction workers blacklisted by the Consultancy Association were awarded damages of £10 million: amounting to between £25,000 and £200,000 per worker depending upon loss of earnings and the seriousness of the defamation.

Keith Ewing, Professor of Public Law at King's College London, has described the blacklist of The Consultancy Association as 'the worst human rights abuse in relation to workers' in the UK in 50 years (cited in GMB, 2012). It is also clear that this activity, as well as helping employers to control their workforce led directly to work-based harm both in relation to health and safety breaches and in relation to the psychological wellbeing of those workers on the blacklist. Whether or not the new procurement strategy towards companies engaged in blacklisting will deter the activity remains to be seen. What is clear is that blacklisting in the UK – at least until the 2014 House of Commons inquiry (House of Commons, 2014b) – has had an almost uninterrupted history since the First World War. The head of The Consultancy Association, for instance, Ian Kerr was previously involved with the Economic League. This organisation operated between 1919 and 1993 and kept files on thousands of workers it considered subversive. The Consultancy Association effectively continued the work of the Economic League after 1993 and demonstrates the lengths some employers, even in so-called developed economies, will go to in order to suppress union activity.[45]

In my own research into exploitative low-wage migrant employment in the UK (Geddes et al, 2013) I uncovered many barriers to union membership:

> "The companies use anti-union tactics. It's difficult for us to organise. So one of the main tactics ... [pause] ... They brought in the [X] Group. They were, for want of a better phrase, brainwashing and scaring, intimidating the workers to vote no [to union recognition]. On top of this, they moved 70 agency workers into full-time positions. Now they said to these 70 agency workers 'Right, you're one of the agency workers, you vote no for union recognition, you've got your full-time job, keep your job.' Third, you would get threats from gangmasters. These would be something along the lines of 'You went against our wishes, talking to a union and so you are out of the house.'" (Unite representative)

> "There isn't union recognition. It's very, very difficult to apply a trade union model to extremely vulnerable, transient, temporary, exploited workers, because twos and threes, handfuls of people living in atrocious conditions, working for three months on very, very low wages, you're telling them to organise themselves and pay subscriptions and elect a shop steward and all that stuff that we take for granted, it's just not a model that would work! We're never gonna get away from the fact that in some of these labour markets, it's such that the trade union model is very difficult to apply." (TUC representative)

Thus, alongside murder and intimidation (Guatemala Maquila system) and destroying people's working lives (UK blacklisting) there are a host of more subtle ways in which unions find it impossible to organise those workers who are most in need of collective representation.

Not all countries draw on anti-union strategies, however, and there are instances where union representation remains strong or where unions are fighting back. One key aspect of the social contract in Nordic social democratic countries (with the exception of Norway), for example, is what is known as the 'Ghent system'.[46] This involves unions, albeit subsidised by the state, paying workers and former workers their welfare benefits, most notably in the event of unemployment. Although apparently less omnipotent than in the past (Lorentzen et al,

2014) the union-driven Ghent system adheres to the basic principle that work qualifies one for better benefits and ensures earnings-related unemployment relief. The benefits to those entitled to unemployment insurance under the Ghent system are relatively generous (especially when compared to a country like the US or UK – see Esser et al, 2013) and can temper the rising inequality that results from rising or persistent unemployment.

The Ghent system is important not just for understanding high union density in social democratic countries, but also for appreciating the ways in which welfare policies can protect the unemployed by providing them with an income guarantee that is well above the subsistence level. For instance, recent evidence suggests that the unemployed receive 80% to 90% of their previous income in unemployment benefits across the Nordic countries (Woolsey, 2008). Such a guarantee means that laid-off workers are, arguably, less vulnerable than those in other countries on residual level benefits (like the UK). The guarantee also has implications for levels of community cohesion and inequality that in turn can affect both social and workplace norms. Crucially, security during times of temporary unemployment also makes workers less vulnerable to exploitation and work-based harm.

Beyond the well-established Ghent system, there are grounds for some optimism with respect to union support in liberal and neoliberal countries. Specifically, there has been the emergence of new modes of organising (often called community unionism) beginning first in the USA (Fine, 2005). Most notable in this respect is the 'Justice for Janitors' campaign of the Service Employees International Union (SEIU). This began in Los Angeles in 1994 and by 1995 the SEIU had won a master contract covering janitors across Los Angeles County (Waldinger et al, 1998; Milkman, 2000; 2006; Cranford, 2005; Lerner et al, 2008). The campaign combined top-down and bottom-up approaches, employed 'social-movement' style tactics, pressurised high profile businesses at the head of supply chains, and has influenced union organising in other countries especially the UK (Wills, 2001; 2005; Simms et al, 2012; Holgate, 2015). Crucially, it was not simply dependent upon traditional models of worker organising and member recruitment.

Questions remain, however, around the extent to which this new mode of organising is genuinely able to succeed in the way that the high union density model of the social democratic countries has. The basic fact is that private sector union member density is below 8% in the US (Weil, 2009, 412) despite two decades of this alternative community union approach. Perhaps there really are new and progressive methods, at the community level, to tackling declining workplace collectivism?

More pessimistically, however, one might interpret the side-stepping of the union membership issue, in countries like the UK and US, as a classic neoliberal response.

Capital–labour relations: worker inequality[47]

Solutions to work-based exploitation and harm arise when social structures become less hierarchical and the power imbalance between labour and capital is reined in. This is not a case for completely flat societies, simply a case for fairer societies where the gap between those controlling and those being controlled is a humane one. In general, the evidence points towards flatter societies being less harmful (Kondo et al, 2009; Wilkinson and Pickett, 2009; Dorling, 2011) and towards atomised societies being more likely to engage in individualised victim blaming (Pemberton, 2015, 59).

As far as work is concerned, the 'income inequality hypothesis' posits that beyond a certain level of per capita GDP the distribution of income across a society is the factor that explains mental and physical health outcomes (Layte, 2012). These appear to be linked to what has been termed 'status anxiety' whereby income inequality is harmful because: 'it places people in a hierarchy that increases status competition and causes stress, which leads to poor health and other negative outcomes' (Rowlingson, 2011, 6). These 'other outcomes' can include reduced trust/communality and increased crime (Elgar and Aitken, 2011; Oishi et al, 2011).

Unfortunately, given this evidence, there is a capitalist logic in dividing labour markets along both class and cultural lines with exploitation and harm most intense in certain sectors and among certain groups of workers. Brass (2014, 8), for instance, argues that workers are 'unfree' at the bottom rungs of the capitalist ladder and form a deproletarianised reserve army of labour 'on which profitability and competitiveness depend'. Using a slightly different language, Piore (1979) talks of primary and secondary segmented labour markets along class lines, while Bonacich (1972) identifies split labour markets according to cultural nuances. In all cases there is a 'divide and rule' logic hard-wired into capitalist accumulation and challenging this is, by definition, seen as economically problematic (even if it is socially desirable).

Recently, the OECD (2013) has noted a relaxation in employment protection legislation leading to the emergence of dual labour markets between those on regular and those on temporary and flexible contracts. The 'divide and rule' logic, then, appears to be intensifying as labour markets become more laissez-faire and neoliberal in nature. The question, given that growing labour market inequality is likely to facilitate greater exploitation and work-based harm, is what can be done to arrest such polarisation?

One of the biggest issues since the global economic crisis of 2008 has been the pay of top managers and executives, the apparent degree to which this pay has increased irrespective of performance, and the way in which it is becoming increasingly removed from most people's notion of a fair or normal income. The richest 1% are set to own over half of the world's wealth by 2016 (Hardoon, 2015) with tax systems in many countries adding to this inequality. In the UK, for example, the Equality Trust (2014) has found that the poorest 10% of the population actually pay proportionally more in tax than the richest 10% (43% of income as opposed to 35%). The richest 10% also have not only accelerated away from the lowest earners but also from the squeezed middle-class. Thus, when a KPMG senior partner received a bonus of £683,000 in January 2012 and then, in March 2012, used a voicemail to inform staff of potential redundancies (White, 2012) the gap between his lifestyle and that of workers below him arguably made this rather crass act possible.

Beyond the UK, the picture of a growing chasm between the elite and the rest of society is clear in many nation-states, especially those that are liberal or neoliberal. Long-term analysis by Atkinson et al (2009), for example, shows that since the early 1970s income growth among the top 5% (particularly the top 1%) of US earners has far outpaced the rest of the US population. This trend, both of income and wealth inequality, is mirrored across the developed world and is particularly acute in Anglophone economies (Hoeller et al, 2012, 18).[48]

Concerns with what has been labelled 'executive pay' led to the 'Buffet Rule' in the US (named after the billionaire investor Warren Buffet). In 2011, Buffet stated that he believed it was wrong that the world's richest people often paid less in tax as a portion of income than middle earners.[49] The 'Buffet Rule' rule argues that no US-based millionaire should pay less than 30% of their income in taxes and is designed to address the fact that the tax paid by the highest earners in the USA has reached an historic low (see National Economic Council, 2012) and that tax evasion by the elite is also common. The Buffet Rule proposals were defeated, however, though their symbolic impact remains. Similar attempts to increase the tax burden for top earners occurred in the UK at around the same time. In 2010, the top rate of income tax was increased from 40% to 50%. However, it was then reduced to 45% three years later, and remains well below the levels of the 1970s and 1980s (on coming to power in 1979, Margaret Thatcher cut the top rate of income tax from 83% to 60%).

If it has proved difficult to rein in the global elite post-crisis, it has proved equally difficult to tie the pay of top earners to that of middle and lower earners. According to the OECD, in the average advanced economy, the income of the richest 10% of the population is roughly nine times that of the poorest 10% (OECD, 2011a, 1). Among academic researchers there is a general consensus that income inequality has increased since the 1970s (Smeeding and Thompson, 2011) and this appears true even in traditionally egalitarian countries: with the income gap between rich and poor expanding from 5:1 in the 1980s to 6:1 today in Germany, Denmark and Sweden (OECD, 2011a, 1).[50]

In liberal and neoliberal economies pay ratios are much more dramatic and once again there has been pressure to act. In the US, the 2010 Dodd–Frank Wall Street Reform and Consumer Protection Act, for instance, contains within it a requirement (under Section 953b) for publicly owned firms to disclose the ratio of CEO compensation to compensation of the average (median) worker.[51] Although slow to act initially, the Securities and Exchange Commission (from September 2013) now enforces this rule and it is possible to rank US companies according to levels of pay inequality.[52] The EU is also looking to increase corporate pay transparency and in April 2014 proposed that publicly traded firms publish the ratio between average employees' and top executives' pay, with shareholders entitled to an explanation of why this ratio is considered appropriate.[53] Although there is considerable opposition from business over this proposal (see Barker, 2014), there is also equal pressure to act given the US Dodd–Frank Act and the rising levels of pay inequality across the EU.

The question of how much is too much as far as pay inequality and worker exploitation is concerned goes back a long way. In ancient Greece, Plato is said to have argued that the incomes of the wealthiest Athenians should never exceed five times those of the poorest Athenians (though Plato was also said have owned a number of slaves – who would have been excluded from this calculation as non-citizens). More recently, in the 1970s, the world's most famous management consultant Peter Drucker (Drucker, 1977) argued that the maximum compensation for corporate executives should be capped at around 15–25 (15 for SMEs and 25 for larger Transnational Corporations) times the income of the lowest paid regular full-time employees.

Unfortunately, there is little reliable data on the CEO to lowest paid worker ratio at present. The US AFL–CIO union has published some data, estimating that in 2013 this CEO to lowest paid (that is, minimum wage) worker ratio for the USA as an average was 774:1 (AFL-CIO, 2014). However, most data takes the measure of CEO to typical (usually median) worker. Table 8.9 indicates how this typical worker ratio varies according to country, based once again on AFL-CIO (2013) data. There are clearly wide geographical variations. Moreover, there are also significant temporal variations. Mishel (2013), for instance, has found that the ratio of CEO (of the 350 largest US corporations) to typical worker earnings was 20:1 in 1965 but that by 2012 it had risen to 273:1: a trend that is outlined in more detail by Mishel and Sabadish (2013, 3). This trend of corporate inequality is evident beyond the USA. In the UK, for instance, the FTSE's 100 chief executives' average total pay in 2013 was 120 times the average earnings of their employees: up from 47 times in 1998 (Groom, 2014). This trend has even caused the Director General of the pro-business CBI to raise concerns (Finch et al, 2010).

Table 8.9: CEO to average worker pay ratios in selected developed world economies, 2012[1]

Country	CEO to Average Worker Pay Ratio
USA	354:1
Canada	206:1
Switzerland	148:1
Germany	147:1
Spain	127:1
Czech Republic	110:1
France	104:1
Australia	93:1
Sweden	89:1
UK	84:1
Japan	67:1
Norway	58:1
Portugal	53:1
Denmark	48:1
Austria	36:1
Poland	28:1

Source: AFL-CIO (2013)

Note: [1] Note this is only the CEO to average worker ratio. In 2013 the CEO to lowest paid (i.e. minimum wage) worker pay ratio for the USA was estimated at 774:1 (AFL-CIO, 2014).

In terms of concrete policies to respond to calls for maximum pay ratios the UK mooted the idea of a 20:1 pay ratio for public sector workers in an interim review of fair pay in the public sector (Hutton, 2010) only to then reject this proposal in the final report (Hutton, 2011). The ratio was seen as unworkable because: it would affect only 70 senior public sector managers; could become a perverse target for executives earning less than 20 times the lowest paid worker; and would produce different top pay limits for differently structured organisations without any clear rationale. The report concluded that 'a single maximum pay multiple would quickly become meaningless' (Hutton, 2011, 28). Similarly, the UK NCVO explored the use of pay ratios in the charity sector but noted that: 'Ratios are not always helpful. There is not a pay ratio that is right for all charities or indeed within particular sub-sectors, as charities operate in very different ways...The Inquiry heard of one instance where a charity had a salary ratio of 1:12, with a cleaner being the lowest-paid member of staff. If the charity outsourced its cleaners its ratio would be reduced to 1:8' (NCVO, 2014, 26). The NCVO did, however, call on charities to be transparent about their pay ratios in line with the sentiments of the Dodd–Frank Act and 2014 EU proposal.

This rejection of the principle of maximum pay ratios in the UK has not deterred others. In 2013 the Swiss 'Young Socialists' managed to secure the 100,000 signatures necessary to trigger a referendum on their '1:12' initiative. This was designed to limit bosses pay to a maximum of 12 times the size of the most junior employees' salaries in a given organisation. Those behind the 1:12 initiative campaigned by arguing that income inequality was running out of control in Switzerland. The Swiss Trade Union Federation, for instance, argued that the gap between the highest and middle earners in Switzerland (a country known for income equality: see Hoeller et al, 2012, 11–13) had grown from 1:6 in 1984, to 1:13 in 1998, and to 1:43 by 2011, and that the gap between highest and lowest earners was up at 93:1. Despite these trends, the November 2013 referendum saw Swiss voters reject the proposal 65.3% to 34.7%.

Notwithstanding the general lack of appetite for statutory pay restraint at the workplace level, there are isolated instances of maximum pay ratios being adopted voluntarily. Most stringently, *Médecins Sans Frontières* (MSF) operates a policy of not paying anyone in the organisation more than three times that of the lowest paid worker. Slightly more generously, but still well below the norm, the Basque-based Mondragon Cooperative has a policy that its top salary must be a maximum of six times that of the lowest worker, except for a few

CEOs where the ratio is a maximum of 1:9 (Flecha and Santa Cruz, 2011). Similarly, an initiative by the Wagemark Foundation certifies employers who pledge to keep the ratio of highest to lowest earners at 8:1 or less stating that: 'we chose an 8:1 ratio based on past precedents as well as recent research concerning optimal wage structures within organizations'.[54] Moving further up the pay spectrum, but still below the norm (see Table 8.9), the UK's John Lewis Partnership has a policy where the highest paid member of staff cannot earn more than 75 times the average wage of a shop floor salesperson.

Beyond targeting top earners and the use of maximum pay ratios, a number of countries also try to maintain more egalitarian society through public transparency (and pressure). Income inequality, for instance, is lowest among Nordic countries (OECD, 2011a) and it is in these countries (Norway, Sweden and Finland) where income and tax details of all citizens are published. This is the exception, however, and in most countries the norm appears to be non-disclosure and the use of minimum wage legislation to prevent those at the bottom end of the income spectrum from experiencing working poverty. In other words, the policy emphasis in most countries is on wage safety-nets to prevent exploitation and harm rather than on overall equality.

Minimum wage guarantees are not evident in all countries. Indeed, and this may seem counter-intuitive, in societies where labour relations are healthy and inequality between workers low, such safety-net style legislation is often deemed unnecessary. Put another way, the fact that state action is needed, through a mechanism such as a minimum wage guarantee, in order to protect workers from declining pay and conditions is seen by some as a worrying sign or a: 'bad equilibrium, characterized by distrustful labour relations, low union density and strong state regulation of the minimum wage' (Aghion et al, 2008, np). This said, it is difficult to imagine strong union activity and cooperative labour relations emerging in many countries/sectors and the minimum wage has certainly filled an important gap. For example, it is simply not possible to achieve the type of collective agreements in the USA or UK that are evident in many Nordic countries. Union density is not high enough and the creation of state-based regulations such as the minimum wage act to further residualise the role of unions and reduce the need for formal cooperation and trust between low-wage workers and their employers.

The above is not intended as a criticism of national minimum wage policies *per se* but as an observation concerning the gap that such policies are often used to fill. To elucidate, where union-driven self-regulation of labour markets is not possible the state must intervene to prevent the power imbalance between labour and capital becoming even more exploitative. This intervention in turn can further reduce the role of and need for union-driven self-regulation with safety-net state regulation becoming the only real protection for a largely deproletaranised workforce. Thus, minimum wage policy is ostensibly a fine solution to addressing exploitation and harm but in countries where labour–capital relations are healthy and where inequality between workers and their employers is low it is often not so essential.

One of the most noteworthy minimum wage policies from a socio-geographical perspective comes from the USA. A national minimum wage has existed in the USA since Roosevelt's 1938 Fair Labour Standards Act (FLSA) (for a review of the FLSA see Grossman, 1978). This established both a minimum wage ($0.25 per hour) and a maximum working week (44 hours) but at the time only applied to about one-fifth of the US labour force. It also banned oppressive child labour. An interesting feature of the US system today is the way in which there are now often three tiers of minimum wage legislation: nation-wide, state-wide (in most but not all states) and city-wide (in some cities).

As of 2014 the federal minimum wage was $7.25 per hour but in certain states and in certain cities it is considerably higher. For instance, Washington state had a 2014 minimum wage of $9.32, the highest of all US states, while the city of San Francisco had a minimum wage of $10.74, the highest of all US cities. What Washington state and San Francisco have in common is that they have indexed their minimum wage rates to inflation via the Consumer Price Index (CPI). This directly addresses the criticism of the federal minimum wage: that it has declined dramatically in real value (Reich et al, 2014). In fact, evidence shows that by 2007 the federal minimum wage reached a 50-year low in terms of its real value (Autor et al, 2010).

One of the criticisms of the more generous state and city-wide minimum wage policies has been that they damage the competitiveness of businesses in the areas covered by such policies. However, Card and Krueger (1994) examined in some detail the employment of fast-food workers across New Jersey and Pennsylvania after New Jersey raised the state minimum wage. Crucially, they found no measurable negative impact on employment. Similarly, Reich et al's (2014) work on San Francisco shows how, following the 2003 vote in favour of an index-linked city minimum wage, private sector employment actually grew faster than surrounding areas and staff turnover decreased. True, there was an impact in terms of prices but overall economic growth was not undermined and lower rates of staff turnover actually benefited businesses economically.[55]

The US case is interesting, then, not only in terms of how long a national minimum wage has been in existence but also in terms of the geographical variations in the minimum wage through the combination of federal, state and city policies. There are certain areas – most notably on the affluent and economically buoyant West Coast – where very progressive minimum wage policies have been pursued often in opposition to, and due to frustration with, the increasingly devalued federal minimum wage. Crucially, in areas with a high minimum wage prosperity does not appear to have been undermined (with lower staff turnover actually acting as a boon to business) and competiveness has been retained. Moreover, the Washington and San Francisco cases also suggest that public support (see below) can be key to achieving a fairer system of work and reward.

Capital–labour relations: social movements

There are a host of ways in which people are able to act to contest pay and working conditions if they deem these to be exploitative or harmful. This final chapter section, before the conclusion, will profile six examples of movements designed to empower workers. These are centred on: 1) online employee-driven rating systems; 2) 'living wage' campaigns; 3) zero-hours contract campaigns; 4) calls for the reform of 'McJobs'; 5) firm-specific pressure; and 6) sector-specific pressure.

It is now possible to rate employers online through the 'Glassdoor' career community platform. This allows workers to pass comment on company culture, wages and give messages to management. This information can then be viewed by potential employees. Glassdoor was launched in 2007, operates (in 2016) in 12 countries, and is now a highly-valued source of information among would-be workers (Frith, 2015). There have been some independent attempts to 'name and shame' the worst employers on Glassdoor. Typically, those employers ranked low down on the satisfaction scale that Glassdoor operates are criticised for the excessive pressures they put staff under, bureaucracy, and for the insecurity of employment.[56] Glassdoor itself prefers to praise the good employers and operates an awards system in various countries.[57]

Recently, grass-roots campaigns for 'living wages' across advanced economies have been organised by a combination of community groups, faith groups and trade unions (Wills et al, 2009; Lopes and Hall, 2015). These campaigns have had highly symbolic, though isolated, successes and demonstrate that a new form of grass-roots worker politics can emerge among traditionally non-unionised and relatively deferential workers to challenge the relationship between capital and labour.

In the UK, the living wage initiatives emerged from TELCO (The East London Communities Organisation) in 2001, building on US success in this area. TELCO was concerned with the problem of people on low pay in Canary Warf (London) finding it difficult to make ends meet and the campaign garnered cross-party support. In 2005 a Living Wage Unit was established by the Mayor of London and the campaign then went national with UK Citizens announcing the first National Living Wage in 2011. In 2016 the UK government adopted a 'national living wage' for workers aged over 25 years of £7.20 that replaced the 'national minimum wage' of £6.70.

The move in the UK to a 'living wage' from a 'minimum wage' was in part about raising workers' pay. It was also in part, however, a re-branding exercise as the difference between the minimum and living wage was only, in actual fact, 50 pence. The analogous US 'living wage' campaign at present is the arguably more ambitious 'Fight for $15' movement that is designed to challenge the erosion of the US federal minimum wage identified above.

Aside from the living wage movements in the UK and US, New Zealand recently witnessed a mass outcry directed towards zero-hours contracts. Once again union involvement was important in the gathering of momentum. The Unite union, allied with workers on zero-hours contracts, began to build grass-roots support for a change in the law. In the event, and following a supportive media campaign via TV3's 'Campbell Live' current affairs show, the New Zealand parliament voted unanimously to support new restrictions on the use of zero-hours contracts. The key concession in this respect involved restricting situations where the obligation on employees to be available for work exceeded employers' obligations to offer work. Employers must now guarantee a minimum number of hours each week to their workers, and, workers are able to refuse extra hours without repercussions. These new laws limiting zero-hours contracts came into force in 2016.

Similar pressure to limit zero-hours contracts has been evident elsewhere in the developed world. Most notably, there has been campaigning to improve what are often terms 'McJobs' in the fast-food restaurant franchise McDonald's. McDonald's employs an estimated 1.8 million workers across 118 countries (Wong, 2014). Only Walmart employs more private sector workers globally. The company has, however, come under pressure in relation to the way it treats its workers and what has been termed the 'low-road Americanization' of work (Royle, 2010). Particular concern, and protest, has been directed towards the zero-hours contracts on which staff are employed, the failure of the company to pay a living wage, and the difficulty workers face in joining trade unions:

1. Zero-hours contracts: The McDonald's Chief Executive in the UK recently said that his circa 80,000 staff on zero-hours contracts (workers find out about shifts two weeks in advance) 'love the flexibility' of these (Farrell, 2015).[58] The McDonalds official website goes on to say: 'We pride ourselves on being a flexible employer and for the majority of our employees, flexibility is one of the main things that they value about their job at McDonald's.'[59] Nevertheless, following pressure from campaign groups like Fast Food Rights[60] and unions, and in light of the events restricting zero-hours contracts in New Zealand, McDonald's UK recently trialled fixed-term contracts in 2016 (Ruddick, 2016).

2. Low wages: In the US McDonald's has come under pressure from the 'Fight for $15' living wage movement (backed by the Service Employees International Union) to raise the wages of its staff above local minimum wage levels. There have been protests since 2012 (Wong, 2014) but business leaders have so far ignored workers' calls and argued that a rise in wages would simply lead to job losses, mainly through relatively cheaper automation (Kasperkevic, 2016).

3. Limiting union activity: McDonald's official website states that: 'Employees are free to join a union if they wish. However, McDonald's does not currently work specifically with any one trade union because we have a number of internal methods that we use to speak to our employees on a regular basis. We believe in honest and open dialogue between employees and the company and we work with employees and franchisees to make sure this happens both in restaurants and within our business as a whole.'[61] In other words, the company is relatively opposed to trade unions and does not want to see large numbers of staff join a union (though see Royle and Urano, 2012). In the US this has culminated in former McDonald's workers filing cases against McDonald's alleging they were: 'fired or intimidated for participating in union organising and in a national protest movement calling for higher wages' (Wilkinson, 2016). In the UK an Early Day Motion was tabled in Parliament in 2016 calling for greater union recognition at McDonald's.[62]

Similar to the 'McJobs' debate, there have been various other firm and sector-specific movements in response to pay rates and working conditions. The Foxconn–Apple example already discussed (see Chapter Two) is a classic instance of this. Initially, the response to worker suicides was to focus attention on the deficiencies of the workers themselves. As has been noted elsewhere: 'It is much easier to ignore, minimise, or blame the victim for a work related negative psychological health outcome than it is to do the same for a work-related physical injury' (Duffy and Sperry, 2012, 142). Solutions focused on anti-suicide nets and an anti-suicide workers' pledge. The pledge was rescinded in the face of pressure from the public and the nets – dubbed '*ai xin wang*' or 'nets of a loving heart' – were eventually seen as simplistic. In response to pressure, spiritual and mental healing for victims was prescribed. Pressure continued, however, and, in February 2013, Foxconn proclaimed that workers could hold direct elections for union representatives. There are obviously still issues with independence as far as unions are concerned and so transnational social media campaigns have also been used to try to improve conditions at Apple–Foxconn factories. For instance, sites such as Change.org and SumOfUs.org have collected hundreds of thousands of signatures for petitions to improve working conditions. This campaigning has also led to the criticising of Foxconn's 'independent' internal social auditing process via the Apple-commissioned Fair Labour Association (China Labor Watch, 2012; SACOM, 2011). Thus, even in a country known for labour discipline, it is possible for social movements to persuade business of the need for reform in order to reduce exploitation and harm.

Beyond specific firms, some campaigning has focused on a sector/industry. The development of the CSR movement, for instance, and in particular the emergence of multi-stakeholder NGOs, has been especially orientated towards the garment/apparel manufacturing industry (see Box 8.5). Related to this, further along the textile supply chain, there has been recent interest in cotton harvesting. Anti-Slavery International (ASI), for example, has formed a 'Clean Cotton' campaign designed to draw attention to, and end, state-based forced labour in the Uzbekistan cotton harvest.[63] This campaign forms part of a wider movement spearheaded by the multi-stakeholder NGO 'Cotton Campaign'.[64]

The latest NGO research from Uzbekistan indicates that that there are now more than 1 million victims of state-imposed forced labour in the country being used to get in the cotton harvest (UGF, 2016). Moreover, global financial organisations like the World Bank have been accused of being complicit in this situation. In fact, in 2016 a petition, signed by 120,000 people, was delivered to the World Bank president to ask the Bank to suspend its US$500 million of agricultural payments to the Uzbekistan government until the government stops state-imposed forced labour. This drew a response from the World Bank, which argued that: 'During the 2015 cotton harvest, monitoring, conducted by the ILO, has not found conclusive evidence that beneficiaries of World Bank-supported projects used child or forced labor.'[65]

Whatever the reality in the Uzbekistan cotton harvest – a country where the number of modern slavery victims has been put at 1.2 million or 3.97% of the total population (Walk Free Foundation, 2016) – it is clear that multi-stakeholder NGOs, and resultant public pressure, can play a role in raising awareness of labour issues even in elite global institutions such as the World Bank. It is important, therefore, not to lose sight of the potential for NGOs and the broader public to affect change from below. The Glassdoor initiative, the living wage campaign, the pressure to end zero-hours contracts, the campaigning around McJobs, the movements to reform Foxconn, and the multi-stakeholder textile supply chain alliances are all indicative of this. Moreover, they build on the long-established traditions and legacies of worker protest from previous eras (see Chapter Three).

Conclusion

Passing laws to criminalise certain forms of work-based exploitation and harm, whether at a transnational or national level, is not especially easy. Nevertheless, there is now ample evidence of legal baselines protecting, in theory at least, the world's workers from severe exploitation and associated harms. These developments are to be welcomed at one level, but also to be viewed critically. Most obviously, legal frameworks are often ratified but not enforced, and over recent years they have been ratified at a time when there is ever-greater labour market deregulation and job degradation. To this extent, legal baseline solutions to work-based exploitation and harm may actually be part of a process of neoliberal impression management rather than part of a genuine attempt to create good and better work for the masses.

Genuine attempts to combat work-based exploitation and harm must also involve a critical appraisal of capitalism and a recognition that there are more or less harmful varieties. In addition, the power (im)balance between capital and labour should be examined within the context of declining union membership, rising worker inequality, and numerous worker-based social movements. This is not to argue that legal baselines are not a solution to exploitation and harm. It is to argue that they are only part of the solution. This is important, given how little attention has been directed towards structural critiques of capitalism and capital–labour relations by those purporting to be interested in solving problems such as modern slavery, forced labour and human trafficking.

We

Your hands are factory-dried and you have
feet that have not rested for eighteen years

when the conveyor rolls, you are one hundred years of fear
of what would happen if it did not

when you lay down your work and feel how we elevate each other
you are one hundred years of obvious victory over that very fear

people like you write the stories
about how we became
humans

NINE

Conclusions

This book began by posing four inter-related questions: 1) How is the distribution of power between labour and capital changing?; 2) How is labour now controlled?; 3) What are the negative outcomes of control?; and 4) How can these negative outcomes be reduced? It has addressed these four questions through eight chapters.

In Chapters One and Two the scope of the book was established and, specifically, I argued that legal baselines associated with issues such as fatalities at/through work, chattel slavery, modern slavery, human trafficking, forced labour and child labour are only a part of a much broader social problem. This broader problem is best understood through reference to labour exploitation and work-based harm, problems that exist 'beyond criminology' (Hillyard et al, 2004). In Chapter Three selected lessons of history were identified to show both how labour has been exploited in the past, and to underline the point that labour–capital relations can change for the better as far as workers are concerned through both radical action and incremental change. Chapters Four, Five and Six looked at different types of largely legal and non-coercive controls which labour now faces. The purpose of these three chapters was to show not only how labour is controlled *per se*, but also to link this control infrastructure to the problem of labour exploitation and work-based harm. Chapter Seven tackled some of the difficult, and sometimes provocative, issues that surround the question of what constitutes the excessive and oppressive control of labour. Finally, Chapter Eight examined three types of solution to labour exploitation and work-based harm and made the case, consistent with the social harm agenda, for looking at structural solutions as well as criminal–legal baselines.

If there is one unifying narrative to this book, it is that the legal approach to problems at work is deficient, and it has been shown to be deficient in four important respects. First, even when legal baselines exist to purportedly protect workers from exploitation and harm they are rarely invoked and are ill-equipped to enable victims and their families to take on (often powerful) state and corporate interests. This explains why, for example, even when workers die as a result of their employment, employer prosecution is still far from commonplace (Slapper and Tombs, 1999). Overall, then, legal protections (especially those focused on criminal law) tend to exist in a *de jure* more than a *de facto* sense. They give workers protection in theory rather than in practice, and this allows states to be seen to be tackling a problem while not actually posing a threat to capital.

Second, legal frameworks, especially those based on criminal law, tend to direct attention towards extreme labour market abuse. The problem of work-based exploitation and harm is, therefore, defined in a narrow way with only the most severe employer transgressions rendered worthy of sanction. This overlooks the fact that above these criminal–legal baselines there is a large grey area of exploitation and harm 'beyond criminology'. In fact, most workers who experience work-based problems are not 'official' victims of abuse and their experiences are unlikely to fall within the totemic 'fatalities at/through work', 'chattel slavery', 'modern slavery', 'forced labour', 'human trafficking' or 'child labour' definitions. Criminal–legal lenses, then, can cause myopia among labour market analysts. They can imply that, if totemic problems are limited in nature, and tackled by the state, then workers have nothing to complain about. This can serve vested interests and deny labour legitimacy, and a language and voice, when faced with work-based problems.

The third deficiency in legal framings which a social harm perspective illuminates concerns the issue of causation. To elucidate, the legal system is predisposed towards the identification of individual criminal actors and is unsuited to the apportioning of blame at an institutional or structural level. The legal system also suffers from being ill-equipped to tackle crimes of the powerful (Tombs and Hillyard, 2004; Hillyard and Tombs, 2007; Lasslett, 2010). As a result, issues of labour exploitation and work-based harm are usually only addressed, and possibly only actually problematised, when an individual perpetrator outside of the elite is identifiable. Put another way, legal protections for workers only really work against relatively obvious 'bad-egg' employers. They are rarely used against powerful state or corporate interests and do not challenge the prevailing capitalist structures that may have exploitation and harm hard-wired into them (though see Pemberton, 2015).

Finally, and related to the above, legal frameworks imply that the solution to exploitation and harm lies within a law enforcement approach that first discourages and then criminalises abusive employment relationships. A harm perspective is liberating in this respect because, while acknowledging the value of criminalising employer malpractice, solutions beyond criminology are seen as equally, and often more, important. As Chapter Eight made clear, for example, varieties of capitalism and capital–labour relations help us to understand the social, temporal and geographical rhythms of labour exploitation and work-based harm. In looking 'beyond criminology' one is, inevitably, directed towards a broader set of causal factors and associated solutions. These challenge state and corporate interests in ways that criminal–legal framings often do not.

Having pointed out four important limitations in the dominant legal (especially criminal law) framing of exploitation and harm, it is important to now reiterate what the social problem actually is. Clearly capitalism, via state and corporate structures, is orientated towards, and in some instances obsessed with, the control of the masses. This control is about the production and reproduction of 'good' and 'better' workers (however defined). The problem with control, however, is that it has a tendency, if left unchecked, to become excessive and oppressive. In relation to employment the outcomes of excessive and oppressive control are exploitation and individual, social–communal and environmental harms.

One might imagine that it is relatively straightforward to identify instances of excessive and oppressive control and to therefore address the resultant problems of exploitation and harm. Capital, however, is aware of its inherent tendency to draw too heavily on labour in order to secure a competitive advantage and bolster profitability. It is often concerned, as a result, with the management of exploitation and harm rather than its actual eradication. As part of this management, cause (accumulation) and effect (exploitation) are often distanced and decoupled. For example, we have elongated corporate value-chains with convoluted labour supply systems, which mean that harm and exploitation can often be effectively out-sourced (see Chapter Five). Similarly, and as we saw above, the turn towards criminal–legal baselines, while progressive in one sense, is also about the management of exploitation and harm to construct and constrict the problem in a particular way and for particular ends.

Whether or not there are alternatives to harm management is at the core of this book. The challenge is to identify and address excessive and oppressive control that leads to exploitation and harm not to seek the end to work-based controls *per se*. It is about achieving degrees of control, while enabling space for human flourishing at, through and beyond work. This certainly requires criminal–legal baselines to protect against the worst forms of abuse. Nevertheless, in a wide variety of contexts above the criminal–legal baselines, human flourishing is limited as a result of the relentless search by capital for 'good' and 'better' workers. To be sure, this search can be a valid and understandable one, and can lead to workers experiencing a great amount of job satisfaction.

Nevertheless, it can also be a dogmatic search that undermines human agency and human dignity.

Looking to the future, a main aim should be to reduce the size of problematic employment along the grey area of the exploitation continuum. This can be done in two ways. First, working patterns and relationships that allow people space to be autonomous and give them the opportunity for personal development and human flourishing, both inside and outside the workplace, need to be nurtured. Second, and if this is not possible, then workers need enough quality leisure and family time in order to make their employment pay in a spiritual as well as a narrow pecuniary sense. These two approaches are essentially about freedom, some of the time, from a narrow employment relationship and a definition of workers, for at least some of the time, as more than deferential subjects and mere commodities. They are about recognising individuals' rights to family and social life and valuing workers for more than an ability to follow orders and generate profit.

Rather than managing harm, as an essential feature of capitalist accumulation, capital could re-define the challenge as one of producing and reproducing 'good' and 'better' work. For this project we require much more than criminal–legal baselines, though these are important. Capital needs to apply the creativity of worker control to the problem of harm reduction. It can achieve this through the auditing and evaluation of the controls governing contemporary work and contemporary workers (Chapters Four to Six) and the establishment of best practice (Chapter Eight).

Figure 9.1 outlines the main types of work-based problems in society and the different solutions to these. It is clear from Figure 9.1 that if one is genuinely interested in identifying and combating labour exploitation in its entirety then legal baselines, and their enforcement via labour inspectorates, represent necessary but not sufficient solutions. Other solutions are also required that are 'beyond criminology' related to the modification of capitalism and/or the rebalancing of labour–capital relations. Four particular strategies stand out for addressing the problems of those on the labour exploitation continuum:

1. the modification of capitalism away from a neoliberal and toward a social democratic harm reduction regime (though I note this goes against the current direction of travel);
2. the modification of capitalism so that corporate structures evolve that are more focused on the long term and on the common good and common wealth (though such structures remain the exceptions rather than the norm);

3. a greater rather than lesser (as is the contemporary norm) role for Trade Unions, and a worker's voice, within the workplace;

4. a reduction in income and wealth inequality (though I note this is growing);

5. the right to peaceful protest in the face of exploitation and harm (though I note this is subject to increasing restrictions and surveillance).

The issue with the aim of achieving 'good' and 'better' work is that it actively challenges the growing gap between capital and labour and calls into question, and calls to account, powerful state and corporate interests. It also aligns the treatment of humans as commodities with harm, and thus points to a fundamental flaw in the contemporary capitalist system. The dilemma is to find a way out of valuing people only in so far as they perform certain types of work, and to allow people to find value both within and beyond their work. This dilemma is a far greater challenge than that implied via criminal–legal baseline framings. It is also an eternal challenge, and one where the perpetrators and the victims are bigger than any one individual, and where control, exploitation and harm are bound in a complex, but not incontestable, commodified mesh of work and reward. At the same time, the challenge is an incredibly simple one. To return to the poem that opened this book's first chapter it is about attending to the worker's call...'I am also human'.

Figure 9.1: Main types of work-based problems and solutions to these

PROBLEMS	The labour exploitation continuum					
	Modern slavery				Severe labour exploitation	Labour exploitation
	Chattel slavery	Forced labour	Human trafficking	Child labour		

SOLUTIONS	
Criminal laws	
Civil/labour laws	
Labour inspectorates	
Modify capitalism	
Re-balance labour-capital relations	

Notes

1.   Though note the need for caution, and statistical adjustment, when making international comparisons of fatality numbers and rates (Lilley et al, 2013).

2.   CSR is about supply-chain governance from within, that is, the industry-led policing of the supply chain, usually involving the largest TNCs (transnational corporations) policing their smaller suppliers.

3.   Another example of an apparent suicide 'cluster' is Orange. In both 2008–09 and 2014 concerns were raised over spates of suicides and these were linked to particular processes of corporate restructuring (Lichfield, 2014).

4.   See www.globalslaveryindex.org/.

5.   All the ILO's 190 Conventions (since 1919) are numbered consecutively and allocated a Convention Number.

6.   In 2005, the first forced labour estimate, the analogous figure was considerably lower at 12.3 million (ILO, 2005a).

7.   State imposed forced labour is still prevalent in some countries, however. For example, in Uzbekistan forced labour has been recently used for the cotton harvest according to Anti-Slavery International (ASI) and the organisation has launched a campaign to attempt to end this (see Chapter Eight).

8.   It should be noted that there are issues with all statistics on modern slavery and forced labour and that the ILO (2012b) resolved to improve global statistics in 2012. It then adopted 'Recommendation 203' in 2014 to improve forced labour data globally.

9.   Beyond trafficking, this is also true of the recent labour exploitation agenda. For instance, the focus on labour exploitation in the UK has been accompanied by an emphasis both on immigration control and tackling organised crime (BIS, 2016).

10.   The ILO has established the 'Statistics Information and Monitoring Programme in Child Labour' (SIMPOC) to improve global data on child labour. See www.ilo.org/ipec/ChildlabourstatisticsSIMPOC/lang--en/index.htm.

11.   See www.censusindia.gov.in/Census_Data_2001/India_at_Glance/scst.aspx.

12.   From *Apology for Smectymnuus* (1642).

13.   Details of those compensated as a result of the ending of slavery can be found at www.ucl.ac.uk/lbs/.

14.   Details of the plan can be found at www.caricom.org/reparations-for-native-genocide-and-slavery.

15.   Servile is derived from *servus*, which is Latin for slave. There were three Serville (slave) rebellions in the late Roman Republic.

16.   The Swing Rebellion of 1830 involved popular opposition and violence towards the lowering of wages and increased mechanisation in agriculture in England. Acts against land owners and employers were accompanied by a letter signed by a 'Captain Swing'.

17.   See www.tolpuddlemartyrs.org.uk/.

18.   Prior to the nineteenth century trade union movement, craftsman's guilds were prevalent throughout Europe. These drew workers together and this collectivism was used to maintain working conditions, ensure appropriate skill levels and standards were met, and provide for the sick and bereaved. The guilds were largely eroded by the development of industrial capitalism.

[19] Details of the Parliamentary requests for Mike Ashley to give evidence are available at www.parliament.uk/documents/commons-committees/scottish-affairs/Sports-direct-correspondence-040315.pdf.

[20] See www.parliamentlive.tv/Event/Index/4f084a41-dade-49d6-ab3d-506c62328124.

[21] From the Uber website, https://get.uber.com/cl/search/?type=bos_brand&city_name=boston.

[22] Workplace 'bullying' refers to systematic and persistent (for example, minimum six months) exposure to negative acts at work (Einarsen, 2000). These acts may be psychological, physical or sexual in nature and may concern work-related (for example, withholding documentation) as well as personal issues (for example, insulting and humiliating acts) (Baillien and De Witte, 2009, 349).

[23] Following the Modern Slavery Act 2015, the UKHTC evolved into the Modern Slavery Human Trafficking Unit (MSHTU).

[24] See http://alanwainwright.blogspot.co.uk/.

[25] Figure taken from www.cia.gov/library/publications/the-world-factbook/rankorder/2004rank.html.

[26] Dubai (UAE) has the highest migrant share of the working population that I am aware of at 96% (Cooper, 2013, 67).

[27] In Qatar the specific kafala sponsorship system was enshrined in Law Number 4 of 2009 Regulating the Entry and Exit of Expatriates, their Residency and Sponsorship.

[28] Though, as Baldwin-Edwards (2011, 43) notes, this issue of domestic workers being excluded from basic labour laws and protections is mirrored across the Arab world.

[29] Enshrined within 'Decision Number (79) for 2009 Regarding the mobility of foreign employee from one employer to another'.

[30] See www.ons.gov.uk/employmentandlabourmarket/peopleinwork/earningsandworkinghours/articles/contractsthatdonotguaranteeaminimumnumberofhours/march2016.

[31] www.gov.uk/au-pairs-employment-law/au-pairs.

[32] The bracero programme (named after the Spanish term bracero, meaning manual labourer) was initiated in 1942 and involved a series of laws and diplomatic agreements between the US and Mexico in order to supply US farm businesses with temporary harvest labour from Mexico. The scheme ran from 1942 to 1964, during which time 4.6 million contracts were signed. It represents the largest US contract labour program ever created. The H-2A programme is the current visa scheme relating to temporary migrant farm workers in the US. It has replaced the bracero programme and under the H-2A programme workers must have a job offer for seasonal agricultural work in the US and must come from a US approved list of origin countries.

[33] See http://aic.ucdavis.edu/publications/whitepapers/Agricultural%20Workforce.pdf.

[34] These figures are from www.prisonpolicy.org/graphs/raceinc.html.

[35] The ILO is the UN's only tri-partite agency.

[36] Prior to this it should be noted that there was the 'Brussels Act' of 1890 that abolished slavery across 18 European states.

[37] For examples of work-related cases, see www.echr.coe.int/Documents/FS_Work_ENG.pdf.

38   On 6 November 2014 the Irish TV channel RTE aired a documentary on this company, see www.rte.ie/news/player/2014/1106/20677365-the-treatment-of-foreign-workers-by-irish-firms/. The RTE documentary has been used as the basis for this case study. Atlanco-Rimec is effectively made up of a range of different companies (and former companies) registered (and wound up) in different jurisdictions.

39   See the evidence cited at www.publications.parliament.uk/pa/cm201415/cmselect/cmscotaf/272/27206.htm.

40   See *Laval un Partneri Ltd v Svenska Byggnadsarbetareförbundet & ors* Case C-341/05. And: *International Transport Workers' Federation & anor v Viking Line ABP & anor* Case C-438/05.

41   There is still some debate, though, as to exactly where inspections should be allowed. Many countries, for example, prohibit labour inspectors from entering private households to inspect working conditions and safeguard workers (Clark, 2013, 36).

42   One could also include 'informal' harm reduction regimes to cover a number of African countries in particular (see for example Dibben and Williams, 2012).

43   The cover of the Walk Free Foundation (2016) report, for instance, contains the following text: 'We call on governments of the top ten economies of the world to enact laws, at least as strong as the UK Modern Slavery Act 2015, with a budget and capability to ensure organisations are held to account for modern slavery in their supply chains, and to empower independent oversight.'

44   There were many more firms (circa 45) linked to The Consultancy Association (GMB, 2012, 12).

45   Recently, the anti-union sentiment in the UK has been enshrined in law via the Trade Union Act 2016 (see Ewing et al, 2016, 46–50).

46   Named after the Belgian city in which, in 1901, the system of unemployment benefits via public subsidies and a voluntary trade union system was first introduced.

47   Inequality here is used to refer to the gap in incomes between workers in a particular workplace or across a national welfare state regime. It is not used to refer to the gap between different countries of the world: which although wide appears to be declining (Milanovic, 2012).

48   Conversely, across the developing world there has been an increase in affluence among middle-income groups. As Milanovic (2012, 12) notes: 'We find some 200 million Chinese, 90 million Indians, and about 30 million people each from Indonesia, Brazil and Egypt...the middle classes of the emerging market economies (who) are indeed the main winners of globalization'.

49   In August, 2011, Warren Buffet wrote in the *New York Times* that his 2010 federal tax rate of 17.4% was 18.6 percentage points less than the 36.0% average rate paid by the 20 other workers in his office. The exact calculations have since been disputed, though there has been less (though some) argument against the principle of higher earners paying more tax relative to lower earners.

50   The gap is 10:1 in Italy, Japan, Korea and the United Kingdom, 14:1 in Israel, Turkey and the United States, and more than 25:1 in Mexico and Chile (OECD, 2011a, 1). Income inequality among working-age persons has risen faster in the United Kingdom than in any other OECD country since 1975 (OECD, 2011b).

51   There has been debate over whether the ratio should be a highest:lowest or highest:average ratio.

52   See http://go.bloomberg.com/multimedia/ceo-pay-ratio/.

53 EU press release available at http://europa.eu/rapid/press-release_IP-14-396_en.htm.

54 See www.wagemark.org/registry/.

55 Similarly, an independent inquiry in the UK has argued that raising the minimum wage is unlikely to cause economic damage to employers: 'Many sectors in the UK economy could, even now, afford to pay more to their lowest paid workers' (Resolution Foundation, 2012, 12, 57).

56 See, for example, the rankings at www.msn.com/en-us/money/inside-the-ticker/the-12-worst-companies-to-work-for/ar-AAcIMbT#page=13.

57 See www.glassdoor.com/blog/airbnb-best-place-to-work/.

58 See www.bbc.co.uk/news/business-34059976.

59 See www.mcdonalds.co.uk/ukhome/whatmakesmcdonalds/questions/work-with-us/working-hours/does-mcdonalds-use-zero-hour-contracts.html.

60 See https://fastfoodrights.wordpress.com/.

61 See www.mcdonalds.co.uk/ukhome/whatmakesmcdonalds/questions/work-with-us/jobs/are-mcdonalds-employees-allowed-to-join-trade-unions.html.

62 See www.parliament.uk/edm/2015-16/1393.

63 See www.antislavery.org/english/campaigns/cottoncrimes/cotton_crimes_video.aspx.

64 See www.cottoncampaign.org/.

65 www.worldbank.org/en/country/uzbekistan/brief/q-a-world-bank-agriculture-sector-policy-in-uzbekistan-in-the-context-of-child-and-forced-labor-concerns.

References

Academy of Medical Sciences (2012) *Human enhancement and the future of work*, London: The Academy of Medical Sciences.

AFL-CIO (American Federation of Labor and Congress of Industrial Organizations) (2013) *CEO-to-worker pay ratios around the world*, Washington, DC: AFL-CIO.

AFL-CIO (American Federation of Labor and Congress of Industrial Organizations) (2014) *Executive paywatch*, Washington, DC: AFL-CIO.

Aghion, P., Algan, Y. and Cahuc, P. (2008) 'Can policy interact with culture? Minimum wage and the quality of labour relations', *IZA Discussion Paper* 3680, Bonn: Institute for the Study of Labour.

Agustin, L.M. (2007) *Sex at the margins: Migration, labour markets and the rescue industry*, London: Zed Books.

Alberti, G. (2014) 'Mobility strategies, "mobility differentials" and "transnational exit": The experiences of precarious migrants in London's hospitality jobs', *Work, Employment and Society*, 28, 6, 865–81.

Amnesty International (2013) *The dark side of migration*, London: Amnesty International.

Anderson, B. (2007) 'Motherhood, apple pie and slavery: Reflections on trafficking debates', *Working Paper* 07-48, Oxford: COMPAS.

Anderson, B. (2010) 'Migration, immigration controls and the fashioning of precarious workers', *Work Employment and Society*, 24, 2, 300–17.

Anderson, B. (2013) *Us and them?: The dangerous politics of immigration control*, Oxford: Oxford University Press.

Anderson, B. and Rogaly, B. (2005) *Forced labour migration to the UK*, London: TUC.

Andrees, B. (2008) *Forced labour and human trafficking: A handbook for labour inspectors*, Geneva: International Labour Organization.

Andrees, B. and Belser, P. (2009) *Forced labor: Coercion and exploitation in the private economy*, Boulder, CO: Lynne Rienner Publishers.

Appelbaum, R.P. and Lichtenstein, N. (2016) 'Introduction: Achieving workers' rights in the global economy', in R.P. Appelbaum and N. Lichtenstein (eds) *Achieving workers' rights in the global economy*, Ithaca, NY: Cornell University Press.

Arakan Project (2012) 'Forced labour still prevails: An overview of forced labour practices in North Arakan, Burma', Submission to the International Trade Union Confederation (ITUC) for consideration at the International Labour Conference 2012, Ottawa: Canada.

Artazcoz, L., Cortès, I., Escribà-Agüir, V., Cascant, L. and Villegas, R. (2009) 'Understanding the relationship of long working hours with health status and health-related behaviours', *Journal of Epidemiology and Community Health*, 63, 7, 521–7.

Atkinson, A.B., Piketty, T. and Saez, E. (2009) Top incomes in the long run of history', *NBER (National Bureau of Economic Research) Working Paper* 15408, Cambridge, MA: NBER.

Austin, R. (1988) 'Employer abuse, worker resistance, and the tort of intentional infliction of emotional distress', *Stanford Law Review*, 41, 1, 1–59.

Autor, D., Manning, A. and Smith, C. (2010) 'The contribution of the minimum wage to US wage inequality over three decades: A reassessment', *NBER (National Bureau of Economic Research) Working Paper* 16533, Cambridge MA: NBER.

Bailey, M. (2014) *The decline of serfdom in late medieval England: From bondage to freedom*, Suffolk: Boydell and Brewer Ltd.

Baillien, E. and De Witte, H. (2009) 'Why is organizational change related to workplace bullying?', *Economic and Industrial Democracy*, 30, 3, 348–71.

Baldwin-Edwards, M. (2011) *Labour immigration and labour markets in the GCC countries*, London: London School of Economics.

Bales, K. (1999) *Disposable people: New slavery in the global economy*, Berkeley, CA: University of California Press.

Ball, K. (2010) 'Workplace surveillance: An overview', *Labor History*, 51, 1, 87–106.

Banerjee, S.B. (2008) 'Corporate social responsibility: The good, the bad and the ugly', *Critical Sociology*, 34, 1, 51–79.

Baritz, L. (1960) *The servants of power: A history of the use of social science in American industry*, Middletown, CT: Wesleyan University Press.

Barker, A. (2014) 'Brussels plans fresh rules on executive pay', *The Financial Times,* 7 March.

Barratt, C. (2009) *Trade union membership 2008*, London: Department for Business Enterprise and Regulatory Reform.

Barrientos, S. (2008) 'Contract labour: The Achilles heel of corporate codes in commercial value chains', *Development and Change*, 39, 6, 1–14.

Barrientos, S. (2013) 'Labour chains: Analysing the role of labour contractors in global production networks', *The Journal of Development Studies*, 49, 8, 1058–71.

Barrientos, S., Gereffi, G. and Rossi, A. (2011a) 'Economic and social upgrading in global production networks: A new paradigm for a changing world', *International Labour Review*, 150, 3–4, 319–40.

Barrientos, S., Mayer, F., Pickles, J., Posthuma, A. (2011b) 'Labour standards in global production networks: Framing the policy debate', *International Labour Review*, 150, 3–4, 297–317.

Barrientos, S., Kothari, U. and Phillips, N. (2013) 'Dynamics of unfree labour in the contemporary global economy', *The Journal of Development Studies*, 49, 8, 1037–41.

Bath, D.E., Stowers, J.R., Hörmann, D., Poehlmann, A., Dickson, B.J. and Straw, A.D. (2014) FlyMAD: Rapid thermogenetic control of neuronal activity in freely walking *Drosophila*, *Nature Methods*, 11, 7, 756–62.

Bauder, H. (2006) *Labour movement: How migration regulates labour markets*, Oxford: Oxford University Press.

Bauman, Z. (1998) *Work, consumerism and the new poor*, Buckingham: Open University Press.

Beale, D. and Hoel, H. (2011) 'Workplace bullying and the employment relationship: Exploring questions of prevention, control and context', *Work, Employment and Society*, 25, 1, 5–18.

Beck, U. (1992) *Risk society: Towards a new modernity*, London: Sage.

Beck, U. (2000) *The brave new world of work*, Cambridge: Polity Press.

Becker, R. and Selden, G. (1998) *The body electric*, New York: Morrow.

Behling, F. and Harvey, M. (2015) 'The evolution of false self-employment in the British construction industry: A neo-Polanyian account of labour market formation', *Work, Employment and Society*, 29, 6, 969–88.

Bell, T. (2016) 'The Marikana massacre: Why heads must roll', *New Solutions: A Journal of Environmental and Occupational Health Policy*, 25, 4, 440–50.

Belser, P. and de Cock, M. (2009) 'Improving forced labour statistics', in B. Andrees and P. Belser (ed) *Forced labor: Coercion and exploitation in the private economy*, Boulder, CO: Lynne Rienner Publishers, pp 173–94.

Benach, J. and Muntaner, C. (2007) 'Precarious employment and health: Developing a research agenda', *Journal of Epidemiology and Community Health*, 61, 4, 276–7.

Bernhardt, A. and McGrath, S. (2005) 'Trends in wage and hour enforcement by the US Department of Labor, 1975–2004', *Economic Policy Brief* 3, New York: Brennan Centre for Justice.

Bethell, L. (1970) *The abolition of the Brazilian slave trade*, Cambridge: Cambridge University Press.

BIS (Department for Business, Innovation and Skills) (2011) *Resolving workplace disputes: government response to the consultation*, London: BIS.

BIS (Department for Business, Innovation and Skills) (2016) *Tackling exploitation in the labour market*. London: BIS/Home Office.

Black, I., Gibson, O. and Booth, R. (2014) 'Qatar promises to reform labour laws after outcry over "World Cup slaves"', *Guardian*, 14 May.

Black, J. (2011) *Slavery: A new global history*, London: Constable and Robinson.

Blackburn, R. (1988) *The overthrow of Colonial slavery 1776–1848*, London: Verso.

Blowfield, M. and Frynas, J.G. (2005) 'Editorial setting new agendas: Critical perspectives on corporate social responsibility in the developing world', *International Affairs*, 81, 3, 499–513.

Bonacich, E. (1972) 'A theory of ethnic antagonism: The split labor market', *American Sociological Review*, 37, 5, 547–59.

Bourcier, N. (2012) 'Brazil comes to terms with its slave trading past', *Guardian*, 23 October.

Bourdieu, P. (1997) *Pascalian meditations*, Stanford, CA: Stanford University Press.

Bourdieu, P. (2001) *Masculine domination*, Stanford, CA: Stanford University Press.

Bourgois, P. (2001) 'The power of violence in war and peace post-cold war lessons from El Salvador', *Ethnography*, 2, 1, 5–34.

Borjas, G.J. (1987) 'Self-selection and the earnings of immigrants', *The American Economic Review,* 77, 4, 531–53.

Brass, T. (1999) *Towards a comparative political economy of unfree labour: Case studies and debates*, London: Frank Cass.

Brass, T. (2004) 'Medieval working practices? British agriculture and the return of the gangmaster', *The Journal of Peasant Studies*, 31, 2, 313–40.

Brass, T. (2014) 'Debating capitalist dynamics and unfree labour: A missing link?', *The Journal of Development Studies*, 50, 5, 570–82.

Braverman, H. (1974) *Labor and monopoly capital: The degradation of work in the Twentieth Century*, New York: Monthly Review Press.

Brown, P. (2012) 'A nudge in the right direction? Towards a sociological engagement with libertarian paternalism', *Social Policy and Society*, 11, 3, 305–17.

Brown, W. and Nash, D. (2008) 'What has been happening to collective bargaining under New Labour? Interpreting WERS (Workplace Employment Relations Survey) 2004', *Industrial Relations Journal*, 39, 2, 91–103.

Brown, W., Deakin, S., Nash, D. and Oxenbridge, S. (2000) 'The employment contract: From collective procedures to individual rights', *British Journal of Industrial Relations*, 38, 4, 611–29.

Bunting, M. (2005) *Willing slaves*, London: Harper Perennial.

Burawoy, M. (1979) *Manufacturing consent*, Chicago, IL: Chicago University Press.

Burchell, B., Day, D., Hudson, M., Ladipo, D., Mankelow, R., Nolan, J.P., Reed, H., Wichert, I.C. and Wilkinson, F. (1999) *Job insecurity and work intensification*, York: Joseph Rowntree Foundation.

Burchell, B., Sehnbruch, K., Piasna, A. and Agloni, N. (2014) 'The quality of employment and decent work: Definitions, methodologies, and ongoing debates', *Cambridge Journal of Economics*, 38, 2, 459–77.

Burke, J. (2014) 'Rana Plaza: One year on from the Bangladesh factory disaster', *Guardian*, 19 April.

Cappelli, P. (1995) 'Rethinking employment', *British Journal of Industrial Relations*, 33, 4, 563–602.

Card, D. and Krueger, A. (1994) 'Minimum wages and employment: A case study of the fast food industry in New Jersey and Pennsylvania', *American Economic Review*, 84, 4, 772–98.

Carnegie, D. (1936/2010) *How to win friends and influence people*, New York: Simon and Schuster.

Carter, B., Danford, A., Howcroft, D., Richardson, H., Smith, A. and Taylor, P. (2013) 'Stressed out of my box: employee experience of lean working and occupational ill-health in clerical work in the UK public sector', *Work, Employment and Society*, 27, 5, 747–67.

Castles, S. and Kosack, G. (1973) *Immigrant workers and class structure in western Europe*, Oxford: Oxford University Press.

Chamberlain, G. (2014) 'The tea pickers sold into slavery', *Guardian*, 2 March.

Chan, J. and Pun, N. (2010) 'Suicide as protest for the new generation of Chinese migrant workers: Foxconn, global capital, and the state', *The Asia–Pacific Journal*, 37, 2, 1–50.

Chan, J., Pun, N. and Selden, M. (2013) 'The politics of global production: Apple, Foxconn and China's new working class', *The Asia–Pacific Journal*, 28, 2, 100–15.

China Labor Watch (2012) *Beyond Foxconn: Deplorable working conditions characterize Apple's entire supply chain*, New York: China Labor Watch.

Chiswick, B.R. (2000) 'Are immigrants favorably self-selected? An economic analysis', in C.B. Brettell and J.F. Hollifield (eds) *Migration theory*, Routledge: New York, pp 61–76.

Cingano, F. (2014) Trends in income inequality and its impact on economic growth, *OECD Social, Employment and Migration Working Papers* 163, Paris: OECD.

Clark, G.E. (2016) 'From the Panama Canal to Post-Fordism: Producing temporary labor migrants within and beyond agriculture in the United States (1904–2013)', *Antipode*, DOI: 10.1111/anti.12218.

Clark, N. (2013) *Detecting and tackling forced labour in Europe*, York: Joseph Rowntree Foundation.

Clarke, M., Lewchuk, W., de Wolff, A. and King, A. (2007) 'This just isn't sustainable: Precarious employment, stress and workers' health', *International Journal of Law and Psychiatry*, 30, 6, 311–26.

Clinard, M. and Yeager, P. (1980) *Corporate crime*, New Brunswick, NJ: Transaction Publishers, 2011.

Coe, N.M. (2013) 'Geographies of production III: Making space for labour', *Progress in Human Geography*, 37, 2, 271–84.

Coe, N.M., Johns, J. and Ward, K. (2008) 'Agents of casualisation? The temporary staffing industry and labour market restructuring in Australia', *Journal of Economic Geography*, 9, 1, 55–84.

Cohen, R. (1987) *The new Helots: Migrants in the international division of labour*, Aldershot: Gower.

Cohen, L. and Hurd, R.W. (1998) 'Fear, conflict, and organizing', in K. Bronfenbrenner, S. Friedman, R.W. Hurd, R.A. Oswald and R.L. Seeber (eds) *Organizing to win: New research on unions strategies*, Ithaca, NY: ILR Press, pp 181–96.

Cooper, N. (2013) 'City of gold, city of slaves: Slavery and indentured servitude in Dubai', *Journal of Strategic Security*, 6, 3, 65–71.

Craig, G., Gaus, A., Wilkinson, M., Skrivánková, K. and McQuade, A. (2007) *Contemporary slavery in the UK: Overview and key issues*, York: Joseph Rowntree Foundation.

Cranford, C.J. (2005) 'Networks of exploitation: Immigrant labor and the restructuring of the Los Angeles janitorial industry', *Social Problems*, 52, 3, 379–97.

Datta, M.N. and Bales, K. (2013) 'Slavery in Europe: Part 1, estimating the dark figure', *Human Rights Quarterly*, 35, 4, 817–29.

Datta, M.N. and Bales, K. (2014) 'Slavery in Europe: Part 2, testing a predictive model', *Human Rights Quarterly*, 36, 2, 277–95.

Davidson, J.O.C. (2010) 'New slavery, old binaries: Human trafficking and the borders of "freedom"', *Global Networks*, 10, 2, 244–61.

Davies, A.C. (2008) 'One step forward, two steps back? The Viking and Laval cases in the ECJ', *Industrial Law Journal*, 37, 2, pp 126–48.

De Maria, W. (2006) 'Common law – common mistakes?: Protecting whistleblowers in Australia, New Zealand, South Africa and the United Kingdom', *International Journal of Public Sector Management*, 19, 7, 643–58.

Devinney, T. M. (2009) 'Is the socially responsible corporation a myth? The good, the bad, and the ugly of corporate social responsibility', *The Academy of Management Perspectives*, 23, 2, 44–56.

Dibben, P. and Williams, C.C. (2012) 'Varieties of capitalism and employment relations: informally dominated market economies', *Industrial Relations: A Journal of Economy and Society*, 51, S1, 563–82.

Di Ruggiero, E., Cohen, J.E. and Cole, D.C. (2014) 'The politics of agenda setting at the global level: Key informant interviews regarding the International Labour Organization Decent Work agenda', *Global Health*, 10, 1.

Dollard, M.F. and Neser, D.Y. (2013) 'Worker health is good for the economy: Union density and psychosocial safety climate as determinants of country differences in worker health and productivity in 31 European countries', *Social Science and Medicine*, 92, 114–23.

Dorling, D. (2011) *Injustice: Why social inequality persists*, Cambridge: Policy Press.

Dorling, D., Gordon, D., Hillyard, P., Pantazis, C., Pemberton, S. and Tombs, S. (2008) *Criminal obsessions: Why harm matters more than crime*, London: Centre for Crime and Justice Studies, King's College.

Downes, D. and Hansen, K. (2006) Welfare and punishment: The relationship between welfare spending and imprisonment, *Crime and Society Briefing* 2, London: King's College.

Draper, N. (2013) *The price of emancipation: Slave-ownership, compensation and British society at the end of slavery*, Cambridge: Cambridge University Press.

Driver, F. (1993) *Power and pauperism*, Cambridge: Cambridge University Press.

Drucker, P. (1959) *Landmarks of tomorrow*, New York: Harper and Brothers.

Drucker, P. (1977) 'Is executive pay excessive?', *The Wall Street Journal*, 23 May.

Duffy, M. and Sperry, L. (2012) *Mobbing: Causes, consequences and solutions*, Oxford: Oxford University Press.

Dundon, T. (2002) 'Employer opposition and union avoidance in the UK', *Industrial Relations Journal*, 33, 3, 234–45.

Dwyer, P., Lewis, H., Scullion, L. and Waite, L. (2011) *Forced labour and UK immigration policy: Status matters?*, York: Joseph Rowntree Foundation.

Economist (2015) 'The on-demand economy: Workers on tap', *The Economist*, 3 January.

Edwards, R. (1979) *Contested terrain: The transformation of the workplace in the twentieth century*, London: Heinemann.

Ehrenreich, B. (2009) *Smile or die: How positive thinking fooled America and the world*, London: Granta Books.

Einarsen, S. (2000) 'Harassment and bullying at work: A review of the Scandinavian approach', *Aggression and Violent Behavior*, 5, 4, 379–401.

Elgar, F.J. and Aitken, N. (2011) 'Income inequality, trust and homicide in 33 countries', *The European Journal of Public Health*, 21, 2, 241–6.

Elk, M. and Sloan, B. (2011) 'The hidden history of ALEC and prison labor', *The Nation*, 1 August.

Equality Trust (2014) *Unfair and unclear*, London: Equality Trust.

Erimtan, C. (2014) The Soma mine disaster or privatization gone wild in Turkey, *RT News*, 16 May.

Esping-Andersen, G. (1990) *The three worlds of welfare capitalism*, Cambridge: Polity Press.

Esser, I., Ferrarini, T., Nelson, K., Palme, J. and Sjöberg, O. (2013) *Unemployment benefits in EU member states*, Brussels: European Commission.

Eurofound (2014) *Quality of employment conditions and employment relations in Europe*, Dublin: Eurofound.

Eurofound (2015) *Collective bargaining in Europe in the 21st century*, Luxembourg: Publications Office of the European Union.

Evans, R. (2009) 'Alan Wainwright: The lonely life of a construction industry whistleblower', *Guardian*, 15 May.

Evans, R. (2013) 'Construction firms to compensate unlawfully blacklisted workers', *Guardian*, 10 October.

Ewing, K.D., Hendy, J. and Jones, C. (2016) *A manifesto for labour law*, Liverpool: Institute of Employment Rights.

Farrell, S. (2015) 'McDonald's UK boss defends company's use of zero-hours contracts for staff', *Guardian*, 26 August.

Ferrie, J.E. (2001) 'Is job insecurity harmful to health?', *Journal of the Royal Society of Medicine*, 94, 2, 71–6.

Ferrie, J.E., Shipley, M.J., Marmot, M.G., Stansfeld, S. and Smith, G.D. (1995) 'Health effects of anticipation of job change and non-employment: Longitudinal data from the Whitehall II study', *British Medical Journal*, 311, 1264–9.

Ferrie, J.E., Shipley, M.J., Newman, K., Stansfeld, S.A. and Marmot, M. (2005) 'Self-reported job insecurity and health in the Whitehall II study: Potential explanations of the relationship', *Social Science and Medicine*, 60, 7, 1593–602.

Fevre, R. (2007) 'Employment insecurity and social theory: The power of nightmares', *Work, Employment and Society*, 21, 3, 517–35.

Fevre, R., Lewis, D., Robinson, A. and Jones, T. (2012) *Trouble at work*, London: Bloomsbury Academic.

Finch, J., Treanor, J. and Wachman, R. (2010) 'Critics unite over executive pay to force the 'aliens' of business down to earth', *Guardian*, 31 March.

Findlay, A. and McCollum, D. (2013) 'Recruitment and employment regimes: Migrant labour channels in the UK's rural labour markets', *Journal of Rural Studies*, 30, 10–19.

Findlay, A., McCollum, D., Shubin, S., Apsite, E. and Krisjane, Z. (2013) 'The role of recruitment agencies in imagining and producing the "good" migrant', *Social and Cultural Geography*, 14, 2, 145–67.

Fine, J. (2005) 'Community unions and the revival of the American labor movement', *Politics and Society*, 33, 1, 153–99.

Fitzgerald, S.A. (2012) 'Vulnerable bodies, vulnerable borders: Extraterritoriality and human trafficking', *Feminist Legal Studies*, 20, 227–44.

Fitzgerald, S.A. (2016) 'Vulnerable geographies: Human trafficking, immigration and border control in the UK and beyond', *Gender, Place & Culture*, 23, 2, 181–97.

FLA (Fair Labor Association) (2012) *Understanding the characteristics of the Sumangali scheme in Tamil Nadu textile and garment industry and supply chain linkages*, Washington, DC: FLA.

FLA (Fair Labor Association) (2013) *Final Foxconn verification status report*, Washington DC: FLA.

Flecha, R. and Santa Cruz, I. (2011) 'Cooperation for economic success: The Mondragon case', *Analyse and Kritik*, 1, 157–70.

FLEX (Focus on Labour Exploitation) (2016) *Combatting labour exploitation through labour inspection*, London: FLEX.

Forkert, K. and Lopes, A. (2015) 'Unwaged posts in UK universities: Controversies and campaigns', *Triple C: Communication, Capitalism and Critique*, 13, 2, 533–53.

FRA (European Agency for Fundamental Rights) (2015) *Severe labour exploitation*, Vienna: European Agency for Fundamental Rights.

Frith, B. (2015) 'Glassdoor trusted more than employers', *HR Magazine*, 3 August.

Fudge, J. and K. Strauss, K. (2013) *Temporary work, agencies and unfree labour*, London: Routledge.

Galenson, D.W. (1984) 'The rise and fall of indentured servitude in the Americas: An economic analysis', *The Journal of Economic History*, 44, 1, 1–26.

Gallie, D. (2003) 'The quality of working life: Is Scandinavia different?', *European Sociological Review*, 19, 1, 61–79.

Gallie, D. (2007) *Employment regimes and the quality of work*, Oxford: Oxford University Press.

Ganster, D.C. and Rosen, C.C. (2013) 'Work stress and employee health: A multidisciplinary review', *Journal of Management*, 39, 5, 1085–122.

Garnsey, P. (1996) *Ideas of slavery: From Aristotle to Augustine*, Cambridge: Cambridge University Press.

Geddes, A. and Scott, S. (2010) 'UK food businesses' reliance on low-wage migrant labour: A case of choice or constraint?', in M. Ruhs and B. Anderson (eds) *Who needs migrant workers?*, Oxford: Oxford University Press, pp 193–218.

Geddes, A., Craig, G. and Scott, S. (2013) *The scope of forced labour in the UK*, York: Joseph Rowntree Foundation.

Gereffi, G. (2014) 'Global value chains in a post-Washington Consensus world', *Review of International Political Economy*, 21, 1, 9–37.

Gereffi, G. and Korzeniewicz, M. (eds) (1994) *Commodity chains and global capitalism*, Westport, CT: Praeger.

Giddens, A. (1991) *Modernity and self-identity*, Cambridge: Polity Press.

Gill, N. and Gill, M. (2012) 'The limits to libertarian paternalism: Two new critiques and seven best-practice imperatives', *Environment and Planning C: Government and Policy*, 30, 5, 924–40.

GMB (2012) *Blacklisting: Illegal corporate bullying*, London: GMB.

Goodwin, T. (2012) 'Why we should reject nudge', *Politics*, 32, 2, 85–92.

Goos, M. and Manning, A. (2007) 'Lousy and lovely jobs: The rising polarization of work in Britain', *The Review of Economics and Statistics*, 89, 1, 118–33.

Graham, R. (1966) 'Causes for the abolition of Negro slavery in Brazil: An interpretive essay', *The Hispanic American Historical Review*, 46, 2, 123–37.

Green, F. (2001) 'It's been a hard day's night: The concentration and intensification of work in late twentieth century Britain', *British Journal of Industrial Relations*, 39, 1, 53–80.

Green, F. (2004) 'Why has work effort become more intense?', *Industrial Relations: A Journal of Economy and Society*, 43, 4, 709–41.

Groom, B. (2014) 'If only Plato were running Barclays', *The Financial Times*, 10 March.

Grossman, J. (1978) 'Fair Labor Standards Act of 1938: Maximum struggle for a minimum wage', *Monthly Labor Review*, 22–30.

Hämäläinen, P., Saarela, K. and Takala, J. (2009) 'Global trend according to estimated number of occupational accidents and fatal work-related diseases at region and country level', *Journal of Safety Research*, 40, 2, 125–39.

Hammar, T. (1990) *Democracy and the nation state: Aliens, denizens and citizens in a world of international migration*, Aldershot: Avebury.

Hannan, D. (2013) 'The fact that we paid to abolish slavery is a cause for pride, not shame', *Telegraph*, 3 March.

Hansen, Å.M., Hogh, A., Persson, R., Karlson, B., Garde, A.H. and Ørbæk, P. (2006) 'Bullying at work, health outcomes, and physiological stress response', *Journal of Psychosomatic Research*, 60, 1, 63–72.

Hardoon, D. (2015) *Wealth: Having it all and wanting more*, London: Oxfam.

Harrington, J.M. (2001) 'Health effects of shift work and extended hours of work', *Occupational and Environmental Medicine*, 58, 1, 68–72.

Hausman, D.M. and Welch, B. (2010) 'Debate: To nudge or not to nudge', *Journal of Political Philosophy*, 18, 1, 123–36.

Harvey, D. (1974) 'What kind of geography for what kind of public policy?', *Transactions of the Institute of British Geographers*, 63, 18–24.

Harvey, D. (2005) *A brief history of neoliberalism*, Oxford: Oxford University Press.

Heaney, C.A., Israel, B.A. and House, J.S. (1994) 'Chronic job insecurity among automobile workers: Effects on job satisfaction and health', *Social Science and Medicine*, 38, 10, 1431–7.

Heery, E. (2000) 'New unionism research project', *Research Bulletin 8*, Cardiff: Cardiff University.

Hepple, B. and Morris, G. (2002) 'The Employment Act 2002 and the crisis of individual employment rights', *Industrial Law Journal*, 31, 3, 245–69.

Herod, A. (2000) 'Workers and workplaces in a neoliberal global economy', *Environment and Planning A*, 32, 10, 1781–90.

Hillyard, P. and Tombs, S. (2004) 'Beyond criminology?', in P. Hillyard, C. Pantazis, S. Tombs and D. Gordon (eds) *Beyond criminology: Taking harm seriously*, London: Pluto Press, pp 10–29.

Hillyard, P. and Tombs, S. (2007) 'From "crime" to social harm?', *Crime, Law and Social Change*, 48, 1–2, 9–25.

Hillyard, P., Pantazis, C., Tombs, S. and Gordon, D. (eds) (2004) *Beyond criminology: Taking harm seriously*, London: Pluto Press.

Hjarnø, J. (2003) *Illegal immigrants and developments in employment in the labour markets of the EU*, Aldershot: Ashgate.

HM Government (2012) *First annual report of the Inter-Departmental Ministerial Group on Human Trafficking*. London: The Stationery Office.

Hochschild, A.R. (1983) *The managed heart: Commercialization of human feeling*, Berkeley, CA: University of California Press.

Hodal, K., Kelly, C. and Lawrence, F. (2014) 'The supermarket slave trail', *Guardian*, 11 June.

Hodson, R. (2001) *Dignity at work*, Cambridge: Cambridge University Press.

Hoel, H., Glasø, L., Hetland, J., Cooper, C.L. and Einarsen, S. (2010) 'Leadership styles as predictors of self-reported and observed workplace bullying', *British Journal of Management*, 21, 453–68.

Hoeller, P., Joumard, I., Bloch, D. and Pisu, M. (2012) 'Less income inequality and more growth – are they compatible? Mapping income inequality across the OECD', *OECD Economics Department Working Papers* 924, Paris: OECD.

Holgate, J. (2015) 'Community organising in the UK: A 'new' approach for trade unions?', *Economic and Industrial Democracy*, 36, 3, 431–55.

Holgate, J., Pollert, A., Keles, J. and Kumarappan, L. (2011) 'Geographies of isolation: How workers (don't) access support for problems at work', *Antipode*, 43, 4, 1078–101.

Hollister, M. (2011) 'Employment stability in the US labor market: Rhetoric versus reality', *Annual Review of Sociology*, 37, 305–24.

Holmes, S. (2013) *Fresh fruit, broken bodies*, Berkeley, CA: University of California Press.

Home Office (2013) *Draft Modern Slavery Bill*, Cm8770, London: The Stationery Office.

House of Commons (2009) *The trade in human beings: Human trafficking in the UK*, Home Affairs Committee: Sixth Report of Session 2008–09, London: The Stationery Office.

House of Commons (2014a) *Human trafficking: UK responses*, London: The Stationery Office.

House of Commons (2014b) *Blacklisting in employment*, Scottish Affairs Committee: Sixth Report of Session 2013–14, London: The Stationery Office.

House of Commons (2015) 'Apprenticeship statistics: England (1996–2015)', *Briefing Paper* 06113, London: The Stationery Office.

House of Commons (2016a) *Oral evidence: Working practices at Sports Direct*, Business, Innovation and Skills Committee, London: The Stationery Office.

House of Commons (2016b) *Courts and tribunals fees*, Justice Committee: Second Report of Session 2016–17, London: The Stationery Office.

House of Lords (2007) *Select Committee on European Union, Twenty-Second Report*, London: The Stationery Office.

HRW (Human Rights Watch) (2011) *They deceived us at every step*, New York: Human Rights Watch.

HRW (Human Rights Watch) (2012) *Building a better world cup*, New York: Human Rights Watch.

HSE (Health and Safety Executive) (2014a) *Statistics on fatal injuries in the workplace in Great Britain 2014*, London: HSE.

HSE (Health and Safety Executive) (2014b) *European Comparison*, London: HSE.

Hutton, W. (2010) *Hutton review of fair pay in the public sector: Interim report*, London: The Stationery Office.

Hutton, W. (2011) *Hutton review of fair pay in the public sector: Final report*, London: The Stationery Office.

Idowu Salih, I. (2015) 'Slavery in the twenty-first century: A review of domestic work in the UK', in L. Waite, G. Craig, H. Lewis and K. Skrivankova (eds) *Vulnerability, exploitation and migrants*, Basingstoke: Palgrave Macmillan, pp 200–8.

ILO (International Labour Organization) (1998a) *ILO Declaration on fundamental principles and rights at work*, Geneva: ILO.

ILO (International Labour Organization) (1998b) *Forced labour in Myanmar (Burma)*, Geneva: ILO.

ILO (International Labour Organization) (2005a) *A global alliance against forced labour*, Geneva: ILO.

ILO (International Labour Organization) (2005b) *Human trafficking and forced labour exploitation: Guidance for legislation and law enforcement*, Geneva: ILO.

ILO (International Labour Organization) (2009a) *The cost of coercion*, Geneva: ILO.

ILO (International Labour Organization) (2009b) *Fighting forced labour: The example of Brazil*, Geneva: ILO.

ILO (International Labour Organization) (2009c) *International labour migration and employment in the Arab region*, Geneva: ILO.

ILO (International Labour Organization) (2009d) *Forced labour and human trafficking: Casebook of court decisions. A training manual for judges, prosecutors and legal practitioners*, Geneva: ILO.

ILO (International Labour Organization) (2010a) *Accelerating action against child labour, Global Report under the follow-up to the ILO Declaration on Fundamental Principles and Rights at Work*, Geneva: ILO.

ILO (International Labour Organization) (2010b) 'Labour inspection in Europe: undeclared work, migration, trafficking', *Working Document 7*, Geneva: ILO.

ILO (International Labour Organization) (2012a) *ILO indicators of forced labour*, Geneva: ILO.

ILO (International Labour Organization) (2012b) *ILO global estimate of forced labour, results and methodology*, Geneva: ILO.

ILO (International Labour Organization) (2012c) *Stopping forced labour and slavery-like practices: The ILO strategy*, Geneva: ILO.

ILO (International Labour Organization) (2014) *Profits and poverty: The economics of forced labour*, Geneva: ILO.

ILO (International Labour Organization) (2015) *Safety and health at work*, Geneva: ILO.

ITUC (International Trade Union Confederation) (2013) *Countries at risk: Violations of trade union rights*, Brussels: ITUC.

ITUC (International Trade Union Confederation) (2014) *Global Rights Index*, Brussels: ITUC.

Jennings, J. (2013) *The business of abolishing the British slave trade, 1783–1807*, Abingdon: Routledge.

Johnson, H. (1986) 'A modified form of slavery: The credit and truck systems in the Bahamas in the nineteenth and early twentieth centuries', *Comparative Studies in Society and History*, 28, 4, 729–53.

Jones, K. (2014) 'It was a whirlwind. A lot of people made a lot of money: The role of agencies in facilitating migration from Poland into the UK between 2004 and 2008', *Central and Eastern European Migration Review*, 3, 2, 105–25.

Jones, O. (2012) *Chavs: The demonization of the working class*, London: Verso Books.

Jütting, J.P. and Laiglesia, J.R. (2009) 'Employment, poverty reduction and development: What's new?', in J.P. Jütting and J.R. Laiglesia (eds) *Is informal normal? Towards more and better jobs in developing countries*, OECD: Paris, pp 17–26.

Kasperkevic, J. (2016) 'Ex-McDonald's CEO suggests replacing employees with robots amid protests', *Guardian*, 25 May.

Keane, L., Pacek, A. and Radcliff, B. (2012) 'Organized labor, democracy and life satisfaction: A cross-national analysis', *Labor Studies Journal*, 37, 3, 253–70.

Kersley, B., Alpin, C., Forth, J., Bryson, A., Bewley, H., Dix, G. and Oxenbridge, S. (2006) *Inside the workplace*, London: Routledge.

Khaleeli, H. (2016) 'The truth about working for Deliveroo, Uber and the on-demand economy', *Guardian*, 15 June.

Khan, A. and Harroff-Tavel, H. (2011) 'Reforming the kafala: Challenges and opportunities in moving forward', *Asian and Pacific Migration Journal*, 20, 3–4, 293–313.

Killick, E. (2011) 'The debts that bind us: A comparison of Amazonian debt-peonage and US mortgage practices', *Comparative Studies in Society and History*, 53, 2, 344–70.

Kimber, M. (2003) 'The tenured "core" and the tenuous "periphery": The casualisation of academic work in Australian universities', *Journal of Higher Education Policy and Management*, 25, 1, 41–50.

Kleppa, E., Sanne, B. and Tell, G.S. (2008) 'Working overtime is associated with anxiety and depression: The Hordaland Health Study', *Journal of Occupational and Environmental Medicine*, 50, 6, 658–66.

Kondo, N., Sembajwe, G., Kawachi, I., van Dam, R.M., Subramanian, S.V. and Yamagata, Z. (2009) 'Income inequality, mortality, and self-rated health: Meta-analysis of multilevel studies', *British Medical Journal*, 339.

Kraemer, K.L., Linden, G. and Dedrick, J. (2011) *Capturing value in global networks: Apple's iPad and iPhone*, Berkeley, CA: University of California.

Krinsky, J. (2008) *Free labor: Workfare and the contested language of neoliberalism*, Chicago, IL: University of Chicago Press.

Large, M. (2010) *Common wealth*, Stroud: Hawthorn Press.

Lasslett, K. (2010) 'Crime or social harm? A dialectical perspective', *Crime, Law and Social Change*, 54, 1, 1–19.

Layte, R. (2012) 'The association between income inequality and mental health: Testing status anxiety, social capital, and neo-materialist explanations', *European Sociological Review*, 28, 4, 498–511.

LeBaron, G. (2008) 'Captive labour and the free market: Prisoners and production in the USA', *Capital and Class*, 32, 2, 59–81.

LeBaron, G. (2014) 'Reconceptualizing debt bondage: Debt as a class-based form of labor discipline', *Critical Sociology*, 40, 5, 763–80.

LeBaron, G. (forthcoming) *Unfree labour and the free market: Prisoners, production and the American state*, Chicago, IL: The University of Illinois Press.

Lenard, P.T. and Straehle, C. (eds) (2012) *Legislated inequality: Temporary labour migration in Canada*, Montreal: McGill-Queen's University Press.

Lennane, K.J. (1993) 'Whistleblowing: A health issue', *British Medical Journal*, 307, 667–70.

Lennane, K.J. (2012) 'What happens to whistleblowers, and why', *Social Medicine*, 6, 4, 249–58.

Lerche, J. (2007) 'A global alliance against forced labour? Unfree labour, neo-liberal globalization and the International Labour Organization', *Journal of Agrarian Change*, 7, 4, 424–5.

Lerche, J. (2012) 'Labour regulations and labour standards in India: Decent work?', *Global Labour Journal*, 3, 1, 16–39.

Lerner, S., Hurst, J. and Adler, G. (2008) 'Fighting and winning in the outsourced economy: Justice for janitors at the University of Miami', in A. Bernhardt, H. Boushey, L. Dresser and C. Tilly (eds) *The gloves-off economy: Workplace standards at the bottom of America's labor market*, Champaign, IL: Labour and Employment Relations Association, pp 243–67.

Lewchuk, W., Clarke, M. and De Wolff, A. (2008) 'Working without commitments: Precarious employment and health', *Work, Employment and Society*, 22, 3, 387–406.

Lewis, D. (2004) 'Bullying at work: The impact of shame among university and college lecturers', *British Journal of Guidance and Counselling*, 32, 3, 281–300.

Lewis, H., Dwyer, P., Hodkinson, S. and Waite, L. (2015a) *Precarious lives: Forced labour, exploitation and asylum*, Bristol: Policy Press.

Lewis, H., Dwyer, P., Hodkinson, S. and Waite, L. (2015b) 'Hyper-precarious lives: Migrants, work and forced labour in the Global North', *Progress in Human Geography*, 39, 5, 580–600.

Leymann, H. (1990) 'Mobbing and psychological terror at workplaces', *Violence and Victims*, 5, 2, 119–26.

Leymann, H. and Gustafsson, A. (1996) 'Mobbing at work and the development of post-traumatic stress disorder', *European Journal of Work and Organizational Psychology*, 5, 2, 251–76.

Lichfield, J. (2014) 'Mobile giant Orange hit by "suicide epidemic" as 10 employees take their own lives in seven weeks', *Independent*, 21 March.

Likic-Brboric, B., Schierup, C.-U. (2015) 'Labour rights as human rights?', in C.-U. Schierup, R. Munck, B. Likic-Brboric and A. Neergaard (eds) *Migration, precarity, and global governance: Challenges and opportunities for labour*, Oxford: Oxford University Press, pp 223–44.

Lillie, N. (2016) 'The right not to have rights: Posted worker acquiescence and the European Union labor rights framework', *Theoretical Inquiries in Law*, 17, 1, 39–62.

Lilley, R., Samaranayaka, A. and Weiss, H. (2013) *International comparison of International Labour Organisation published occupational fatal injury rates: How does New Zealand compare internationally?*, Injury Prevention Research Unit, Department of Preventive and Social Medicine, Dunedin School of Medicine, Dunedin: University of Otago.

Logan, J. (2002) 'Consultants, lawyers, and the "union free" movement in the USA since the 1970s', *Industrial Relations Journal*, 33, 3, 197–214.

Logan, J. (2006) 'The union avoidance industry in the United States', *British Journal of Industrial Relations*, 44, 4, 651–75.

Lopes, A. and Dewan, I. (2014) 'Precarious pedagogies? The impact of casual and zero-hour contracts in higher education', *Journal of Feminist Scholarship*, 7, 8, 28–42.

Lopes, A. and Hall, T. (2015) 'Winning a living wage: the legacy of living wage campaigns', in L. Waite, G. Craig, H. Lewis and K. Skrivankova (eds) *Vulnerability, exploitation and migrants*, Basingstoke: Palgrave Macmillan, pp.230–43.

Lorentzen, T., Angelin, A., Dahl, E., Kauppinen, T., Moisio, P. and Salonen, T. (2014) 'Unemployment and economic security for young adults in Finland, Norway and Sweden: From unemployment protection to poverty relief', *International Journal of Social Welfare*, 23, 1, 41–51.

Lucas, K., Kang, D. and Li, Z. (2013) 'Workplace dignity in a total institution: Examining the experiences of Foxconn's migrant workforce', *Journal of Business Ethics*, 114, 1, 91–106.

Lund-Thomsen, P. and Lindgreen, A. (2014) 'Corporate social responsibility in global value chains: Where are we now and where are we going?', *Journal of Business Ethics*, 123, 1, 11–22.

Lynd, R.S. and Lynd, H.M. (1929) *Middletown: A study in contemporary American culture*, New York: Harcourt Brace and Company.

McCarthy, L.A. (2014). 'Human trafficking and the new slavery', *Annual Review of Law and Social Science*, 10, 221–42.

McGrath, S. (2012) 'Many chains to break: The multi-dimensional concept of slave labour in Brazil', *Antipode*, 45, 4, 1005–28.

McGrath, S. (2013) 'Fuelling global production networks with slave labour?: Migrant sugar cane workers in the Brazilian ethanol GPN', *Geoforum*, 44, 32–43.

McGrath, S. and Strauss, K. (2014) 'Unfreedom and workers' power: Ever-present possibilities', in K. van der Pijl (ed) *Handbook of the international political economy of production*, Cheltenham: Edward Elgar, pp 299–317.

McIntosh, A. (2001) *Soil and soul: People versus corporate power*, London: Aurum Press Limited.

MacKenzie, R. and Forde, C. (2009) 'The rhetoric of the "good worker" versus the realities of employers' use and the experiences of migrant workers', *Work, Employment and Society*, 23, 1, 142–59.

Maguire, E.A. and Mullally, S.L. (2013) 'The hippocampus: A manifesto for change', *Journal of Experimental Psychology: General*, 142, 4, 1180–9.

Manning, S. (2013) 'Britain's colonial shame: Slave owners given huge payouts after abolition', *Independent*, 24 February.

Mantouvalou, V. (2013) 'What is to be done for migrant domestic workers?', in B. Ryan (ed) *Labour migration in hard times*, Liverpool: Institute of Employment Rights, pp 141–56.

Martin, B. (2003) 'Illusions of whistleblower protection', *UTS Law Review*, 5, 119–30.

Martin, B. and Rifkin, W. (2004) 'The dynamics of employee dissent: Whistleblowers and organizational Jiu-Jitsu', *Public Organization Review*, 4, 3, 221–38.

Martin, P. (2002) 'Mexican workers and US agriculture: The revolving door', *International Migration Review*, 36, 4, 1124–42.

Martin P. (2003) *Promise unfulfilled: Unions, immigration and the farm workers*, Ithaca, NY: Cornell University Press.

Mason, P. (2007) *Live working or die fighting*, London: Vintage.

May, R., Peetz, D. and Strachan, G. (2013) 'The casual academic workforce and labour market segmentation in Australia', *Labour and Industry*, 23, 3, 258–75.

Mayer, R. (2005) 'Guestworkers and exploitation', *The Review of Politics*, 67, 2, 311–34.

Meltzer, M. (1993) *Slavery: A World History*, Boston, MA: Da Capo.

Mesini, B. (2014) 'The transnational recruitment of temporary Latino workers in European agriculture', in J. Gertel and S.R. Sippel (eds) *Seasonal workers in Mediterranean agriculture: The social costs of eating fresh*, Abingdon: Routledge, pp 71–82.

Metcalf, D. (2008) 'Why has the British national minimum wage had little or no impact on employment?', *Journal of Industrial Relations*, 50, 3, 489–512.

Mezzadri, A. (2014) 'Indian garment clusters and CSR norms: Incompatible agendas at the bottom of the garment commodity chain', *Oxford Development Studies*, 42, 2, 238–58.

Midgley, C. (1996) 'Slave sugar boycotts, female activism and the domestic base of British anti-slavery culture', *Slavery and Abolition*, 17, 3, 137–62.

Miers, S. (2003) 'Slavery: A question of definition', *Slavery and Abolition*, 24, 2, 1–16.

Milanovic, B. (2012) *Global income inequality by the numbers: In history and now*, The World Bank Development Research Group Poverty and Inequality Team, Washington, DC: World Bank.

Miles, R. (1987) *Capitalism and unfree labour: Anomaly or necessity*, London: Tavistock.

Milkman, R. (2000) 'Immigrant organizing and the new labor movement in Los Angeles', *Critical Sociology*, 26, 1–2, 59–81.

Milkman, R. (2006) *LA story: Immigrant workers and the future of the US labor movement*, New York: Russell Sage Foundation.

Ministry of Justice (2011) *Reform of legal aid in England and Wales: The government response*, London: The Stationery Office.

Ministry of Justice (2013) *Legal aid statistics in England and Wales*, London: The Stationery Office.

Mishel, L. (2013) *The CEO-to-worker compensation ratio in 2012 of 273 was far above that of the late 1990s and 14 times the ratio of 20.1 in 1965*, Economic Policy Institute, Economic Snapshot, 24 September.

Mishel, L. and Sabadish, N. (2013) CEO pay in 2012 was extraordinarily high relative to typical workers and other high earners, *Economic Policy Institute Brief* 367, Washington, DC: Economic Policy Institute.

Mitchell, D. (1996) *The lie of the land: Migrant workers and the California landscape*, Minneapolis, MN: University of Minnesota Press.

Mitchell, D. (2011) 'Labour's geography: Capital, violence, guest workers and the post-World War II landscape', *Antipode*, 43, 2, 563–95.

Munusamy, R. (2015) 'The Marikana massacre is a tale of utter shame for South Africa', *Guardian*, 26 June.

Nadolny, A. and Ryan, S. (2015) 'McUniversities revisited: A comparison of university and McDonald's casual employee experiences in Australia', *Studies in Higher Education*, 40, 1, 142–57.

National Economic Council (2012) *The Buffet Rule*, Washington, DC: The Whitehouse.

NCVO (National Council for Voluntary Organisations) (2014) *Inquiry into charity senior executive pay and guidance for trustees on setting remuneration*, London: NCVO.

New, S.J. (2015) 'Modern slavery and the supply chain: The limits of corporate social responsibility?', *Supply Chain Management: An International Journal*, 20, 6, 697–707.

Newburn, T. (2002) 'Atlantic crossings: Policy transfer and crime control in the United States and Britain', *Punishment and* Society, 4, 2, 165–94.

Newsome, K. (2010) 'Work and employment in distribution and exchange: Moments in the circuit of capital', *Industrial Relations Journal*, 41, 3, 190–205.

Niedl, K. (1996) 'Mobbing and well-being: Economic and personnel development implications', *European Journal of Work and Organizational Psychology*, 5, 2, 203–14.

OECD (2011a) *Divided we stand: Why inequality keeps rising*, Paris: OECD.

OECD (2011b) 'Divided we stand: Why inequality keeps rising', *Country note*, UK, Paris: OECD.

OECD (2013) 'Protecting jobs, enhancing flexibility: A new look at employment protection legislation', in OECD *Employment Outlook 2013*, Paris: OECD, pp 65–107.

Oishi, S., Kesebir, S. and Diener, E. (2011) 'Income inequality and happiness', *Psychological Science*, 22, 9, 1095–100.

ONS (Office for National Statistics) (2014) *Analysis of employee contracts that do not guarantee a minimum number of hours*, London: ONS.

Otabor, C. and Nembhard, J. (2012) 'The Great Recession and land and housing loss in African American communities', *Centre on Race and Wealth Working Paper*, Washington, DC: Howard University.

Pande, A. (2013) 'The paper that you have in your hand is my freedom: Migrant domestic work and the sponsorship (Kafala) system in Lebanon', *International Migration Review*, 47, 414–41.

Patterson, O. (1982) *Slavery and social death: A comparative study*, Cambridge, MA: Harvard University Press.

Peck, J. (1996) *Workplace: The social regulation of labour markets*, New York: Guilford Press.

Peck, J. and Theodore, N. (1998) 'The business of contingent work: Growth and restructuring in Chicago's temporary employment industry', *Work, Employment and Society*, 12, 4, 655–74.

Peck, J. and Theodore, N. (2001) 'Contingent Chicago: Restructuring the spaces of temporary labor', *International Journal of Urban and Regional Research*, 25, 3, 471–96.

Peck, J. and Theodore, N. (2007) 'Flexible recession: The temporary staffing industry and mediated work in the United States', *Cambridge Journal of Economics*, 31, 2, 171–92.

Pemberton, S. (2007) 'Social harm future(s): Exploring the potential of the social harm approach', *Crime, Law and Social Change*, 48, 1–2, 27–41.

Pemberton, S. (2015) *Harmful societies: Understanding social harm*, Bristol: Policy Press.

Pemberton, S., Tombs, S., Chan, M.M.J. and Seal, L. (2012) 'Whistleblowing, organisational harm and the self-regulating organisation', *Policy and Politics*, 40, 2, 263–79.

Phillips, N. (2013) 'Unfree labour and adverse incorporation in the global economy: Comparative perspectives on Brazil and India', *Economy and Society*, 42, 2, 171–96.

Phillips, N. (2015) 'Private governance and the problems of trafficking and slavery in global supply chains', in L. Waite, G. Craig, H. Lewis and K. Skrivankova (eds) *Vulnerability, exploitation and migrants*, Basingstoke: Palgrave Macmillan, pp 15–27.

Phillips, N. and Mieres, F. (2011) 'The issue of poverty in global policy debates on forced labour: A critical perspective', *Chronic Poverty Research Centre Working Paper* 178, Manchester: University of Manchester.

Phillips, N. and Mieres, F. (2015) 'The governance of forced labour in the global economy', *Globalizations*, 12, 2, 244–60.

Phillips, N., Bhaskaran, R., Nathan, D. and Upendranadh, C. (2014) 'The social foundations of global production networks: Towards a global political economy of child labour', *Third World Quarterly*, 35, 3, 428–46.

Pijpers, R. (2010) 'International employment agencies and migrant flexiwork in an enlarged European Union', *Journal of Ethnic and Migration Studies*, 36, 7, 1079–97.

Piore, M. (1979) *Birds of passage*, Cambridge: Cambridge University Press.

Pitta, T. (2015) *Catastrophe: A guide to the world's worst industrial disasters*, New Delhi: Alpha Editions.

Piven, F. and Cloward, R. (1993) *Regulating the poor: The functions of public welfare*, New York: Vintage Books.

Plant, R. (2009) 'Foreword', in B. Andrees and P. Belser (eds) *Forced labor: Coercion and exploitation in the private economy*, Boulder, CO: Lynne Rienner Publishers, pp ix–xii.

Polanyi, K. (1944) *The great transformation*, Boston, MA: Beacon Press, 2001.

Pollert, A. (2005) 'The unorganised worker, the decline in collectivism and the new hurdles to individual employment rights', *Industrial Law Journal*, 34, 3, 217–38.

Pollert, A. (2006) 'The unorganised worker', *Working Lives Working Paper* 6, London: London Metropolitan University.

Pollert, A. (2007) 'Individual employment rights: Paper tigers, fierce in appearance but missing in tooth and claw', *Economic and Industrial Democracy*, 28, 1, 110–39.

Pollert, A. (2010) 'The lived experience of isolation for vulnerable workers facing workplace grievances in 21st-century Britain', *Economic and Industrial Democracy*, 31, 1, 62–92.

Portes, A., Castells, M. and Benton, L.A. (eds) (1989) *The informal economy: Studies in advanced and less developed countries*, Baltimore, MD: Johns Hopkins University Press.

Purcell, J., Purcell, K. and Tailby, S. (2004) 'Temporary work agencies: Here today, gone tomorrow?', *British Journal of International Relations*, 42, 4, 705–25.

Quinlan, M., Mayhew, C. and Bohle, P. (2001) 'The global expansion of precarious employment, work disorganization, and consequences for occupational health: a review of recent research', *International Journal of Health Services*, 31, 2, 335–414.

Raynor, C., Hoel, H. and Cooper, C.L. (2002) *Workplace bullying*, London: Taylor and Francis.

Reich, M., Jacobs, K. and Dietz, M. (eds) (2014) *When mandates work: Raising labor standards at the local level*, Berkeley, CA: University of California Press.

Reid, A. and Brewster, J. (1983) *Slavery, bondage, and dependency in Southeast Asia*, Basingstoke: Palgrave Macmillan.

Resolution Foundation (2012) *Gaining from growth: The final report of the Commission on Living Standards*, London: Resolution Foundation.

Rogaly, B. (2008a) 'Intensification of workplace regimes in British horticulture: the role of migrant workers', *Population, Space and Place*, 14, 6, 497–510.

Rogaly, B. (2008b) 'Migrant workers in the ILO's global alliance against forced labour report: A critical appraisal', *Third World Quarterly*, 29, 7, 1431–47.

Rogaly, B. (2009) 'Spaces of work and everyday life: Labour geographies and the agency of unorganised temporary migrant workers', *Geography*, Compass, 3, 6, 1975–87.

Roscigno, V.J., Hodson, R. and Lopez, S.H. (2009) 'Workplace incivilities: The role of interest conflicts, social closure and organizational chaos', *Work, Employment and Society*, 23, 4, 747–73.

Rowlingson, K. (2011) *Does income inequality cause health and social problems?*, York: Joseph Rowntree Foundation.

Royle, T. (2010) 'Low-road Americanization and the global "McJob": A longitudinal analysis of work, pay and unionization in the international fast-food industry', *Labor History*, 51, 2, 249–70.

Royle, T. and Urano, E. (2012) 'A new form of union organizing in Japan? Community unions and the case of the McDonald's "McUnion"', *Work, Employment and Society*, 26, 4, 606–22.

Ruddick, G. (2016) 'McDonald's offer staff the chance to get off zero-hours contracts', *Guardian*, 15 April.

Ruhs, M. (2012) 'The human rights of migrant workers: Why do so few countries care?', *American Behavioral Scientist*, 56, 9, 1277–93.

Ruhs, M. (2015) *The price of rights*, Princeton, NJ: Princeton Press.

Rushe, D. (2015) 'Apple passes gas firms with record $18bn quarterly profit', *Guardian,* 30 January.

Ryan, B. (2013) 'From labour migration to labour reform', in Ryan, B. (ed) *Labour migration in hard times*, Liverpool: Institute of Employment Rights, pp 60–74.

SACOM (Students and Scholars Against Corporate Misbehaviour) (2011) *iSlave behind the iPhone Foxconn workers in central China*, Hong Kong: SACOM.

Savulescu, J. and Bostrom, N. (2009) *Human enhancement*, Oxford: Oxford University Press.

Scheper-Hughes, N. and Bourgois, P. (2003) 'Making sense of violence', in N. Scheper-Hughes and P. Bourgois (ed) *Violence in war and peace: An anthology*, Malden, MA: Blackwell, pp 1–31.

Schierup, C.U., Munck, R., Likic-Brboric, B. and Neergaard, A. (eds) (2015) *Migration, precarity, and global governance: Challenges and opportunities for labour*, Oxford: Oxford University Press.

Schlosser, E. (1998) 'The prison–industrial complex', *Atlantic Monthly*, December, pp 51–77.

Schneider, F., Buehn, A. and Montenegro, C.E. (2010) 'Shadow economies all over the world: New estimates for 162 countries from 1999 to 2007', *World Bank Policy Research Working Paper Series* 5356, Washington, DC: World Bank.

Scott, J.C. (1985) *Weapons of the weak: Everyday forms of peasant resistance*, Newhaven, CT: Yale University Press, 2008.

Scott, S. (2013a) 'Labour, migration and the spatial fix: evidence from the UK food industry', *Antipode*, 45, 5, 1090–109.

Scott, S. (2013b) 'Migrant–local hiring queues in the UK food industry', *Population, Space and Place*, 19, 5, 459–71.

Scott, S. (2013c) 'Migration and the employer perspective: Pitfalls and potentials for a future research agenda', *Population, Space and Place*, 19, 6, 703–13.

Scott, S. (2015a) 'Making the case for temporary migrant worker programmes: Evidence from the UK's rural guestworker ("SAWS") scheme', *Journal of Rural Studies*, 40, 1–11.

Scott, S. (2015b) 'Venues and filters in managed migration policy: The case of the UK', *International Migration Review*, DOI: 10.1111/imre.12189.

Scott, S. (forthcoming) 'Informalization in low-wage labour markets: A case-study of the UK food industry', *Population, Space and Place*.

Scott, S. and Geddes, A. (2015) 'Ethics, methods and moving standards in research on migrant workers and forced labour', in D. Siegel and D. de Wildt (eds) *Ethical concerns in research on human trafficking*, New York: Springer, pp 117–36.

Scott, S., Craig, G. and Geddes, A. (2012) *Experiences of forced labour in the UK food industry*, York: Joseph Rowntree Foundation.

Sehnbruch, K., Burchell, B., Agloni, N. and Piasna, A. (2015) 'Human development and decent work: Why some concepts succeed and others fail to make an impact', *Development and Change*, 46, 2, 197–224.

Selinger, E. and Whyte, K. (2011) 'Is there a right way to nudge? The practice and ethics of choice architecture', *Sociology Compass*, 5, 10, 923–35.

Sennett, R. (1998) *The corrosion of character: The personal consequences of work in the new capitalism*, London: W.W. Norton.

Shade, L.R. and Jacobson, J. (2015) 'Hungry for the job: Gender, unpaid internships, and the creative industries', *The Sociological Review*, 63, S1, 188–205.

Sharma, B. (2006) *Contemporary forms of slavery in Bolivia*, London: ASI (Anti-Slavery International).

Shildrick, T., MacDonald, R. and Webster, C. (2012) *Poverty and insecurity: Life in low-pay, no-pay Britain*, Bristol: Policy Press.

Siebert, S. and Wilson, F. (2013) 'All work and no pay: Consequences of unpaid work in the creative industries', *Work, Employment and Society*, 27, 4, 711–21.

Simms, M., Holgate, J. and Heery, E. (2012) *Union voices: Tactics and tensions in UK organizing*, Ithaca, NY: Cornell University Press.

Skogstad, A., Matthiesen, S.B. and Einarsen, S. (2007) 'Organizational changes: A precursor of bullying at work?', *International Journal of Organizational Theory and Behavior*, 10, 1, 58–94.

Skrivánková, K. (2010) *Between decent work and forced labour: Examining the continuum of exploitation*, York: Joseph Rowntree Foundation.

Slapper, G. (1999) *Blood in the bank: Social and legal aspects of death at work*, Aldershot: Ashgate.

Slapper, G. and Tombs, S. (1999) *Corporate crime*, Harlow: Longman.

Smeeding, T.M. and Thompson, J.P. (2011) 'Recent trends in income inequality', *Research in Labor Economics*, 32, 1–50.

Smith, D. and Chamberlain, P. (2015) *Blacklisted: The secret war between big business and union activists*, Oxford: New Internationalist.

Soederberg, S. (2013) 'The US debtfare state and the credit card industry: Forging spaces of dispossession', *Antipode*, 45, 2, 493–512.

SOMO (Centre for Research on Multinational Corporations)/ICN (India Committee of the Netherlands) (2011) *Captured by cotton*, Amsterdam: SOMO.

Sporton, D. (2013) 'They control my life: The role of local recruitment agencies in East European migration to the UK', *Population, Space and Place*, 19, 5, 443–58.

Standing, G. (2010) 'The International Labour Organization', *New Political Economy*, 15, 2, 307–18.

Standing, G. (2011) *The precariat: The new dangerous class*, London: Bloomsbury Academic.

Standing, G. (2014) 'Understanding the precariat through labour and work', *Development and change*, 45, 5, 963–80.

Steinbeck, J. (1939) *Grapes of wrath*, New York: The Viking Press.

Stevens, S. (2001) 'A social tyranny: The Truck system in colonial Western Australia, 1829–99', *Labour History*, 80, 83–98.

Strauss, K. (2012) 'Coerced, forced and unfree labour: Geographies of exploitation in contemporary labour markets', *Geography* Compass, 6, 3, 137–48.

Strauss, K. and Fudge, J. (2013) 'Temporary work, agencies and unfree labour', in J. Fudge and K. Strauss (eds) *Temporary work, agencies and unfree labour*, London: Routledge, pp 1–25.

Strauss, K. and McGrath, S. (2017) 'Temporary migration, precarious employment and unfree labour relations: Exploring the "continuum of exploitation" in Canada's Temporary Foreign Worker Program', *Geoforum*, 78, 199–208.

Stringer, C., Simmons, G., Coulston, D. and Whittaker, D.H. (2014) 'Not in New Zealand's waters, surely? Linking labour issues to GPNs', *Journal of Economic Geography*, 14, 4, 739–58.

Sunstein, C. and Thaler, R. (2008) *Nudge*, New Haven, CT: Yale University Press.

SYNDEX (2012) *A mapping report on Labour Inspection Services in 15 European countries*, A SYNDEX report for the European Federation of Public Service Unions (EPSU), Brussels: EPSU.

Tailby, S., Pollert, A., Warren, S., Danford, A. and Wilton, N. (2011) 'Under-funded and overwhelmed: The voluntary sector as worker representation in Britain's individualised industrial relations system', *Industrial Relations Journal*, 42, 3, 273–92.

Taylor, F. (1911) *The principles of scientific management*, New York: Harper and Brothers.

Taylor, M. and Hurst, W. (2013) 'Met police launch inquiry into construction worker blacklisting', *Guardian*, 21 February.

Taylor, P., Cunningham, I., Newsome, K. and Scholarios, D. (2010) 'Too scared to go sick: Reformulating the research agenda on sickness absence', *Industrial Relations Journal*, 41, 4, 270–88.

Theodore, N. (2007) 'Closed borders, open markets: Day labourers' struggle for economic rights', in H. Leitner, J. Peck and E. Sheppard (eds) *Contesting neoliberalism: Urban frontiers*, Guilford: New York, pp 250–65.

Thompson, E.P. (1993) *Customs in common*, New York: New Press.

Thompson, P. (2002) 'Fantasy island: A labour process critique of the age of surveillance', *Surveillance and Society*, 1, 2, 138–51.

Thompson, P. (2003) 'Disconnected capitalism: Or why employers can't keep their side of the bargain', *Work, Employment and Society*, 17, 2, 359–78.

Thompson, P., Newsome, K. and Commander, J. (2013) 'Good when they want to be: Migrant workers in the supermarket supply chain', *Human Resource Management Journal*, 23, 2, 129–43.

Tinker, H. (1974) *A new system of slavery*, London: Oxford University Press.

Tombs, S. (1999) 'Death and work in Britain', *The Sociological Review*, 47, 345–67.

Tombs, S. (2007) 'Violence, safety crimes and criminology', *British Journal of Criminology*, 47, 4, 531–50.

Tombs, S. (2008) 'Workplace harm and the illusions of law', in D. Dorling, D. Gordon, P. Hillyard, C. Pantazis, S. Pemberton and S. Tombs (eds) *Criminal obsessions: Why harm matters more than crime*, London: Centre for Crime and Justice Studies, King's College, pp 43–64.

Tombs, S. and Hillyard, P. (2004) 'Towards a political economy of harm', in P. Hillyard, C. Pantazis, S. Tombs and D. Gordon (eds) *Beyond criminology: Taking harm seriously*, London: Pluto Press, pp 30–54.

Tombs, S. and Whyte, D. (2010) 'A deadly consensus: Worker safety and regulatory degradation under New Labour', *British Journal of Criminology*, 50, 1, 46–65.

Tomlins, C. (2001) 'Reconsidering indentured servitude: European migration and the early American labor force, 1600–1775', *Labor History*, 42, 1, 5–43.

TUC (2007) *New EU members*, London: TUC.

TUC (2008) *Hard work, hidden lives: The full report of the Commission for Vulnerable Employment*, London: TUC.

TUC (2016) *UK employment rights and the EU*, London: TUC.

UGF (Uzbek–German Forum for Human Rights) (2016) *The cover-up: Whitewashing Uzbekistan's white gold*, Berlin: Uzbek–German Forum for Human Rights.

UN (United Nations) (2013) *Total migrant stock at mid-year by origin and destination*, New York: United Nations Department of Economic and Social Affairs, Population Division.

UNDP (United Nations Development Programme) (2013) *Human development report 2013*, New York: UN.

US Department of State (2014) *Trafficking in persons report, 2014*, Washington, DC: Department of State.

Vertovec, S. (1995) 'Indian indentured migration to the Caribbean', in R. Cohen (ed) *The Cambridge survey of world migration*, Cambridge: University of Cambridge Press, pp 57–62.

Virtanen, M., Kivimäki, M., Joensuu, M., Virtanen, P., Elovainio, M. and Vahtera, J. (2005) 'Temporary employment and health: A review', *International Journal of Epidemiology*, 34, 3, 610–22.

Virtanen, M., Singh-Manoux, A., Ferrie, J.E., Gimeno, D., Marmot, M.G., Elovainio, M. and Kivimäki, M. (2009) 'Long working hours and cognitive function the Whitehall II Study', *American Journal of Epidemiology*, 169, 5, 596–605.

Virtanen, M., Ferrie, J.E., Singh-Manoux, A., Shipley, M.J., Stansfeld, S.A., Marmot, M.G. and Kivimäki, M. (2011) 'Long working hours and symptoms of anxiety and depression: A 5-year follow-up of the Whitehall II study', *Psychological Medicine*, 41, 12, 2485–94.

Visser, M.A. (2016) 'A floor to exploitation? Social economy organizations at the edge of a restructuring economy', *Work Employment and Society*, DOI: 10.1177/0950017016638020.

Wagstaff, A.S. and Lie, J.A.S. (2011) 'Shift and night work and long working hours: A systematic review of safety implications', *Scandinavian Journal of Work, Environment and Health*, 37, 3, 173–85.

Waite, L. (2009) 'A place and space for a critical geography of precarity?', *Geography Compass*, 3, 1, 412–33.

Waite, L., Craig, G., Lewis, H. and Skrivankova, K. (2015) *Vulnerability, exploitation and migrants*, Basingstoke: Palgrave Macmillan.

Wakley, T. (1841) *The Lancet*, 1 May, 922, 193–6.

Waldinger, R. and Lichter, M.I. (2003) *How the other half works*, Berkeley CA: University of California Press.

Waldinger, R., Erickson, C., Milkman, R., Mitchell, D., Valenzuela, A., Wong, K. and Zeitlin, M. (1998) 'Helots no more: A case study of the Justice for Janitors Campaign in Los Angeles', in K. Bronfenbrenner, S. Friedman, R.W. Hurd, R.A. Oswald and R.L. Seeber (eds) *Organizing to win: New research on unions strategies*, Ithaca, NY: ILR Press, pp 102–120.

Walk Free Foundation (2013) *The Global Slavery Index 2013*, Western Australia: Walk Free Foundation.

Walk Free Foundation (2016) *The Global Slavery Index 2016*, Western Australia: Walk Free Foundation.

Walker, C., Burton, M., Akhurst, J. and Degirmencioglu, S.M. (2015) 'Locked into the system? Critical community psychology approaches to personal debt in the context of crises of capital accumulation', *Journal of Community and Applied Social Psychology*, 25, 3, 264–75.

Walker, J. (1993) *The Black Loyalists: The search for a promised land in Nova Scotia and Sierra Leone, 1783–1870*, Toronto: University of Toronto Press.

Walshe, S. (2012) 'How US prison labour pads corporate profits at taxpayers', expense, *Guardian*, 6 July.

Walzer, M. (1983) *Spheres of justice: A defense of pluralism and equality*, New York: Basic Books.

Weber, A., Musiolek, B., Maher, S. (2015) 'False promises and movements of contestation in the global garment industry', in C.-U. Schierup, R. Munck, B. Likic-Brboric and A. Neergaard (eds) *Migration, precarity, and global governance: Challenges and opportunities for labour*, Oxford: Oxford University Press, pp 245–60.

Weber, M. (1930) *The Protestant ethic and the spirit of capitalism*, London: Allen and Unwin.

Weeks, J. (2005) 'Inequality trends in some developed OECD countries', *Working Paper* 6, New York: UN.

Weil, D. (2009) 'Rethinking the regulation of vulnerable work in the USA: A sector-based approach', *Journal of Industrial Relations*, 51, 3, 411–30.

Western, B. and Rosenfeld, J. (2011) 'Unions, norms, and the rise in US wage inequality', *American Sociological Review*, 76, 4, 513–37.

White, A. (2012) 'KPMG voicemail: Dial this number to hear your job is at risk', *Telegraph*, 8 March.

Wilkinson, A. (2016) 'Labour's ban on McDonald's in no snobbery', *Guardian*, 22 April.

Wilkinson, R. and Pickett, K. (2009) *The spirit level: Why more equal societies almost always do better*, London: Penguin.

Wills, J. (2001) 'Community unionism and trade union renewal in the UK: Moving beyond the fragments at last?', *Transactions of the Institute of British Geographers*, 26, 4, 465–83.

Wills, J. (2005) 'The geography of union organising in low-paid service industries in the UK', *Antipode*, 37, 1, 139–59.

Wills, J. (2009) 'Subcontracted employment and its challenge to labor', *Labor Studies Journal*, 34, 4, 441–60.

Wills, J., Datta, K., Evans, Y., Herbert, J., May, J. and McIlwaine, C. (2009) 'Religion at work: The role of faith-based organizations in the London living wage campaign', *Cambridge Journal of Regions, Economy and Society*, 2, 3, 443–61.

Wills, J., Datta, K., Evans, Y., Herbert, J., May, J. and McIlwaine, C. (2010) *Global cities at work: New migrant divisions of labour*, London: Pluto Press.

Wong, J.C. (2014) 'You want fries with your poverty wages and exploited McDonald's workers?', *Guardian*, 15 May.

Woolsey, M. (2008) 'World's best places for unemployment pay', *Forbes*, 27 June.

Wrangborg, J. (2013) *Kallskänken*, Stockholm: Ordfront.

Wright Mills, C. (1951) *White collar: The American middle classes*, Oxford: Oxford University Press.

Yea, S. (2015) 'Trafficked enough? Missing bodies, migrant labour exploitation, and the classification of trafficking victims in Singapore', *Antipode*, 47, 4, 1080–100.

Index